NEW VIEWS
OF CO-OPERATION

EDITED BY STEPHEN YEO

ROUTLEDGE
London and New York

First published 1988
by Routledge
11 New Fetter Lane, London EC4P 4EE
29 West 35th Street, New York, NY 10001

©1988 in editorial matter, Stephen Yeo
©1988 in all other material, Routledge

Typeset by BookEns, Saffron Walden, Essex
Printed in Great Britain by T J Press (Padstow) Ltd, Padstow, Cornwall

British Library Cataloguing in Publication Data
New views of cooperation.
1. Great Britain. Cooperatives
I. Yeo, Stephen
334′.094

ISBN 0-415-02523-0

Library of Congress Cataloging in Publication Data
Also available

FOR JOHN HARRISON, SOCIAL HISTORIAN

CONTENTS

CONTENTS

NOTES ON CONTRIBUTORS

ANDY DURR is co-ordinator of Continuing Education in the Faculty of Art, Design and Humanities at Brighton Polytechnic. He teaches History there, and is working on a study of freemasonry and related associations among working people for a doctorate at Sussex University.

ROBIN THORNES works for the Royal Commission on the Historical Monuments of England, as head of the Northern office of its Threatened Buildings Section. He was a postgraduate student at Sussex from 1976 to 1979, completing a doctoral thesis on 'The early development of the co-operative movement in West Yorkshire, 1827–1863'.

PETER GURNEY is a doctoral research student at Sussex who will submit a thesis soon on aspects of the co-operative movement during the late nineteenth and early twentieth centuries. He does part-time teaching when he can get it.

MICK REED is at present a temporary WEA organizer in West Sussex. He is working on a doctorate at Sussex on small farmers and trades-people. He is on the editorial advisory board and acts as the reviews editor of the *Journal of Peasant Studies*.

KEITH HARDING recently completed a doctorate at Sussex on 'The Irish issue in the British labour movement, 1900–22'. He now teaches English in North London and is married with a son.

ALISTAIR THOMSON comes from Australia but now lives in Brighton where he is finishing a doctorate about the memory of the Great War in Australia and the use of memory by oral historians.

He works for the community publisher, QueenSpark Books, and teaches in adult and tertiary education.

GILL SCOTT has recently completed a D. Phil. thesis at Sussex University on the history of the Women's Co-operative Guild. She lives in London and works as a lecturer, doing part-time teaching in different institutions of adult and higher education.

SALLY MULLEN is now a full-time mother living in Bristol. While studying at Bristol Polytechnic in 1979 she wrote a dissertation on socialist culture in Bristol which has formed the basis of her article. She became an English teacher at Highwood Secondary Modern School in Gloucestershire during which time she had several articles published by Bristol Broadsides, an affiliate of the Federation of Worker Writers and Community Publishers.

LAWRENCE MAGNANIE graduated from Sussex University with a first-class honours degree in History in 1983, followed by an MA in Social History in 1984. A supermarket worker, his *History of Football in Eastbourne* is due to be published in 1988 and reflects a continuing interest in the role of sport and leisure in modern British History.

PADDY MAGUIRE was a D.Phil. student at Sussex from 1975 to 1978 after taking his first degree at York. He now teaches History at Brighton Polytechnic. He continues to work on relations between government, employers, and trade unions during the twentieth century, to assist in the organization of History Workshops, and to play bar billiards.

NEIL KILLINGBACK graduated from Sussex in 1975 and in 1980 completed his doctorate on the organization, political behaviour, and economic activities of small businessmen in Britain during the 1930s. He taught adult education classes, collaborated with Keith Middlemas in his work on the post-war consensus, worked for local government in Islington, and is now manager for business development and information with Throgmorton Investment Management Services Ltd in the City of London.

EILEEN YEO was educated at Brandeis University, the University of Wisconsin, and the University of Sussex where she now teaches History, including the MA course in Keywords. She has written on popular culture and is currently finishing a book on 'Social Science, Class and Gender in Britain, 1789–1914'.

STEPHEN YEO teaches at Sussex. He is interested in the history of Co-operation and other forms of working-class association, in the history and class position of different kinds of socialism, in all forms of voluntary organization, and in autobiography alongside the historiographical question 'Whose Story?' about which he is currently writing.

PREFACE

This book arose from a wish to honour J. F. C. Harrison, Professor of History at the University of Sussex from 1970 to 1982 and author, among many other works of social history, of the classic *Robert Owen and the Owenites in Britain and America* (1969). The work represented here comes out of the graduate programme in History at Sussex of which all of the authors but one (and she has strong connections) have been part, and to which John Harrison has been so central. We owe a great debt to John as an historian, as well as liking him enormously as a person.

There are many other Sussex faculty and ex-students whose work-in-progress could have been included, even restricting the book, as we chose to do, to *New Views of Co-operation* in order to give it a thematic unity close to one of John Harrison's main interests. Malcolm Chase's work on early nineteenth-century radicalism and the land question, Ian Dyck on William Cobbett, Alun Howkins on nineteenth- and twentieth-century working-class rural history, and Barbara Taylor on feminism and Owenism spring to mind, in a school of early modern and modern social history at Sussex which continues to be fecund. The book is also intended to celebrate social history at Sussex which remains very much alive. It is part of the sad history of the last decade that very few of the authors of this book have professional History jobs of any kind, and quite a number have no secure jobs at all.

The book's other aim is more obvious. It is to contribute to the reinterpretation of the changing place of working-class association in capitalist Britain, with particular reference to co-operation and the co-operative movement, which our present political culture makes quite urgent. It is designed to be read in sequence rather than as a random collection. The introductory paragraphs to chapters 2–13 are by the editor.

Chapter One

INTRODUCTORY: RIVAL CLUSTERS OF POTENTIAL: WAYS OF SEEING CO-OPERATION

STEPHEN YEO

Association (as, for instance, in co-operatives and in the co-operative movement itself) may be regarded as labour's own capital. It may be seen as what, in the end, constitutes labour's power: what labour has to work with and to work for – free association.

Indeed, as more and more people are deprived of ownership and of control over the dominant means of producing and exchanging in modern societies, association may even become all that labour has left. For those who 'only have their labour force to depend on', 'social combinations' have been a unique opportunity for struggle on their own behalf, and therefore also a particular site for struggle against them on behalf of superior interests.[1] Class conflict within and against Co-operation is a major theme in all the chapters of this book. 'Everyone who had nothing brought it together and it made a lot': 'the mighty power of the million pence'[2]: 'make yourselves powerful by your united strength if you cannot be powerful by your separate strength'.[3] Getting together, union, combination, co-operation, association . . . may be seen as part of the power inherent in (human) labour power, potentially usable for itself, for labour, as well as being a matter for deliberate organization on capital's behalf in the era of large-scale industry.

Co-operators in Britain have known about this for two hundred years. In a speech at the Co-operative Union Congress of 1894, Catherine Webb spoke of 'association' alongside 'machinery' as the 'modern methods of production' needing to be applied to women's domestic work. The vision of the main body of the movement has been that through associations for exchange (co-operative societies/stores) members would use what they produced and produce what they used, making capital into a hired servant of theirs

1

rather than their continuing as hired servants of capital. In their living critique of competition, which they saw as a cancer on the body politic, they favoured the language of 'association'.[4] Among their journals of the 1820s was one called *The Associate* (for which see Chapter 2). The subtitle of *The Co-operative News* from 1886 onwards was *and Journal of Associated Industry*. The CWS magazine, *The Millgate Monthly*, founded in 1905, was to be 'A Popular Magazine devoted to Association, Education, Literature and General Amusement'. 'Is it not true to say', asked T. W. Mercer in 1920, 'that whereas members of the Labour Party are collectivists, co-operators are associationists.'[5] Their favourite slogan was 'each for all and all for each',

> The Co-operative ideal may be expressed thus:- By means of mutual association to eliminate the present competitive industrial system, and to substitute mutual Co-operation for the common good as the basis of all human society . . . by the principle of service for service, the instinct of self-interest is made to promote the common good.[6]

CWS own-brand seeds were called 'One and All'. Through co-operative membership, members would unite capital and labour, and producers and consumers, in a single (their own) body: members one of another. Or, as the first two principles agreed at a co-operative conference in Rochdale in 1855 (recorded by Holyoake in his *Self-help by the People: The History of the Rochdale Pioneers*) expressed it:

I. That human society is a body consisting of many members, the real interests of which are identical.
II. That true workmen should be fellow workers.

'This is the simple difference between competitive and co-operative production and trading,' explained a piece (probably by Dr John Watts) in the CWS *Almanac and Diary* for 1881, 'under competition everyone strives to benefit himself alone, whilst under co-operation everyone works for the common good.' The whole was the precondition of the health of the part: as Brighton co-operators expressed it in the late 1820s, members should 'never eat or drink . . . wear or consume any article the profit of which goes to enrich any single individual, if such an article can be procured of any society where the whole receive the equal benefit' (see Chapter 2). The Co-operative Wholesale Society was a direct continuation of this commitment to 'equal benefit' well into the twentieth century. The

CWS journal, *The Wheatsheaf* (started in 1896) explained its name to readers in July 1900:

> The essential part performed in our life by wheat symbolises the importance of Co-operative principles. The inability of the grain to stand upright unless bound up with its fellows illustrates the power of association.

Pulling capital back into their own hands – money, machines, knowledge, organization – has been the project for which working-class co-operators have sought adequate language, adequate activity, adequate associational forms. Language, as always, was indicative. Key words like 'profit' and 'consumers' went into inverted commas because in a co-operative context they meant something different. 'Profits as understood by the ordinary economist have no existence in the co-operative movement'; 'the real reason why the control of industry, as regards the owning and managing of factories should be in the hands of the "consumers" is because they are ultimately *the whole community*, and they work for the interest of all'[7] (my emphasis; see Chapter 13). The phrase for the Pioneers' 'world-making' project was a more active one than 'nationalizing the means'. It was 'arranging the powers', 'powers of production, distribution, education and government'[8] (see Chapter 3). This project involved finding forms of association which did without masters, an independence which stuck in the gullet of many would-be patrons of Co-operation all through the second half of the nineteenth century: 'the working class', as Holyoake explained, in their defence, in his *History of the Rochdale Pioneers*, 'are not considered to be very rich in the quality of self-trust, or mutual trust. The business habit is not thought to be their forte. The art of creating a large concern, and governing all its complications, is not usually supposed to belong to them' (see Chapter 2). Working-class co-operators experienced relations of production as integrated with the forces thereof, but also as imbricated in wider social or less-than-social relations. They therefore sought to transform them, as a whole, from competition to Co-operation through deliberate, conscious construction, towards a commonwealth or 'close community'.[9] 'Association', in George Jacob Holyoake's view, was 'a moral art as well as a new form of economy'[10] (see Chapter 4).

'They had the power of organisation and understood the requirements of their fellow men.'[11] In the nineteenth- and early twentieth-century co-operative movement in Britain, it sometimes seemed so simple. They had the power of association. Legal rights might be a problem. Much of what they did was, in the first instance, illegal. The Rochdale Pioneers had a long struggle with Tidd Pratt, the responsible Registrar under the Industrial and Provident Society Acts, over the illegality of setting aside funds for educational purposes.[12] But legislation seemed, as it came, to confirm their capacities rather than to deny them. It thus appeared transparent, rational, and progressive, that large-scale co-operation was the future form, competition the past. 'The members have now a great lever within their reach', 'the complete emancipation of the workers of this country is assured'.[13] A truly social economy would, because it could, replace the existing political one. This social economy would recuperate some of the characteristics of an older, moral economy. It was already available: 'the alternative society does exist': it took the form of flour mills, for instance, as well as ideas.[14] In the phrase of an Owenite author of a series of 'Letters on Associated Labour' in 1834, they had resolved 'to constitute the society for which we work'.[15] And because of the inventiveness of their resolution, expressed in clock towers as well as on bits of paper, in jubilee teapots as well as in mid-town buildings which dwarfed town halls, in Congresses, 'Parliaments of Labour', as well as in packets of biscuits . . . its potential was attacked. The attacks came as conflicts from within – as they are bound to do in a movement of any size – as well as in the form of struggle by hostile interests from outside (see Chapters 9, 11, 12 and 13).

For at least three hundred years in Britain there has been manifest conflict over associational form, private ('economic') conflict as well as public ('political') conflict. The question for capital and for labour has been: how can dominant forms of association – factories, schools, entertainments, as well as 'voluntary associations' like sects, co-ops, unions – how can such forms be contrived so that they work in *our* interests more than *theirs*? This may sound like a crude way of putting it. In practice, however, it has rarely been a matter of either/or – either capital's or labour's interests – but of both, to differing degrees, and within the same associations. The most interesting associations, such as unions and co-operative societies, have been sites of (class) conflict rather than unambiguous instruments of either side. It has also only rarely been a matter of explicit intention, conspiracy, or conscious struggle, on

4

either side. But there have been two tendencies in conflict, two opposed clusters of potential. And one of the interesting things about co-operators which will become evident in this book, has been the extent to which they articulated them as such.

The chapters which follow will point towards working-class potential – potential for the material development of labour as a class for itself, able to construct, or so many people thought, a whole 'society' – embodied in a wide and linked array of associational forms, and strong by the turn of the nineteenth and twentieth centuries. This potential was even located in the most 'basic' area of all, that of material production. One estimate has it that co-operative production was at its strongest in relation to the rest of the economy *circa* 1905.[16] Certainly the movement was very large by then, with a million members nation-wide and with the Co-operative Wholesale Society one of the largest businesses in the world. It was early in the twentieth century that W. H. Lever, for instance, became most concerned about the Co-operative Wholesale Society's soap works at Irlam, Silvertown, and Dunston-on-Tyne. He took legal action against co-operative societies' refusal to stock Sunlight Soap, in the Taff Vale of the co-operative movement.[17] Concern by private capital and concern at the level of the state continued well into the twentieth century (see Chapter 12) and is still apparent in 1980s Britain.

Having indicated potential-for-labour, however, and writing during the late 1980s, it is also necessary to emphasize its non-realization, even destruction. In a prolonged and general crisis which is still with us, but which was at its most acute between about 1870 and 1930, a broadly successful vaccination programme was undertaken by capital, against labour's associated potential. This programme has not been easy to see, let alone to interpret. It was carried out by would-be friends (for instance in the Labour Party) as well as by obvious enemies, by class warriors (from above) as well as by gentler folk who disliked the language of class, preferring, for instance, 'community' (see Chapter 13). Bodies and antibodies fought over visions as well as over practical facts, dreams as well as numbers: reinterpreting impulses so that they returned unrecognizable to those whose energy they first had been. Thomas Rigby, co-operator, author of Bury Co-operative Society's Jubilee History in 1905, had a vision of 'the general transference of the spirit of association from a political into an industrial form'. For him there was a time to 'look forward to . . . when all distinctions, except those of merit and high attainment in the cause of progress, shall be abolished'.[18] This was in line with J. T. W. Mitchell's commitment to human equality as Chairman of the CWS from 1878 to 1895.[19] It was also in line with the revolutionary side of Samuel Smiles's vision, in his book on *Character* (1871), that 'all men might become what some men are'.[20] It was in line with 'one of the remarkable facts about the Wholesale Societies, that the men to whom is entrusted the executive control of this vast organisation are all workers who have risen from the ranks of Co-operation, having won the respect and confidence of the Movement by years of service'.[21] But it was not in line with a more characteristic twentieth-century utterance on 'the spirit of association' in a book with that title published in 1913, in which the author purported to praise co-operatives, trade unions and friendly societies but in which the project was in fact to police them:

> The attitude of mind which conceives that any one person can do a given job as well as another, has often accounted for a pitiable misconception of the facts of daily life. There will be differences in capacity so long as this world revolves upon its axis.[22]

Giving such differences psychological, theological, biological, educational, material, managerial . . . (facts of life) bases, and then using them to determine (limit and contain) mutuality, has been a large part of what has been done to the co-operative movement in our time. Defeat has not been total – it never can be – but its processes are probably now, during the late 1980s, as important to draw attention to as the many partial, preliminary victories achieved. An articulated working-class movement which was cheap enough to be generally available but high in class dividend; which was geographically and socially accessible but also patient of universalization; and which was independent but also engaged with allies and against enemies – such a formation did not, it now appears (1988), come into being in twentieth-century Britain. It was immanent during the late nineteenth and early twentieth centuries, for instance in the co-operative movement, but blocked. The processes of blockage or prevention may be a fruitful way of looking at twentieth-century British social history from labour's point of view.

A sense of federal, open-ended aspiration and activity at a personal and an associational level; identification of *class* with creativity and confidence rather than with submission (see Chapters 9 and 10), with a future rather than with a past, with capacity rather than with apathy; serious inventiveness about the cultural and political and social components of 'democracy' if ever that new order of society was to be universalized (see Chapters 4, 6, and 7); determination to go through civil society to the state, through private spaces into the reconstruction of the public sphere; recognition of human differences as reasons for co-operation rather than justification for competition . . . all these ran away into the earth. Large possibilities – involving labour doing away with masters, and doing its own, associated production and allocation of would-be dominant forms and spaces – have been channelled into underground streams, waiting for creative politics to divine them again.

This is to anticipate. Defeat remains as a direction, not a finished result. To the extent that defeat has occurred, moreover, it need not be blamed upon earlier working-class initiatives. These can only be diminished (or inflated) by being seen as the causes, in a simple sense, of later happenings. The fact that the world did not go their way should not be allowed to conceal what Holyoake called the 'world-making' project of co-operators: results need not be allowed to erase struggles, nor need defeat be equated with failure. The rest of this book will attempt to seize what is perhaps the social historian's main opportunity, namely to get behind effects into processes or struggles. 'We have to develop modes of analysis which, instead of reducing works to finished products, and activities to fixed positions, are capable of discerning, in good faith, the finite but significant openness of many actual initiatives and contributions.'[23] 'The whole in Co-operation is better than a part, but it would be unwise not to accomplish in part what we desire and stand so much in need of, because we cannot at once realise it perfectly.'[24] One of the two main opposed tendencies or clusters of potential in nineteenth- and twentieth-century Britain, namely private capital (often referred to within the co-operative movement as 'competition'), could have developed and can only develop through subordinating the other. The other tendency, namely private labour (often signified, during the nineteenth century, with words like 'co-operation' or 'mutuality'), could have developed and can only develop towards universalizing the most generous possibilities disclosed within capitalism through superseding private capital, thus shaping a whole 'associated mode' of production.[25]

The two clusters of potential are locked hopefully (or tragically) together.

How did the struggle go? In what did the struggle consist? Who, in less abstract terms than 'capital' and 'labour', 'competition' and 'co-operation', were some of the protagonists? What did they believe and dare and do? The rest of this book consists of attempts to find out. Each chapter will be linked by a few paragraphs of editorial introduction.

NOTES

1 The phrases are those of E. R. T. Morse, a Reading co-operator, in *Reading Co-operative Record*, 17 February 1904, and Thomas Rigby, a Bury co-operator, in *The Origin and History of Co-operation in Bury, 1855–1905*, Bury, 1905.

2 The phrases are from W. H. Brown, *The Co-operative Manager*, Manchester, National Co-operative Managers' Association, 1937, p. 15, and *Co-operative News*, 25 April 1891, the opening of CWS Flour Mills, Dunston on Tyne.

3 *The Co-operator*, March 1863, Address to Co-operators from Rochdale Pioneers, accompanying a set of model rules they issued following the passing of the Industrial and Provident Societies Act of 1862.

4 The cancer image is in W. T. Carter, *Co-operation a Remedy*, a pamphlet, Manchester, Co-operative Union, 1885.

5 T. W. Mercer, *The Co-operative Movement in Politics*, a pamphlet, Manchester, Co-operative Union, 1921.

6 Catherine Webb (ed.), *Industrial Co-operation: The Story of a Peaceful Revolution*, 1st edn, Manchester, Co-operative Union, 1904; 8th edn, 1919, p. 2.

7 From an article in the CWS *Annual* for 1902. In this article even the word 'sold', as in buying and selling, is put into inverted commas as being not quite appropriate for co-operative exchanges. The whole movement at this time was a living critique of the commodity form itself.

8 G. J. Holyoake, *Self-help by the People: The History of the Rochdale Pioneers*, 10th edn, revised and enlarged, London, Swan Sonnenschein, 1907, p. 12.

9 The 'close community' phrase is from the article cited in n. 7 above.

10 At the Congress of 1874, see *Co-operative News*, 25 April 1874, p. 230. I owe this reference to Peter Gurney.

11 From a speech made in Reading in 1898 by the Honorary Secretary of the Southern Section of the Co-operative Union, Adam Deans.

12 See Holyoake, op. cit., p. 73.

13 Rigby, op. cit., p. vi.

14 'The Labour Movement must work to show that the alternative society does exist and can be achieved without national catastrophe which

itself could lead to the triumph of a system which is the very opposite of democratic socialism. . . . There will never be a "convenient" time to alter the structure of existing society', Royal Arsenal Co-operative Society, *The Role and Problems of the Co-operative Movement in the 1980's*, a pamphlet, May 1977.

15 Senex, in *The Pioneer*, 22 March 1834, Letter II, 'To the productive classes'.

16 D. C. Jones, 'The economics of British producer co-operation', unpublished PhD thesis, Cornell University, 1974.

17 Percy Redfern, *The New History of the C.W.S.*, London, J. M. Dent and Manchester, CWS, 1938, p. 55. I shall be dealing with this case at length elsewhere.

18 Rigby, op. cit., pp. 7 and vi.

19 I will be publishing a separate essay on J.T.W. Mitchell which was intended for this volume but grew too long for it.

20 Samuel Smiles, *Character*, London, 1871.

21 Webb, op. cit., p. 122.

22 M. Fothergill Robinson, *The Spirit of Association*, London, John Murray, 1913, p. 350.

23 Raymond Williams, *Marxism and Literature*, London, Oxford University Press, 1977.

24 CWS, *Annual*, 1886, p. 115.

25 For which see K. Marx, *Capital*, vol. 3, Harmondsworth, Penguin Books, 1981, pp. 571-2.

Chapter Two

WILLIAM KING OF BRIGHTON: CO-OPERATION'S PROPHET?

ANDY DURR

As well as being the place from which this book of essays comes, Brighton has an old and honourable place in the history of Co-operation. 'It may seem strange', wrote G. D. H. Cole in his *A Century of Co-operation*, published in 1944 to celebrate the centenary of the Rochdale Pioneers, 'that Brighton, the fashionable watering-place and residence of George IV, should have been thus forward in accepting Owenite doctrines; but the town was in fact very much to the fore in those days in many progressive movements.'

The Brighton Society came at an important moment. Robert Owen had acquired New Harmony in Indiana in 1825; Abraham Combe, author of *Old and New Systems* (1823), founded Orbiston in Lanarkshire as an Owenite 'Village of Co-operation' in 1826. These were all-at-once communities, as new *systems*, founded by prophets driven by notions of reform, from above. There were, however, other more bit-by-bit ways of co-operating, also interested in community but through the trades and exchanges of working people, building means into ends rather than starting all at once at the end. Such a bit-by-bit approach had been represented by London printers around George Mudie and the first co-operative journal *The Economist* from 1821, and it was to characterize the Brighton initiatives from 1827. These initiatives were not primarily those of the 'poor man's Doctor', King, as this chapter shows. There has been a continual tension in the history of Co-operation, fully evident in the first series of Co-operative Congresses during the early 1830s, between prophets (often claiming monopoly over the principles of 'true Co-operation') and working people's practices (often in the moral economy tradition of, for example, co-operative flour mills), necessarily messy and necessarily 'failing' on the way to any kind of possible success. As the *Quarterly Review* commented in November 1829, 'all resolve themselves into the fear that the working classes might become so independent that the unworking classes would not have sufficient control over them, and would be ultimately obliged to work for themselves'. It is this tension that co-operative manu-facture and exchange, as opposed to other ways through to a society better than competitive capitalism, is specifically about.

Andy Durr explores the tension as it affected the immediate practice but also the subsequent historiography of Co-operation in Brighton, using William Bryan the cabinet maker and William King the doctor. Through the monthly journal *The Co-operator*, written by King and 'devoted to a sys-tematic exposition of the principles of Co-operation' between 1828 and 1830, the Brighton Society had an influence which 'extended far beyond what it immediately achieved'. *The Co-operator* was reprinted in 1947, edited by T. W. Mercer and, with a Life and Letters of King, published by the Co-operative Union (which also commissioned the Cole book) in an early example of labour history archive retrieval. In its first issue it recorded the existence of four Societies, two in Brighton, one in Worthing, and the sur-viving London Society. In the final number, the estimate was of 300 Societies. By that time there was also an extraordinary flowering of working-class and Radical and co-operative journalism, with *The Associate* and *The British Co-operator* in 1829, *The Co-operative Miscellany* and *The Chester Co-operator*, *The United Trades Co-operative Journal*, the *Herald to the Trades Advocate* in 1830, and so on. The co-operative movement has, ever since, been characterized by its literacy and educational invention. Writing and reading seem to have been an essential part of its practice. It is from these other papers and from ephemera like handbills that the role of prophets can, to some extent, be qualified by the activities of more or less anon-ymous people. Andy Durr has tried to get some way beyond Cole's dramatic

> But in 1830 Bryan, the treasurer, departed suddenly to America, and with Dr King withdrawing owing to family difficulties the movement began to break up. It disappeared in 1832, and a few of its members, taking out their capital, bought a boat and set up as share-fishermen. The rest is silence.

The centenary of the Brighton Equitable Co-operative Society Limited (for which see W. Henry Brown, *Brighton's Co-operative Advance*, 1938, and Sir William Richardson, *The People's Business*, 1986), was celebrated during 1988.

The Brighton co-operatives became a model for many of the early-nineteenth-century co-operative ventures in Britain. William King, writing to Henry Brougham in December 1828, said 'I have had the opportunity of watching every step of the [Brighton] Society, I consider their case proved.'[1]

The Brighton Society was supported by Robert Gooch in an article in the *Quarterly Review*. Robert Southey talked of 'a slip of Owenism grafted upon a sound source of stock'. William King, who largely wrote and published *The Co-operator* from Brighton between May 1828 and August 1830 has been given the mantle of 'Co-operation's Prophet'.[2]

The ideology of *The Co-operator* at its beginning had inspirations quite other than King. It expanded on a Brighton handbill that owed much to a pamphlet written by an American boot-maker, William Heighton – *An Address to the Members of Trade Societies and to the Working Classes Generally*. The handbill was produced by 'some persons of various occupations and trades' in October 1827 by the Brighton Co-operative Benevolent Fund Association:

> Their attention has been directed to the fact that their labour is becoming really more valuable by increased skill, and their power astonishingly multiplied when assisted by the recent contrivances of art; and yet they observe at the same time that the difficulties and uncertainty of procuring a moderate supply of the necessaries of life are gradually increasing.
>
> They see that the real cost of all commodities is the amount of labour employed in preparing them for use; that it is their interest, both as producers and consumers, that there should be the greatest possible quantity of useful articles made with the greatest possible saving of labour; and that different kinds of labour are equally valuable, when they are employed in producing articles that are equally necessary to support life with decency and comfort.
>
> They see that the process called trade, by which commodities now reach the consumer, conceals from every one as much as possible the real cost of production, the quantity of labour bestowed on them.
>
> They see that those engaged in distributing commodities can become rich only by a profit on cost price, and that they are compelled to seek their own exclusive advantage by buying cheap and selling dear: which practice is the very opposite of doing as they would be done by, and has introduced competition into all the transactions of life.

They see that this general competition has the effect of putting human labourers on the same footing as the inanimate objects they work upon, and of subjecting human labour, the source of all wealth, to rise and fall in price, just as the employment of labourers may or may not be found conducive to the profit of those engaged in trading with the produce of their labour.

They have experienced too many changes in the demand for their labour from these causes not to feel alarmed at the uncertainty of obtaining constant employment; and they dread the alternative of claiming the legalized pittance of parish relief.[3]

Parts of King's *Co-operator* were drawn from his observations of the Brighton Society. However, towards the end of the journal's short life, King moved away from the thinking and practice of the Brighton co-operators and allowed other views to develop which would be reflected by Robert Owen in the mid-1830s:

the working classes never did direct any permanently successful operation. . . . Whenever the working class have attempted any important measure that required unity, patience and perseverance to bring it to a successful issue, they have failed in every instance as soon as they have taken direction of it.[4]

King himself claimed that it was his 'paper which raised the societies' throughout Britain in the early nineteenth century. By and large the Brighton story has been seen through King's eyes. But it was not just *The Co-operator* that told the Brighton story; there was a whole range of co-operative journals being published at this time. Here we want to revise King's version of events and see them through the eyes of common people like the cabinet maker William Bryan, the secretary of the Brighton Society. The Brighton co-operatives were born out of the working-class trades societies, the failure of the Mechanics' Institute, and the friendly societies, rather than through the vision of a professional such as Dr King.[5]

I

As Brighton expanded and the different crafts and trades became established during the early nineteenth century, journeymen formed trades clubs, branches of national unions took root in the

13

town, and, in the second decade of the nineteenth century, the different journeymen organizations formed the Committee of Brighton Trades.

During the twenty years following 1808 the Boot and Shoe Makers Society, the Society of Tailors, the United Benevolent Sawyers, the Hearts of Oak Society of Carpenters, the Society of Cabinet Makers, the Society of Bricklayers, the Society of Painters, the Brighton Tin Plate Workers Society and combinations of coach makers, smiths, stonemasons, and plasterers were establishing themselves in Brighton.[6]

During the period of the Combination Acts the picture is necessarily sketchy. The Brighton Tin Plate Workers Society were in dispute with their masters in 1823. The Boot and Shoe Makers was the only society the masters brought to court. In February 1824, just before the repeal of the Act, eight journeymen shoemakers were charged, including James Bellingham, the local secretary. The Blacksmiths Arms in North Street and The Carpenters Arms in West Street were houses of call for journeymen on the tramp, and The Carpenters Arms was used for meetings for most of the building workers in the town. The Brighton Tin Plate Workers Society was part of a national union of tin plate workers, a federation of local societies from 1821 which equalized the union's funds. The Brighton Society supported the tinmen of Wolverhampton during their strike of 1822. The Hammers in North Street was the tinmen's house of call, and men from Brighton tramping, looking for work, turned up in Liverpool. The Brighton tailors, on the death of the Duke of York, came out on strike to gain extra payment during the three weeks following his death, as did the London tailors, and gave the impression of national action to the local press.[7]

The Committee of Brighton Trades was formed in October 1825 with William Bryan, who was to be the leader of the co-operators two years later, as chairman. The Committee of Brighton Trades was composed of delegates drawn from the different trade societies: the sawyers, carpenters, etc. The ideology behind the committee was simple enough: 'no class of mechanic can stand against their masters . . . without pecuniary aid of his fellows, and this can only be done by combination'. The Committee was seen by the local press 'as just one Brighton Union – individual Trade Societies no longer exist'. The Brighton Union in their eyes would force wages higher than the 'income of many clerks and persons in the middling classes of life, who with means much more limited have to support the appearance of gentlemen'. However, when the committee took on board the wider role of co-ordinating the collection of funds for the Bradford weavers, holding meetings of over three hundred journeymen in their support, we find the local establishment saying: imagine Brighton workmen 'subscribing to the funds of workmen who have struck in Yorkshire and imagine how extensive must be the ramifications, and how powerful the machine which can produce effects like these'.[8] Teachers at the new Mechanics' Institute argued at one public meeting, called by the Committee of Brighton Trades, against supporting the Yorkshire men. Philips, a botanist, a member of the committee of the Mechanics' Institute, said 'that most persons present were journeymen, and he would take for granted that they had all the ambition to become masters . . . if, when they were masters [would they like] their servants should thus turn upon them'. Ricardo, another teacher, 'cautioned them against any combination of any kind'. Dr William King agreed with the local press that no union men should be members of the Mechanics' Institute. In his view their 'objects and principles, and proceedings [were] essentially and fundamentally opposed' to those of the Mechanics' Institute. King said of Bryan that meetings of working men 'decide upon pointed evidence . . . judge without inquiry . . . teach without knowledge . . . rouse the angry passions of our nature'.[9]

II

The Brighton Mechanics' Institute had been opened in August of 1825, part of a fast-growing movement started in Yorkshire. At the opening of Brighton's Mechanics' Institute, the aspirations were clear enough; it 'would be [a] beneficial experience, in settling those important discussions now in agitation between the employers and the employed' by the mechanic being educationally 'assimilated with his employer and a partaker of those advantages which his master enjoys'.[10] The Institute was situated in West Street in a converted house. The conversion and equipping of the Institute at first placed it in debt. There were formal classes in writing, mathematics and natural philosophy, geography and the use of the globe, drawing, and modelling in clay; also general lectures were offered in natural philosophy and the use of the air pump, botany, the origin and progress of knowledge, and the gas light. William King, a Vice-President, taught mathematics and natural philosophy. In general, the main thrust of the Institute was useful knowledge, technical and vocational education. In the first few years it was a success.[11] By 1827 there were just under three hundred members; only fifty of these were drawn from the professional and commercial classes, the remainder being skilled journeymen. By far the largest group came from the building trades – bricklayers, carpenters, gas fitters, painters, plasterers, plumbers, etc. Once the Brighton Mechanics' Institute was founded, the expenditure already undertaken, the equipping of the building and the general educational thrust established, the Institute democratized itself. Two-thirds of the committee were drawn from the journeymen. This caused immense problems, as the journeymen had to help manage an organization which they had had no part in establishing. By late 1827 the committee dwindled, leaving mainly the journeymen. By March 1828 the experiment was over and the journeymen issued a little circular:

> that their finances are in a great state of embarrassment. This circumstance . . . does not arise from any defalcations in the present members' payment, or weakness in numbers, but sundry heavy expenses, incurred at the outset of the Institute, by general gentlemen, who at that time constituted the Committee, but who have since been succeeded.[12]

III

By the 1820s most towns and villages in Sussex had self-help organizations of the labouring and artisan classes, with a developed form of democracy and self government, rules of behaviour, and a social life of their own. Such organizations touched the lives of an estimated four thousand families. In Rye the town council borrowed from the Friendly Society; in Worthing the Town Commissioners in the 1820s had a £100 mortgage paying £5 a year interest to the Worthing Friendly Society.[13] In Brighton the general picture was of organizations of charity being provided for the labouring poor, in which they were intended to comply and receive: organizations not of their own, but organized and administered by a kindly and caring group drawn from the middling classes; Elizabeth Fry's District Society, for example, had William King as an important member.[14]

However, Brighton also had a network of organizations of self-help; the Freemasons first opened a lodge – the Royal Clarence – in 1789 and the Royal York opened in 1822. The United Fisherman's Society was started in 1813 to support its members when they could not fish; the Brighton Society of Carpenters, Joiners and Cabinet Makers was a registered friendly society in 1823. There were three other friendly societies formed from 1813 and the friendly society that met at the Old Ship in 1818 had over one hundred members.[15] In 1822 the Brunswick Lodge of Oddfellows was formed and four years later, in 1826, a new lodge in William Street at The Artichoke Inn. The second Brighton Oddfellows lodge was known as the Co-operative Lodge, the first five people being initiated by the Brunswick Lodge in 1826 to form the new one. The Brighton Oddfellows were in the habit of selecting a member of the lodge to open an account at the Savings Bank in Middle Street where lodge funds grew in £10 blocks. The individual account books were then kept in the lodge chest. It was to be over the price of initiation and the use of the Savings Bank that the Co-operative Lodge would come into dispute with the other Lodges of the Unity. In 1827 'the names of all brothers who belonged to the lodge [were] sent to Manchester [and] expelled'. In the same year the new independent Brighton Co-operative Benevolent Fund Association was founded in West Street.[16]

IV

The new Brighton co-operative at first looked to London. They took advantage of the link that many members had with the failed Mechanics' Institute, developed co-operative shopkeeping, set up producer co-operatives and put into practice the concept of exchange. They maintained the role of the friendly society, and continued the work of Brighton Trades Committee, supporting other workers in the country who were in dispute.

The expelled oddfellows started to meet in the Mechanics' Institute, leaving the Artichoke Inn and forming the Brighton Co-operative Benevolent Fund Association, 'the name assumed by workmen of Brighton, who were the first to unite and raise a sum in aid of any one among them who might stand in want of friendly assitance with a small contribution of one penny to threepence a week'. Printers, working men in London, had first embraced the ideas of community that Robert Owen was pursuing during the early 1820s. 'In the pages of the journal, the *Economist* (1821–22) correspondents were continually searching for an answer to the question of how to implement Owen's ideas.' In 1825 a plan was published to establish a community within 50 miles of London at an estimated cost of £20,000. Owen himself launched the scheme which relied on taking out £100 shares. By 1827 it was clear from the pages of *The Co-operative Magazine* that an auxiliary fund set up to fund the project was meeting with little success. However, William Bryan, writing from Brighton, proposed a far less ambitious form of finance through the Co-operative Benevolent Fund Association collective saving. The plan was to save, over a four-year period, with the clear aim of gaining a place for their members in a community.[17]

The Brighton scheme soon attracted over two hundred members: 'persons of either sex', 'agricultural labourers, house carpenters, bricklayers, printers, cabinet makers, turners, painters, gardeners, dress makers, bakers, tailers, tinmen, coppersmiths, shoemakers, bookbinders, grocers, sextants etc' drawn, as Bryan put it, in an early use of class language, from 'the working class in the town'.[18] The co-operators held weekly meetings and in June 1827 a Co-operative Trading Fund Association was started. Members contributed in small payments to buy £5 shares, seventy contributing members in all. At first money was 'laid out in candles, nearly at cost price, and brought the usual profit, by being sold in retail to the subscribers and their families'. They went on to sell mutton, beef, butter, bread and tea. For six months the two organizations, the Benevolent Fund Association and the Trading Fund Association, worked side by side.[19] Between June and December 1827 there were moves by some members of the Benevolent Fund to convert these funds into £5 shares in the Trading Association. This debate caused a split within the Benevolent Fund Association. Some members retained the original position of the association, others the idea of co-operative trading with the collective ownership of the profits for new investment. By the end of December 1827 the latter won the day. Membership dropped off as the subscriptions were raised to meet the new concept of co-operative trading. The two associations merged to form the Brighton Co-operative Society, maintaining the function of self-help born out of the Co-operative

Oddfellows Lodge two years before together with co-operative trading and ideas about producer co-operatives.[20]

In commercial terms the Trading Association started with a turnover of 2s. 6d. and operated out of a room in the Mechanics' Institute. It soon rose to a weekly turnover of £38. By February 1828 the new Brighton Co-operative Society employed their first full-time worker, William Bryan, as agent or storekeeper at the shop; he was paid £1 a week plus his lodging.[21] At the end of February 1828 the Mechanics' Institute failed. The Co-operative Society took over the building two months later, afterwards moving to new premises at 37 West Street 'at a rent of fifty pounds per annum all rates and taxes included'. On taking stock three months later the co-operators

> found, after paying rent, salary and all expenses of meeting-rooms, lights, books and incidental expenses arising from postage of letters etc., that the sum of money we had employed to obtain those results would have yielded us in the Saving Bank less than five pounds and now yielded us thirty pounds.

The *Weekly Free Press* said of the Brighton Society, 'starting twenty-one months ago [it] is now possessed of property by deposits and profits, to the amount of nearly one thousand pounds'.[22] The practice of co-operative trading quickly spread in Sussex. The second store was opened at Worthing in Marine Place, a street where the Freemasons met and the Mechanics' Institute would have its first home. Within a few months there was a branch store at Findon, just north of Worthing. Allen Hide, the secretary, who lived a few houses up from the shop and had lived in Marine Place for many years, wrote of the store in its boom in March 1829 as having fifty-six members, a capital of £150, with a quarterly profit of just under £9. In George Street, Hastings, it was reported, after thirteen weeks' trading, that they had shown a clear profit of £79 and by July 1828 the two hundred members were trading with a weekly turnover of £100.[23]

In Brighton the co-operators were not standing still but setting up producer co-operatives. These were based on ideas long preceding Owen's concept of Utopian communities and nearer to eighteenth-century isolated co-operative ventures at Hull, Oldham, Woolwich, Chatham, Sheerness, and so on, where co-operative bakeries and mills had been formed.[24] Under the watchful eye of the parent body – the Brighton Co-operative Society – the Sussex General Co-operative Trading Association, the Garden Society, Brighton Marine Co-operative Society and the Female Co-operative society were formed.

From the early days of the Benevolent Fund Association the co-operators were men and women labourers, journeymen, artisans and small masters. The different co-operative ventures reflected the needs of the members. A theme that ran throughout was independence from the non-productive classes. For the labourer and journeyman the need was to become his own collective master; for the artisan and small master the need was to do away with middle men. The artisans and small masters first talked about a store where they could exchange articles produced by their own labour at the real cost of production in November 1827. In practice they opened a small shop at 10 Queens Place, which later moved to Cavendish Street, known as the Sussex General Co-operative Trading Association, with the concept of 'unity in business and the general transactions of life'. The co-operators agreed to

> register the names etcetera of all those members who shall
> transact any business with me, at expiration of each quarter,
> allow a discount at the rate of five per cent, from the result of
> such unity, to be given in aid of funds of the association.

In the first month there were a butcher, tea dealers, bakers, shoemakers, and both letterpress and copper-plate printers.[25] The Brighton Society then leased 28 acres of land at Albourne, 9 miles outside Brighton, known as the Garden Society. The land had a small cottage. The Garden Society employed a man and his wife permanently on the land and they lived in the cottage. The man was paid 14s a week, which was 4s above the Sussex rate for agricultural labourers. On different occasions four to five other members of the society were employed at the same rate. They owned 'two cows, two horses and carts and many pigs'.[26] Other co-operators formed the Marine Society and in early 1828 'they built a fishing boat, and employed their own members in fishing. The boat cost them one hundred and forty pounds, has produced at the rate of about four pounds per week clear profit, after deducting all expenses and losses.' The Marine Society concentrated on mackerel fishing; by the end of the first season they started to build another boat; by February 1831 'the co-operative societies of the town [had] . . . three fishing boats which regularly sail from this place'. And the fishing boat *The Co-operator* was still working out of Brighton in 1842.[27] A Female Co-operative Society was formed early in 1829 'consisting of milliners and stain-stitch makers, who had clubbed together and got a shop of their own, at which, when any of them were out of employment they went and worked at baby linen and other articles'. The society was still active three years later.[28]

It would be wrong to imply that all was smooth sailing; the rapid expansion of the different co-operative ventures had its financial strains. The Worthing store was founded with little or no funds. The renting of a shop and the employment of a full-time store-keeper in the first few months, and the added expense of stocking the Findon branch at a cost of £70, nearly brought the co-operative venture in West Sussex to an early end. In Brighton the starting of producer co-operatives drew heavily on the capital; the laying out of £150 for the land of the Garden Society, the early withdrawal of some of their members and their capital to form the Marine Co-operative, all caused temporary financial crises. There were certainly problems in trading when credit was given which upset the cash flow of stores. In 1829 there were bad debts on the trading account of £20 for that quarter, but this has to be seen against the assets of the Brighton Society of over £1,000. In economic terms the Brighton Society required that each member 'spend at least two shillings a week . . . never eat or drink, to wear or consume any article, the profit of which goes to enrich any single individual, if such an article can be procured of any society where the whole receive the equal benefit.'[29]

The Sussex co-operative ventures were in the business of building co-operative communities (Societies) within established society. The Brighton Society was far broader than trading and producer co-operation. Their concept of community included benefits funds 'for the relief of sick and distressed members'. Apart from quarterly business meetings, they met each week; at these meetings they concerned themselves with matters such as collecting money for the striking Kidderminster carpet weavers and complaining about the use of troops as a weapon to 'crush the working classes still lower into poverty and distress'. The co-operative in West Street was open in the evening with a library. They employed a librarian who acted as teacher. They had a social life; the Christmas party 'consisted of a tea party and dance'. The Hastings co-operators held feasts above their store in George Street, eating 'onions in steamed mutton'.[30]

It was on this model of a broad-based movement – women and men, labourer and small master, the shop, distribution of goods, producer co-operatives, relief of the sick and distressed, availability of education, debate on working-class issues and an active social life – that the other English co-operatives based themselves. Two years after the start of the Brighton co-operative, in 1827, William Bryan left for America to form one of the first co-operatives in New York. By June 1829, just before Bryan went to America, societies were formed or forming in Kent, Middlesex, Hampshire, Dorset, Gloucester, Northampton, Worcester, Cheshire, Leicester, Nottingham, Derby, Cambridge, Lancashire and Yorkshire, all acknowledging Brighton as the parent body.[31]

V

A week or so after Bryan left for New York, a process started to write him out of the history of the co-operative movement. The local press implied that he had left in a hurry, defrauding the Society. John Evelyn, writing in 1830, tried to use Bryan as an example to show that working people could not be trusted to run their own affairs. William King would write of Bryan that 'he lost courage and went to America'. Holyoake, in his classic history of Co-operation, picked up this theory which has been used by most historians ever since.

The Brighton Society had an audit of accounts soon after Bryan left for America and stated publicly that there was 'no defalcation in his accounts'. John Evelyn and others had to withdraw their statements. Bryan was writing from America to encourage Brighton folk to join his new co-operative in New York long after William King had given up the idea of co-operation.[32]

A mythology has grown up about William King as the father of the Brighton Society and 'Co-operative Prophet'. In the latest history of the Brighton co-operative movement, *The People's Business* (1936), we are given the picture of Bryan sitting at the feet of King at the Mechanics' Institute. But Bryan was never a student of the Mechanics' Institute and was in conflict with King over trade unions at this time. Attree, who had been a student at the ill-fated Mechanics' Institute and a member of the Brighton Society, at the first anniversary dinner of the Birmingham Co-operative Society in January 1830, 'spoke in high terms of the patient perseverance of Mr W. Bryan' and concluded by proposing his health as the 'Founder of the first co-operative Trading Association in England'. William Thompson, writing in 1830, was clear enough:

> the people themselves took up the idea of co-operative industry, and under the benevolent, enlightened, and unremitting efforts of William Bryan, himself one of the hard-working industrious classes, established in Brighton, Sussex, an incipient modification of co-operative industry, under the name of a Trading Fund Association.[33]

The place of King and Bryan in the history of the common people is classic. King has been given a leading role partly because he claimed one and had a journal in which he could write himself into the story, and partly because he was educated at Ipswich Grammar School, then went to Westminster School, for a short while to Oxford, and then to Cambridge University and then took medicine at St Bartholomew's Hospital.[34] Bryan had little formal education and learnt his trade at the cabinet maker's bench. Bryan by popular vote was an officer of Brighton Vestry; King gained a place on Brighton Town Commission, through internal election. King was part of a caring group of middling people who administered charity on their terms to the poor; Bryan was active in the friendly societies and trade unions. King was comfortable with an income six times larger than Bryan's. King was never a member of any of the Brighton co-operatives; Bryan was. In a nutshell, Bryan was part of the common people and their associations; King was an observer who flirted with the idea of Co-operation as a means of self-improvement of the labouring poor on his terms.

In one of the later editions of King's *Co-operator* he published an article by Rickman, where 'he emphasized the supreme importance of business-like management, proper accountancy, and ready money trading'. He was keen that co-operators should get a 'patron . . . either one of the clergymen of the parish, a resident magistrate or . . . some other respectable and intelligent individual'. The British Association for Promoting Co-operative Knowledge responded,

> Beware of Patrons of any sort – but particularly a clergyman or the magistrate! Beware of such insidious plans for divesting

the members of a co-operative society of all control over their capital and their affairs. These dangerous propositions must be blotted out from the pages of the *Co-operator*, or all future communications in that little pamphlet must be looked on as wolves in sheep's clothing.

William King would write of the movement that: 'the Chartists of the day, the Red Republicans got hold of it, and perverted it to their own purpose'.[35] In reality no one had 'perverted' his ideas, they but maintained the original ideas and practices of 'agricultural labourers, gardeners, bakers, grocers, dressmakers, tailors, shoe-makers, servants, cabinetmakers, turners, printers, bookbinders, tinners, coppersmiths, carpenters, bricklayers and house-painters'. 'The working class in the town', as articulated by Bryan the cabinet maker, resolved that 'we shall do for ourselves', as 'the real cost of all commodities is the amount of labour employed'. This was ideology that had caused them to be called 'Communists or Socialists' by some, a year before King put pen to paper.[36]

NOTES

1 William King to Henry Brougham, 12 December 1828, printed in T. W. Mercer, *Dr William King and the Co-operative Movement 1828-1830*, Manchester, The Co-operative Union, 1922, pp. 199-202.

2 *Quarterly Review*, November 1829, pp. 365-75, Robert Southey to John Rickman, 9 July 1829, printed in C. C. Southey, *The Life and Correspondence of Robert Southey*, London, Longman, 1850, vol. VI, p. 50; T. W. Mercer, *Co-operation's Prophet: The Life and Letters of Dr William King of Brighton with a Reprint of the Co-operator 1828-1830*, Manchester, Co-operative Union, 1947. There have been many accounts of the Brighton story, for example W. Henry Brown, *Brighton's Co-operative Advance 1828-1938*, Manchester, Co-operative Union, 1938; W. Richardson, *The People's Business: A History of Brighton Co-operative Society*, Brighton, Brighton Co-operative Society, 1986.

3 *The Co-operative Magazine and Monthly Herald* vol. II, no. XI, 1827, p. 508, A Fellow Labourer, *An Address to the Members of Trade Societies, and to the Working Classes Generally*, London, Co-operative Society, 1827. The handbill was reproduced in the *Brighton Gazette*, 1 November 1827.

4 Robert Owen, in *New Moral World*, 1837, cited by Mercer, *Co-operation's Prophet*, p. 183.

5 *The Weekly Free Press*, 31 January 1829, 14 March 1829, 28 March 1829, 11 April 1829; *The Birmingham Co-operative Herald*, 1 April 1830;

The Lancashire Co-operator, 25 June 1831; W. Thompson, *Practical Directions for the Speedy and Economical Establishment of Communities on the Principle of Mutual Co-operation, United Possessions and Equality*, London, Strange, 1830, p. 2.

6 *The Trades Newspaper and Mechanics' Weekly Journal*, 30 September 1825, 6 October 1825, 13 October 1825.

7 T. Brake, *Men of Good Character: A History of the Sheet Metal Workers, Coppersmiths, Heating and Domestic Engineers*, London, Lawrence & Wishart, 1985, pp. 53–4, 58, 77; *Brighton Gazette*, 24 February 1824, 6 May 1824; *Brighton Herald*, 13 January 1827.

8 *The Trades Newspaper and Mechanics' Weekly Journal*, 23 October 1825, 30 October 1825; *Brighton Gazette*, 22 October 1825.

9 *Brighton Gazette*, 20 September 1825; *Brighton Herald*, 22 October 1825.

10 *Brighton Herald*, 17 September 1825.

11 *Brighton Herald*, 29 September 1827; *Brighton Gazette*, 2 June 1825, 16 June 1825, 30 June 1825, 28 July 1825, 8 March 1827; *Brighton Guardian*, 3 September 1827.

12 Brighton Mechanics' Institution Account Book, 1827; MS, Brighton Central Library; *Brighton Herald*, 1 March 1828.

13 F. M. Eden, *Observations on Friendly Societies*, London, J. White, 1801, p. 7; J. Tidd Pratt, *A List of Friendly Societies in the County of Sussex*, London, HMSO, 1856; Worthing Commissioners' Book 1820–1831, MS, Worthing Town Hall.

14 *Memoirs of the Life of Elizabeth Fry*, London, 1847, vol. I, p. 468.

15 T. Francis, *History of Freemasonry in the Province of Sussex*, Portsmouth, Henry Lewis, 1883, p. 30; C. Wright, *The Brighton Ambulator*, London, Sherwood, 1818, pp. 116–18.

16 F. White, *Annals of the Brighton District Independent Order of Odd Fellows*, Brighton, Southern, 1911, p. 40.

17 *The Co-operative Magazine and Monthly Herald*, vol. II, no. IV, 1827, p. 225.

18 ibid., vol. II, no. IX, 1827, pp. 418–20.

19 *The Associate*, no. 1, 1829, p. 3; no. 3, 1829, p. 20.

20 ibid., no. 5, 1829, p. 35; no. 3, 1829, p. 18.

21 ibid., no. 5, 1829, p. 33.

22 *The Weekly Free Press*, 28 March 1829.

23 *The Associate*, no. 3, 1829, p. 14.

24 R. Campbell, *Provident and Industrial Institutions*, Manchester, Rechabite, 1924, p. 220; G.D.H. Cole, *A Century of Co-operation*, Manchester, Co-operative Union, 1944, pp. 14–16.

25 *The Co-operative and Monthly Herald*, vol. III, no. IX, 1828, pp. 67–8; *The Weekly Free Press*, 25 April 1829; *Brighton Gazette*, 12 May 1831; *The Associate*, no. 5, 1829, p. 33.

26 *The Associate*, no. 1, 1829, p. 33; no. 5, 1829, p. 33; *The Co-operative and Monthly Herald*, vol. II, no. IX, 1827, p. 418; *The Weekly Free Press*, 28 March 1829; letter from William King to Henry Brougham, 12 December 1828, printed in Mercer, *Dr William King*.

27 *Quarterly Review*, November 1829, p. 370; *Brighton Herald*, 12 December 1831.

28 *The Crisis*, vol. 1, no. 34, 1832, p. 135.

29 *The Weekly Free Press*, 28 March 1829.

30 *The Associate*, no. 3, 1829, p. 18; *Brighton Gazette*, 31 July 1828; *Brighton Herald*, 2 August 1828; *The Associate*, no. 2, 1829, p. 10; E. C. Mayne, *The Life and Letters of Anne Isabella, Lady Noel Brougham*, London, Constable, 1929, p. 322.

31 *The Weekly Free Press*, 25 April 1829.

32 J. Evelyn, *Co-operation. An Address to the Labouring Classes, on the Plans to be Pursued and the Errors to be Avoided in Conducting Trading Unions*, London, J. Souter, 1830, p. 13; *The Christian Socialist: A Journal of Association*, vol. 2, no. 50, 1851, p. 226; G. J. Holyoake, *The History of Co-operation*, London, T. Fisher Unwin, 1906, p. 481; F. Parker, *The First 125 Years*, American Co-operative League, 1956, p. 3.

33 W. Thompson, op. cit.

34 T. W. Mercer, *Co-operation's Prophet*, Manchester, Co-operative Union, 1947.

35 *The Christian Socialist: A Journal of Association*, vol. 2, no. 50, 1851, p. 226.

36 *The Co-operative Magazine and Monthly Herald* vol. II no. XI, 1827, p. 508.

Chapter Three

CHANGE AND CONTINUITY IN THE DEVELOPMENT OF CO-OPERATION, 1827–1844

ROBIN THORNES

Movements make their own myths and monuments, usable in their life and growth. The twenty-eight Pioneers of Rochdale (1844) have become one of the best known of these, commemorated in the Toad Lane Museum (well supported by the Japanese Co-operative movement), a street name in Moscow, bottles of *vin de table* sold in Northern French Co-ops, huge amounts of commemorative pottery, influential all over the world. Their 150th anniversary in 1994 will be a world event. There is a famous picture of thirteen of them taken more than twenty years later, in 1865, which has stood in as an icon for them all. George Jacob Holyoake's much-translated *Self-help by the People: The History of the Rochdale Pioneers*, begun as a serial for the *Daily News* in 1857 (anticipating Samuel Smiles's *Self-help*, 1859), has been the major carrier of the Rochdale story (for its setting within Holyoake's thought, see Chapter 4 of this book). *The History of the Pioneers* has been a usable text, inspiring many societies. The Blaydon-on-Tyne Society began with nightly readings of Holyoake to pitmen and other neighbours of Joseph Cowen: the book features as an inspiration in many of the Jubilee Histories of local societies published around 1900.

Then historians outside movements get interested in them and, for their own reasons, point patiently to what was and was not so. Robin Thornes is one of these, in his Sussex University Doctoral thesis, 'The early development of the co-operative movement in West Yorkshire, 1827–63' (1984). Parallel work has been done by M. Purvis ('Co-operative retailing in England, 1835–1850: developments beyond Rochdale', *Northern History*, XXII, 1986, pp. 198–215). Rochdale was not a discontinuous break: it is possible that Meltham Mills had been giving dividend since 1827 (see G. D. H. Cole, *A Century of Co-operation*, Manchester, Co-operative Union, 1944, p. 67). Paddock certainly did from 1829 and, after the 1840s, every society did not become a carbon copy of the Pioneers. In times which historians like to docket as Political with a big 'P', co-operation went on: in times when co-operation was dominant, politics was still strongly present.

Historians like to flatten changes which flatter activists: this chapter points to real continuities in the detailed history of co-operative formations from the 1820s to the 1840s and beyond.

Getting it straight in a narrative sense, however, is only one of the functions of the historical record. This chapter points in more important directions. Successful movements grow, turn into mighty organizations with their own dominant myths and associational forms. But these have penalties. Big rivers make it appear as though all precedent water is tributary to their own later flood. But it always might have been otherwise: other courses were, and remain, available: other courses, away from the river, will be taken, and may become mainstream. For a long time co-operation as a 'spontaneous', anyway *necessary*, working-class practice was wider than 'The Co-operative Movement' with all its dominant organizations. It remains so today. And all the important conflicts in and around it – about day-to-day dividends versus the whole Co-operative Commonwealth, about humdrum practice *now* versus grand Politics in the interests of *then* ran through the history of Co-operation in Britain from its inception, long before the twenty-eight Pioneers. The practice of working people in the early nineteenth century, as they constructed co-operative forms in impossible, as well as in exciting, political times – and their critique of dominant styles of reform-from-above – remains as an available resource for successors now.

I

It has been usual for historians of the co-operative movement to divide its development into two distinct phases. Sidney Pollard has written that the first phase began

> with the publications of Robert Owen in the second decade of the century, rising to a peak of influence in the years 1828–34 and ending with the failure of Queenwood, in 1846; and the second, heralded by the foundation of the Rochdale Pioneers' Society in 1844, registering an expansion around the year 1850 and becoming established about ten years later.[1]

The first phase is generally regarded as being Owenite; trading and manufacturing ventures being embarked upon for the purpose of raising capital to finance community experiments. The second phase is one of societies trading on the Rochdale system of dividing surplus among the membership according to the amount of their purchases; retaining a commitment to the replacement of competitive society by a co-operative commonwealth.

It is to this version of the history of Co-operation that the movement has adhered for over a hundred years, tracing its line of descent from the Rochdale Pioneers rather than from the societies of the 1820s and 1830s. The consensus regarding the position of these Rochdale co-operators was summed up by Isa Nicholson, in her *Our Story: History of the Co-operative Movement for Young Co-operators* (1924):

> Rochdale is looked upon by co-operators all over the civilised world as the birthplace of co-operation, in the sense of which we know it. . . . Some old societies have claimed that they traded on the same principles as the Rochdale Pioneers many years previous to the opening of the store in Toad Lane; but these were little heard of, and have made no mark in history, and, as it is from the rules and methods of the Rochdale store that the great bulk of present day societies have copied, we quite rightly regard that as our first co-operative society, and the men who started it as the pioneers of modern co-operation.[2]

I shall argue that this division of the early history of the co-operative movement is simplistic. At no time in the first half of the nineteenth century was Co-operation a movement in any but the loosest sense of the word. It was adopted and adapted to meet the specific wants and needs of groups of working men who founded societies. As a result, co-operative ventures took a variety of forms, most of which were, to a greater or lesser extent, represented within the movement at any time in its development.

II

The origins of the co-operative movement are, indeed, traceable to the early writings of Robert Owen. In these Owen formulated a critique of competitive capitalism and advocated the creation of villages of unity and mutual co-operation – communities in which the inhabitants would receive, by direct exchange, the full value of their labour. First advocated as a means of dealing with unemployment and pauperism, he came to see in communities the key to the creation of a rational and equitable society. Co-operation, the act of working together to a common end, was, from the early 1820s onwards, to denote this alternative form of social organization.

Although his schemes were aimed principally at the labouring poor, it was not to them that he looked for the millions of pounds he regarded as necessary to realize his plans for large, rurally located, self-supporting communities, but to wealthy individuals and governments. Owen's conception of community was not shared by all those he influenced. Among these were small groups of working men, not content to play the passive role he had assigned to them. One such was a group of journeymen printers which gathered around George Mudie in London, in 1821.[3] Mudie differed from Owen in that he believed that communities could be built up gradually on limited means. To this end he advocated the purchasing of provisions and other necessities on the wholesale market as a means of saving money, which in turn could be added to a community fund.

These London co-operators argued that the principle of Co-operation, even when employed with the aim of making savings in the purchase of food and clothing, could be of great benefit to the working-class, it being

> susceptible of so many modifications, as to be capable of being brought to bear upon almost any supposed circumstances. In some cases the benefits of such co-operation could only be partially attained; but still something might be gained. Wherever Friendly Societies or Benefit Clubs exist, the members would do well to form themselves into Associations, for the purpose of devising modes in which they can reap any of the advantages held forth in the above plan. In some cases, it might be merely practicable to unite a portion of their earnings for the purchase at the best markets, of certain articles of provisions or clothing.[4]

To these working-class co-operators, Co-operation meant the act of co-operating one with another for mutual benefit, rather than a closely defined system of the kind being evolved by Owen. They saw Co-operation as the means of creating communities and as the principle upon which communities would be conducted. Co-operation could be any collective action on the part of working people to raise and employ a common capital for the purpose of conferring economic benefit on the individuals participating. From this advocacy of co-operative purchasing it was only a short step to the co-operative store.

This step was taken six years later when co-operators in London and Brighton established stores, the profits of which were to finance community experiments. One London co-operator, putting the case for co-operative trading, argued that capital raised 'by profits on trade' had the advantage of not putting 'the parties concerned to any expense'.[5] The advantage of the co-operative store from the point of view of working-class co-operators was that

> it is not an enthusiast calling on the rich to subscribe towards a scheme for amending the condition of the poor but the workmen themselves are the prime movers: and, secondly, the means required are within the power of the labouring-classes in every town in the kingdom.[6]

The spread of Co-operation was assisted by the propaganda of the Co-operators of London and Brighton, through their respective organs, the *Co-operator* and the *Associate*, and through the activities of the London-based British Association for the Promotion of Co-operative Knowledge. The fruit of this activity was a rapid increase in the number of co-operative retail societies. At the close of 1828 the *Co-operator* listed only nine trading associations. By August 1830, when the last number of that journal appeared, it was claiming that there was some three hundred.

In May 1831 the first congress of the co-operative movement was held. The principal objective of the co-operators who organized the congress was community, it being resolved:

> That this congress considers it highly desirable that a community, on the principles of 'MUTUAL CO-OPERATION, UNITED POSSESSIONS, and EQUALITY OF EXERTIONS, and of the MEANS OF ENJOYMENTS' should be established in England as speedily as possible, in order to show the practicability of the Co-operative scheme.[7]

When the delegates of the societies met for their second congress, in Birmingham in October 1831, the question of community was again high on the agenda. On this occasion they went further, resolving 'that a council be now appointed to carry out the resolution of the first congress'.[8] When the committee responsible for arranging the scheme reported back to the London Congress in the following year, only two societies had responded to the committee's circular.[9]

In the view of a large number of societies, particularly those in the Midlands and the North, the priority was to expand their activities from retailing into manufacturing. In a letter to the London Congress the co-operators of Rochdale called for the establishment of 'a national Co-operative manufactory':

> our society wishes to urge the utility of bringing the following subjects before the Congress – first the establishment of a Co-operative woollen manufactory. As the Huddersfield cloth, Halifax and Bradford stuffs, Leicester and Loughborough stockings, Rochdale flannels &c. &c. require in several respects similar machinery and processes of manufacture, might not these societies be brought to work together, on co-operative principles, and procure mutual advantages not attainable by separate establishments.[10]

A selection of goods manufactured by co-operative societies was displayed at the London Congress by Thomas Hirst of Huddersfield, foremost among which were textiles:

> I have on my back a Co-operative shirt, and here's a Co-operative coat, and here's a Co-operative waistcoat (loud laughter). All my friends have Co-operative clothes; and for my own part, I would sooner go without clothes at all, than be clothed in any other way; so strong an advocate am I for co-operation.[11]

Hirst's enthusiasm for the proposed co-operative community, was, in contrast, somewhat lukewarm. That is not to say that Hirst and his fellow northern co-operators were opposed to the idea of community *per se*. Owen's ideal of self-supporting, purpose-built communities in rural settings seems to have been regarded by a significant section of the movement as neither practicable nor desirable. Their preferred version of community was one in which their existing communities evolved into co-operative ones. The society in the West Yorkshire weaving village of Cumberworth, for instance, hoped to see 'a manufacturing community arising up amongst us, as we should have no doubts of its success'. They did not, on the other hand, have such good hopes of an agricultural community succeeding amongst a manufacturing population. Neither did they see the necessity of engaging in agriculture when they would always be able to 'command the produce of land in any market by their manufacturing goods'.[12]

Several delegates to the second congress in 1831 were, like Mandley of Birmingham, worried 'that there were many societies which were clearly not Co-operative', and that these would, in time, 'clash together, and be almost inferior to the common benefit societies'. The Reverend Marriott, of Warrington, put it more bluntly when he declared that 'nearly 99 out of every 100 societies were still ignorant of the principles of Co-operation'. William Thompson, of Cork, believed that 'it is very important that we should not have different doctrines being preached, and for this purpose there should be one code of Co-operative doctrines which may be referred to'. Thompson suggested that the movement's lecturers should be supplied with the works of the communitarian theoreticians, Owen, Morgan, Grey, and himself. This was successfully opposed by Marriott, who argued

> that in the writings of Mr Thompson, as of those of Mr Owen
> and Mr Morgan, there are opinions which we do not hold in
> common, and if they do not give offence to our brethren,
> they do to the rest of mankind, who will be glad by any
> means to strike us down. Many of our societies' laws (as Mr
> Thompson observes), are at variance with each other; for
> instance the absurd laws of dividing, and others among
> societies not favourable to community.

Marriott urged the necessity of the movement's asserting its independence of any individual, Owen included, arguing that he 'would have it go forth to the world what are the opinions, not of Mr Owen or another person, but of the Co-operative Congress'.[13]

Marriott's speech reflected the views of those co-operators who accepted the economic analyses of Owenism but rejected those related to religion and the family. *The Co-operator* and the *Co-operative Magazine* dissociated themselves from Owen's views on those subjects, the former denouncing him for 'having pretended to doubt the real truth of the Gospel', and the latter failing to understand what it saw as his 'religio phobia'.[14] Thomas Hirst 'thought the less Co-operation associated with peculiar abstract doctrines, the better'. He felt sure 'that many were driven from Co-operation by supposing it to be a system of infidelity'.[15] Some were angered by Owen's undemocratic behaviour. Benjamin Warden, of the first Western Union Society (London), contrasted the democratic constitutions of the co-operative societies with Owen's autocratic rule of his Institution – the former being 'based upon a perfect equality of rights among their members; and every officer was chosen by universal suffrage, through the medium of the ballot', while the latter was 'a perfect despotism . . . whose movements depended entirely on the will of one man'.[16]

By the autumn of 1832 the first flush of enthusiasm for Co-operation had already faded. The growing number of failures resulted in a weakening of the influence of those remaining over the communitarian movement as a whole.

As the influence of the trading societies dwindled, labour exchanges were advocated as a means of inculcating into working men the practice of Co-operation, and as sources of finance for communitarian experiments. Initially they were not advocated as an alternative strategy to the stores, but as complementary to them. The question of labour exchanges was discussed at the London Congress of April 1832. The delegates resolved in favour of them. It is significant, though, that only thirteen of the fifty-three societies at Congress had ever discussed the principles of exchange.

One of the most influential champions of the labour exchange was Owen. As early as 1820 he had suggested that labour be made the standard of value, and currency based on the labour standard had been used in his community at New Harmony, Indiana, in 1826. In September 1832 he opened a labour exchange in Gray's Inn Road, London, the profits from which were to be used to finance a community. Owen was later to dismiss the exchanges as having been a mere bagatelle. But it was probably with some relief that he took the opportunity offered by the labour exchange to take a leading role in the movement again and, more particularly, to achieve the personal power which the co-operators had denied him. The delegates of those societies which supported the congresses had successfully established them as a mouthpiece for their movement, a mouthpiece which was democratic and independent of all other contemporary movements. But with the decline in the number and, therefore, the influence of the trading societies, the congresses became less a reflection of the views of those societies which survived. Henceforth the paths of the co-operative societies and those

of Owen and hs followers were to diverge, as these two strands of
the communitarian movement developed along different lines.

III

The decline in the fortunes of the co-operative movement was par-
alleled by that of the agitation for Radical (parliamentary) reform.
The co-operative movement was divided on the question of Radical
reform, including in its ranks those who believed reform to be a
precondition of a more sweeping transformation of society, and
those who felt that it would treat only the symptoms of society's ills.
Speaking at the London Congress, in April 1832, the Reverend
Marriott expressed the latter view, arguing that

> whatever views a Radical Reformer might entertain relative to
> the benefiting of society, it was morally impossible he could
> ameliorate the condition of mankind so far as the Co-operator,
> who acted upon a system that embraced the whole human
> race; a system that acknowledged all men to be the creatures
> of circumstance, and forgave the failings of every one, from
> the king to the poorest peasant.[17]

The belittling of the importance of political agitation by co-
operators like Marriott annoyed the Radicals and provoked the
Poor Man's Guardian to declare 'our opinions of Co-operation are
well known. We admire the principle, but we despise the shallow
conceit which would carry it into practice, without pre-existing
materials.' Co-operation, it claimed, 'was utterly impracticable
under the existing laws, or any form of Government other than a
Government of the people'.[18] Such criticism did not, however, prevent co-operators and Radicals from working together at a local
level, overlaps of membership between Radical associations and
co-operative societies being common. In Yorkshire, the case of Peter
Bussey, of Bradford, who combined involvement in the agitations for
parliamentary and factory reform with his posts of land official in the
National Association for the Protection of Labour and secretary of
Bradford Moor Co-operative Society, was probably not untypical.[19]
The officers of one society in the Halifax area went as far as to ask
prospective members 'Are you a real Radical Reformer?'[20]

With the passing of the Reform Bill the Radicals were left without any immediate objective. In this malaise they sought to map out new battle lines of class interest. The Reform Act had brought enfranchisement to sections of the shopkeeping community, and it was towards these new voters, characterized as the 'shopocracy', that the Radicals now turned their attention.

> All that is mean, and grovelling, and selfish, and sordid, and rapacious, and hard, and cold, and cruel, and usurious, belongs to this huxtering race. . . . To screw all they can out of poverty and weakness, and to seduce all they can out of powerful vice, is the grand business of their lives.[21]

It was suggested in the Radical press that shopkeepers should be asked if they were members of political unions, and if not then they should be boycotted – a variation on the already tried and tested weapon of exclusive dealing. It was not uncommon in the early nineteenth century for groups of working men to exert pressure on shopkeepers, particularly in local and parliamentary elections, to follow an approved course of action, on threat of their businesses being boycotted if they failed to comply. In the Oldham election of 1832, for example, Radicals used this threat to secure the election of their candidates:

> The enemies of reform are everywhere alarmed at the non-electors adopting exclusive dealing. The nation and your enemies know the immense power of the working classes. . . . Therefore, working men, if you wish well to yourselves, lay out your money with those electors of Oldham who support . . . Fielden and Cobbett. . . . The electors franchise is a trust to be used for your benefit; and not a right to be used against you.[22]

A new twist was given to the campaign, however, by the announcement, in September 1833, that at a meeting in London it had been decided 'to form a Co-operative Body of one hundred members for Exclusive Dealing and helping each other in sickness'.[23] One correspondent to the unstamped *Voice of the West Riding* took up the idea:

> The evil that I complain of is people buying their groceries and all other kinds of goods at the shops of their enemies, for such they have proved themselves to be, nearly on every

occasion, they are the enemies of the Trade Union. They have opposed the enfranchisement of the people, they are the foes of Co-operation, and when a contest takes place between the aristocracy and the working-classes we always find the shopocrat in the ranks of the aristocrat. . . . Now Co-operative shops at Halifax and Huddersfield have all kinds of goods necessary for the people, and at reasonable prices.[24]

Through their campaign against the 'shopocracy' the Radicals provided the working-class with another motive for forming co-operative societies. It was to bring Radicals, in substantial numbers, into the co-operative movement, with important consequences for that movement's future development.

There were those in both the Radical and co-operative camps who regarded the stagnation which had set in within their respective movements by 1833 as a purely temporary phenomenon, and who looked forward to an imminent revival of their fortunes with millennial anticipation.

Some imagine that all is still, the stillness is not death but transformation: the new 'movement' is almost invisible, but yet a little while and it will burst on an astonished world like another moon rising at mid-noon. . . . Co-operation and political knowledge are about to give a glorious emancipation to the producers of wealth, and really conduct us into a new age.[25]

In their debilitated state the co-operators and Radicals came to pin their hopes on the trade unions. The rapid growth of the movement, and its apparent preparedness to acknowledge him as its leader, impressed Owen, who soon came to see it as a vehicle which he could use to bring about the transformation of society. The often proposed and long-awaited general trade union became a reality in February 1834 with the founding of the Grand National Consolidated Trade Union. The GNCTU was, however, weakened from its inception by the numerous strikes and lock-outs which it inherited. In the face of the difficulties experienced by the union in supporting members already on strike, it soon became evident that concerted action in the form of a general strike was out of the question.

The co-operators had from the outset been opposed to the use of the strike weapon, which they believed to be a costly and inefficient way of utilizing union funds. It would, they argued, be better for unions to use their funds to finance co-operative manufacturing ventures. Thomas Hirst summed up this view when he told an audience that he disapproved of strikes 'except the men turned out for good, in order to work for themselves'.[26]

In 1834 the idea of adopting co-operative manufacturing as a means of combating unemployment or sustaining striking workers appeared an attractive proposition. On 24 May the *Leeds Times* printed an account of such a co-operative among the textile workers of Huddersfield:

> the men of Huddersfield are forming themselves into a society for the express purpose of manufacturing on their account. Indeed, it may be a consolation to those who think a redundancy of hands an evil, that many men who have been turned out of employment have clubbed their savings, and commenced on their own account, and have orders from various parts of the country for more cloth than they with their present arrangements can supply.[27]

The article concluded with a call to the Leeds textile workers to follow the Huddersfield men's example. This they were not slow to do. The *Leeds Times* reported a fortnight later on a similar scheme called the United Joint Stock Trading Company.

Nationally, sectional strikes took their toll of the GNCTU. Owen's fundamental opposition to the methods employed by the unions, and his often-stated belief that the interests of masters and men were one and the same, made him a far from ideal leader for a body which was fighting for its very existence. Increasingly vocal among his critics at this time were the editors of the *Pioneer* and his own paper, the *Crisis*.[28] Faced with a rapidly collapsing union and mutiny in the *Crisis* office, Owen responded by abandoning the GNCTU, closing down the *Crisis*, founding a new paper (the *New Moral World*), and greeting the dawn of the Millennium.[29]

Owen's lack of concern at the collapse of the labour movement was rooted in his dislike of that which he could not control. In May 1835 he founded the Association of all Classes of All Nations, the object of which was to

> carry into practical operation the system of society propounded by Robert Owen – not the views which this or

that individual may have formed of that system – but Robert Owen's own view of it, and under his immediate direction.[30]

Owen had, to all intents and purposes, washed his hands of the co-operative societies – excluding them from the family circle of Owenism. The *New Moral World* admitted their kinship, as distant relations:

> In recent numbers of this publication we have given accounts of the various societies which have been established, in order to obviate some of the evils of competition; societies wherein community of property has more or less been carried into effect, and where, consequently, the cares of possession, the fears of loss and the grovelling anxieties respecting mere sustenance have been almost utterly annihilated. Societies of this description, which still retain many of the fundamental errors of old society, may now be considered in the relation of extended family circles.[31]

IV

In April 1835 the co-operators of Halifax hosted the last co-operative congress of the first series. Only eleven societies sent delegates, all of whom represented Yorkshire societies.[32] Weakened by the failure of a great number of societies and estranged from Owenism, the movement was by no means dead. Aims were pursued in isolation, or, at best, in loose local association, lacking a national leadership and their own press.

Reports in the Radical press do, however, show that a significant number of societies did survive, and that new societies were established. On 12 August 1834 the *Voice of the West Riding* reported that the committee of the Halifax Society had recommended the immediate purchase of two looms and a spinning jenny and that others be bought when required. In the following month the Knaresborough Society announced that in its first year of trading it had turned over £410.[33] In May 1835 the 1st Bradford Society could still muster eighty to ninety members for its anniversary dinner.[34] In the following March the Clayton Society opened a new shop. The *Leeds Times*, writing of its progress, reported that

> This society consists of one hundred members, 'good men and true', who by the assistance of an agent, purchase and

retail to the members and neighbourhood nearly all the
necessities of life, and its benefits and utility have been
responded to by the grateful feelings of the industrious
poor.[35]

The Huddersfield Society also continued to prosper.[36]

That there continued to be a commitment to the co-operative
idea among sections of the working class is evident from the records
of the Registrar of Friendly Societies. On 30 July 1834 an act of
Parliament was passed amending the law relating to friendly
societies. This act extended the scope of friendly society legislation
to include all societies established for 'any other purpose that is not
illegal', provided that the rules of those societies were certified by
the Registrar as being in conformity with the act. This meant that it
was possible for co-operative societies to enrol under it and gain,
for the first time, legal recognition and a degree of financial security.
The first Yorkshire society to take advantage of the change was the
Huddersfield Co-operative Trading Association, which enrolled on
4 July 1838.[37] In 1839 six Yorkshire societies enrolled, a further six
in the following year, and no less than eighteen in 1841.[38]

The majority of societies in this period divided their profits
according to share capital held. This meant that, as most societies
permitted members to hold only one share, profits were equally
divided between all full members. The most important exception
to this rule was the handful of societies known to have paid their
dividends according to the amount purchased at the society's store
by individual members. The credit for the introduction of dividend
by purchase has been traditionally given to the Rochdale Pioneers,
although by the end of the nineteenth century it was recognized
that a number of societies had employed this method of distributing
profits prior to the establishment of the Rochdale society. At a
meeting of the 1st Western Union Society (London) in April 1832,
those present discussed 'the propriety of altering their laws so as to
allow a percentage to every member in proportion to the amount
of his dealings'.[39] In West Yorkshire at least four societies, all
within the Huddersfield district, were dividing their profits according
to purchases a number of years before the establishment of the
Rochdale Society. The rules of the Paddock Society (enrolled in
1839) are the oldest surviving Yorkshire ones which state that dividend
on purchase was employed.[40] This society anticipated the Rochdale

40

Pioneers in their making interest (at a rate of 5 per cent per annum) on all loans, subscriptions, and donations, the first call on profits; the remainder of the profits, if any, were then 'to be equally divided among the members according to the amount of monies paid for the purchase of goods, by each individual member'.

In attempting to explain the failure of earlier co-operative ventures and the success of the Rochdale Pioneers society it has been usual, since the time of Holyoake, to lay at least part of the blame for the failure of the former on their allowing members credit, and the success of the latter on its insistence on ready money trading. It is certainly true that the majority of societies founded in the 1830s and early 1840s did allow credit; but this was done only in cases of extreme necessity and even then in a strictly controlled way. Most societies would allow a member in need credit up to the amount of his subscription, or, in some cases, up to two-thirds of it. The members were, therefore, only receiving their share of the common capital and did not become debtors to the society. This was no more than a recognition that if members could not get credit when they needed it then they would be forced to withdraw their entire share. The system was one which Holyoake, writing in 1857, professed not to oppose.[41]

The rule books of those societies which survived the collapse of the GNCTU, or were established subsequent to it, give an insight into the reasons those who founded societies had for becoming co-operators. The Ripponden co-operators prefaced their revised and enrolled rules (1839) with a statement of the circumstances which had motivated them to found their society (in 1832).[42] Starting from the premises 'That labour is the source of all wealth', and that 'consequently the working-classes have created all wealth', they concluded 'That the working-classes, although the producers of wealth, instead of being the richest, are the poorest in the community; hence, they cannot be receiving a just recompense for their labour.' In order to rectify this situation they believed it necessary to seek 'the attainment of independence by means of a common capital'. This capital was to be raised, firstly, 'by a weekly subscription to a common fund'; secondly, by co-operative retailing, the profits being added 'to form an undivided stock'; thirdly, 'by employing its members as circumstances admit'; and, lastly, 'by living in community with each other, on the principle of mutual Co-operation, united possessions, equality of exertions, and of the means of enjoyment'. The ultimate objective of the Huddersfield Society (founded 1829, enrolled 1838) also remained that of community, as the preamble to the Society's 1838 rules made clear.[43]

Such commitment was not restricted to societies established in the years before 1834, the rules of a number of societies founded after that date also having the same preamble, verbatim, as that of the Huddersfield Society.

The majority of societies whose rules have survived, however, made no mention of either community or co-operative manufacturing. The rules of the Carr Green Society, for example, saw its purpose in vaguer terms: to promote 'the interest and comfort of the society, individually and collectively'.[44] The two neighbouring societies of Kirkheaton and Colne Bridge (founded in 1835 and 1842 respectively) share identical rules, which declared their objective to be

to raise a capital sufficient for the purpose of food and rainment at the wholesale market and retail them out to the members and other customers at the lowest possible price in order to give to industry as large a share of its products as the present exigencies of the country will admit.[45]

They intended to give to labour a greater share of its 'products' through the distributive rather than through the manufacturing process.

V

The late 1830s witnessed a revival of the labour movement; this being particularly marked in the north of England, where the combination of a severe trade recession, coupled with the ill-timed introduction of the New Poor Law, provided ideal conditions for a new agitation for more sweeping parliamentary reform. The conditions which favoured the growth of Radicalism, and which were, in 1838, to lead to the creation of the Chartist movement, also benefited Owenism. There is evidence that Owenites, at a local level at least, recognized the value of co-operative retailing. In November 1839 the Owenites of Oldham reported to the *New Moral World*:

Some time ago we held several meetings to consider the propriety of establishing a shop, on Co-operative principles, for retailing and distributing wealth. . . . Accordingly we opened an establishment in Yorkshire Street for the general and retail business in groceries and provisions. . . . This was three months since and I am happy to inform you, that so far there is every prospect of success. We shall this week open a branch of it in another part of town. The funds were raised in shares of five shillings each. Since we opened our premises . . . several candidates have joined our branch every week, most of whom have taken shares in the store, which is the best proof that can be afforded, that the unremitting exertions of the socialists to improve the state of society are duly appreciated by the inhabitants of this district.[46]

This was the only report of its kind ever to appear in the paper. The Chartist paper *Northern Star*, on the other hand, carried regular reports on the progress of co-operative ventures. In May 1840 one of its Bradford correspondents announced that 'The socialists of this town have opened a Co-operative provision store, in a large and spacious room under their institution. We wish them every success in their undertaking.'[47] No mention of this store was ever made by the Bradford socialists in their otherwise detailed progress reports to the *New Moral World*. It is possible that these Owenites recognized that co-operative societies no longer had any place in Owen's scheme of things and therefore forebore from making any mention of their store.

The reports of co-operative societies' progress printed in the *Northern Star* showed that some continued to maintain a deep commitment to the cause of social, economic and political reform. The wide scope of the commitment of the Huddersfield Society for example, is illustrated by the range of toasts proposed at the society's annual festival on New Years Eve, 1837:

'The Huddersfield Co-operative society, and may it flourish and increase, and answer the end intended'. 'The people, the producing people; the source of all wealth'. 'The principles of Co-operation', 'Robert Owen, Esq., the Friend of Co-operation'. 'Richard Oastler, Esq., the Persevering Friend of the Factory Child, and the Advocate of the Ten Hours Bill'. 'May Temperance and Sobriety increase till all the People become intelligent'. 'John Fielden, Esq., the patriotic member for Oldham'. 'Feargus O'Connor, Esq., and may the principles of

Radicalism advance'. 'G. S. Buckingham, Esq., the Persevering Advocate of Temperance and Civil and Religious Liberty'. 'The Liberty of the Press'. 'The Friends of Co-operation all over the world'.[48]

Sympathetic as they were towards Chartism, the co-operators of Huddersfield continued to stress that their movement was, potentially, of more importance to the working class than any agitation for political reform. Only through Co-operation, they maintained, could a complete social revolution be achieved. Co-operation, and the welfare of the individual society in particular, still came first. They saw their society as representing continuity, stability of organization, and fixity of purpose, it having

> stood all the changes which have agitated the political and social
> world; while system after system, union after union, have
> risen up and passed away like the fleeting meteor through the
> air showing but a momentary gleam of hope to the care-worn
> and benighted operative, then leaving him more desolate than
> before.[49]

When the Chartist delegates assembled in London in February 1839 for the movement's first National Convention, one of the first problems that faced them was what action to take in the event of Parliament's rejecting their petition for the six points of the Charter. A committee was appointed to examine the question of what 'ulterior measures' should be contemplated. Reporting back in May, the committee recommended a number of measures, including a run on the banks, a general strike, arming, and dealing exclusively with shopkeepers known to be Chartists. At a Chartist meeting in Bradford on 30 June, it was resolved

> That we view with feelings of regret the apathy and
> indifference manifested by the middle-classes of this country
> towards the interests and welfare of the working-classes, seeing
> as we do, that they derive their subsistence from the profits
> arising out of our dealings with them in the necessary articles
> of subsistence, and do solemnly declare that henceforth we are
> determined to give support to those persons only who are
> friendly to the principles of justice for which we contend.[50]

It was inevitable perhaps that Co-operation, as an extension of the principle of exclusive dealing, would recommend itself to the

Chartists, as it had to the Radicals before them. As early as April 1839 the *Northern Star* reported that a co-operative store with Chartist connections had been established at Hull, and that this would 'be the means of bringing the shopocrats to their senses'.[51] At an illegal meeting in Huddersfield in August, members of the co-operative society used the platform to extol the merits of Co-operation. One of them, George Barker, argued that under capitalism the nation's wealth

> went to the money mongers, it went to all the wholesale and retail dealers, to those who live by buying cheap and selling dear. They saw that those were the greatest enemies of liberty, and yet they . . . supported those individuals. His plan would be to cure this, that in every town and village they should establish shops of their own. Let fifty or a hundred of them unite and put their 10/- or 20/- together . . . and with the profits lay them up until they become independant labourers.[52]

In Dewsbury the local Chartists founded a 'Joint Stock Co-operative Society' with the declared intention of securing for its membership 'a commercial independence of the middle man'.[53] The shop premises of this society were to be used in the following five years as one of the principal venues for West Riding Chartist delegate meetings.

The co-operative principle took particularly firm root among the Chartists of the north-east, the local leaders in both Durham and Northumberland becoming enthusiastic advocates of Co-operation. In September 1839 the *Northern Liberator* carried a report of a speech made by the Sunderland Chartist James Williams to the Durham County Charter Association, on the subject of exclusive dealing.[54] Williams used the occasion to recommend to his fellow Chartists the adoption of Co-operation:

> Co-operation is the most practical form of exclusive dealing. This would (if the people had been sufficiently disinterested and determined) have been the speediest means of working out our political regeneration. Let this be employed in establishing grocery and provision, drapery, hardware and book and news stores, it will place us in a position in which we can battle with the wholesale merchants, the great commercial gods.

In Newcastle the council of the Northern Political Union founded the North East of England Joint-Stock Company, which, despite its name, had the characteristics of a co-operative society. The prospectus of the company declared its objective to be to enable the individual member 'to obtain all his necessaries of life of the very first rate quality, at the very lowest price; and at the same time realising a profit to himself'. In order to make it easier for working-men to become full members relatively quickly the capital was to be raised in shares with a fixed value of 10s, with a maximum shareholding of fifty per member. The democratic principle maintained by the voting was not to be according to shares held, each member was to have 'one vote and no more'.[55] Thomas Devyr, speaking at a meeting of the North East Joint-Stock Company, dwelt on the potential of the combination of Co-operation and the Charter for bringing about the emancipation of the working-class:

> They could purchase coalfields in which to employ those men who were persecuted by their present tyrants. They could build ships, employ sailors and give the famishers of London a cheap fire. They could become possessed of estates, and if any of them, through disease or misfortune, came to destitution, it would be easy for the company to locate him in a neat little cottage, with its garden of vegetables, fruits, and flowers . . . and this system be carried out on an extended scale, and it would at once sweep social misery and political tyranny from the face of the land, and make idle schemers do honest labour for their living.[56]

The failure of the Chartist insurrections in Wales and the north of England in the winter of 1839–40 seriously weakened that movement. In the absence of any lead at a national level the Chartists began to formulate their own responses to the new conditions at branch level. The general trend was for branch activities to become increasingly diversified; this diversification leading, in some areas, to the evolution of what amounted to a Chartist subculture. This process was, in part, the result of official harassment and persecution, which had the effect of making Chartists wish to be as self-sufficient as possible. A feature of this subculture was the way it adopted and adapted the institutions of the organized working class for its own ends and needs. It expressed itself in such forms as Chartist chapels, bands, benefit societies, temperance societies, also in the form of Chartist co-operative societies.

There were those in the Chartist body who were sceptical of the value of expending energy in the formation of co-operative societies. The Newcastle Working Men's Association warned

> That neither Trade Unions nor Co-operative societies of any description can be in any measure productive of relief to the suffering millions, unless so far as such unions and societies exercise the advantages of their organisation to obtain the Charter.[57]

Despite such misgivings, interest in Co-operation among the Chartists continued to grow. With the possibility of a renewal of the agitation still remote, and with physical force discredited for the time being, Co-operation remained one of the few avenues of activity still open to them. In the spring of 1840 the *Northern Star* carried an increasing number of reports of co-operative activity. In March it was announced that the Chartists of Stockport had founded a co-operative society, the intention of which was to give 'one half of the clear profits . . . to the Chartists prisoners in Chester, and their families'.[58] In May the paper reported a tea-party held by a co-operative at Stainland, in Yorkshire, at which those present were addressed by a number of speakers, including the Chartist preacher Ben Rushton.[59] The toasts offered on this occasion left no doubt as to where the origins and sympathies of the society lay: 'The Radical Co-operative society of Stainland, and may its principles spread far and wide until the Charter became the law of the land'.[60] A report from Manchester on a recently opened store showed that exclusive dealing continued to be a powerful motive behind Chartist interest in Co-operation:

> it is now well understand the best mode of convincing the shopocrats of the justice of the People's Charter is to keep our money out of their tills; the profits of which have been the lever by which they have long held us in bondage, and which used by ourselves, will in the end work out our salvation.[61]

The same issue of the *Northern Star* carried a report on the progress of the recently founded Bradford Chartist Temperance Co-operative Society, the very name of which exemplifies the fragmentary and diverse nature of Chartism in that period. This Bradford society is of particular interest because it is a rare, possibly unique, example of a co-operative society which also functioned as a Chartist association in its own right, sending delegates to district meetings and acting as local agent for the *Northern Star*.

The year 1840 was the high water mark of the first period of Chartist involvement in Co-operation. In the following five years news of Co-operative societies continued to appear in the Chartist press, although with by no means the same frequency as in the years 1839 and 1840. It is difficult to say whether the *Northern Star*'s near silence on the subject of Co-operation was indicative of a decline in interest in it on the part of the paper, or among Chartists at a grass roots level. A tailing-off of interest among Chartists in 1841 might be explained by the fact that the political agitation was renewed in that year. Reports of the activities of co-operative societies gave way to ones on new Charter Associations. Co-operation, which had owed its success among the Chartists to the political defeat of 1839 may have been a victim of the revival of the agitation in 1841–2.

In the following five years new co-operative societies continued to be founded, but in nothing like the numbers that they had been in the years of active Chartist involvement in the movement. In West Yorkshire, for example, the flood of new co-operative societies founded in 1839 and 1840 was reduced to a trickle, only three societies enrolling under the Friendly Societies Act in 1843, and a further three in 1844.[62]

VI

The year 1844 has gone down in the annals of the English labour movement as the date when modern Co-operation was born. It was in this year that the Rochdale Pioneers opened their now famous Toad Lane store. It is, however, questionable whether the Pioneers' society did, in fact, mark a significant departure from the main trends within Co-operation in the 1820s and 1830s. The idea that the co-operative movement in those decades was essentially different from that of the 1860s is largely based on the misconception that the movement in the early period was an Owenite one, committed to the creation of communities, which died out about the time of the collapse of the GNCTU in 1834, and that the modern movement came about as the result of the founding of the Rochdale Society in 1844. The origins of the present co-operative movement are traceable, without any significant break in the line of descent, back to the societies of the 1820s. Further, the decade 1834–44, far from being one of virtual inactivity, was a period in which Co-operation became more deeply entrenched as a strategy of the labour movement, and one in which the organizational form of retail co-operative later characterized as the Rochdale became firmly established.

NOTES

1 S. Pollard, 'Co-operation: from community building to shopkeeping', in A. Briggs and J. Saville (eds), *Essays in Labour History*, London, Macmillan, 1967, p. 74.

2 I. Nicholson, *Our Story: History of the Co-operative Movement for Young Co-operators*, Manchester, Co-operative Union, 1924, p. 32.

3 See J. M. Bellamy and J. Saville (eds), *Dictionary of Labour Biography*, vol. 1, London, Macmillan, 1972, pp. 249–50.

4 *Report of the Committee Appointed at a Meeting of Journeymen, chiefly Printers, to Take into Consideration Certain Propositions, Submitted to Them by George Mudie*, London, 1821, p. 6.

5 Pollard, op. cit., p. 82.

6 *Fortnightly Review*, November 1829.

7 *Resolutions Passed at the First Meeting of the Co-operative Congress, held in Manchester . . . May, 1831*, bound in *Co-operative Congresses: Reports and Papers, 1831–32*, resolution 7.

8 *Crisis*, 5 May 1832.

9 *Proceedings of the Third Co-operative Congress held in London . . . on the 23rd April, 1832 . . .*, London, 1832, p. 121.

10 ibid., p. 123.

11 ibid., p. 92.

12 ibid., p. 49.

13 *Proceedings of the Second Co-operative Conference held in Birmingham, October 4, 5, and 6, 1831, and Composed of Delegates from the Co-operative Societies of Great Britain and Ireland*, Birmingham, 1831, pp. 6, 5, 8.

14 *The Co-operator*, 1 July 1830; R. G. Garnett, *Co-operation and the Owenite Socialist Communities in Britain, 1825–34*, Manchester, Manchester University Press, 1972.

15 *Proceedings*, London 1832, p. 118. Thomas Hirst was one of the best-known co-operative missionaries of the period. His style of oratory was described as 'peculiar yet animating', capable of creating an 'extraordinary sensation', *Lancashire and Yorkshire Co-operator*, n.s., no. 1. For a fuller account of Hirst's life in the co-operative move-ment see R. C. N. Thornes, 'The early development of the co-oper-ative movement in West Yorkshire, 1827–63', unpublished D.Phil. thesis, University of Sussex, 1984.

16 ibid.

17 *Proceedings*, London 1832, p. 100.

18 *Poor Man's Guardian*, 28 June 1834.
19 Bussey is named as the secretary of the Bradford Moor Society in the statistical tables appended to the proceedings of the Birmingham Congress. Kirby and Musson mention that he was an official of the National Association for the Protection of Labour (R. G. Kirby and A. E. Musson, *The Voice of the People: John Doherty, 1798–1854, Trade Unionist, Radical and Factory Reformer*, Manchester, Manchester University Press, 1975, p. 257).
20 *Proceedings*, London, p. 6.
21 *Poor Man's Guardian*, 17 August 1833.
22 J. Foster, *Class Struggle and the Industrial Revolution*, London, Methuen, 1974, p. 53.
23 *Poor Man's Guardian*, 7 September 1833.
24 *Voice of the West Riding*, 12 October 1833.
25 ibid., 28 September 1833.
26 *Halifax and Huddersfield Express*, 24 March 1832.
27 *Leeds Times*, 24 May 1834.
28 The editor of the *Pioneer* was James Morrison, and that of the *Crisis*, James 'Shepherd' Smith. Owen attempted to gain control of the *Pioneer*, but, having failed, launched his own journal: *The Official Gazette of the Executive Council*. Smith attacked Owen for his handling of the whole affair: 'how miserably have these pecuniary transactions been conducted ever since they were taken out of the hands of the Pioneer. . . . From the day that that paper and its conductors ceased to be the agents of the Unions, everything has been mismanaged', *Crisis*, 12 July 1834.
29 *Crisis*, 23 August 1834.
30 *New Moral World*, 17 October 1835.
31 ibid., 23 April 1836.
32 A. Pahlman, 'The rise and fall of the Northwest of England Co-operative Society', *Co-operative Review*, July 1935, p. 211.
33 *Leeds Times*, 7 March 1835.
34 *Voice of the West Riding*, 24 May 1835.
35 *Leeds Times*, 7 March 1835.
36 O. Balmforth, *The Huddersfield Industrial Society Limited: A History of Fifty Years Progress*, Manchester, Co-operative Wholesale Society, 1910, p. 24.
37 *Rules of the Huddersfield Co-operative Trading Friendly Society*, Huddersfield, 1838.
38 PRO, F.S.2/11, Index of West Riding Friendly Societies.
39 *Poor Man's Guardian*, 7 April 1832.
40 PRO, F.S.1/811, Rules of the Paddock in Huddersfield Co-operative Trading Association.
41 G. J. Holyoake, *Self-help by the People: The History of the Rochdale Pioneers*, 1857, reprinted London, Sonnenschein, 1893, p. 56.
42 J.H. Priestley, *The History of the Ripponden Co-operative Society*, Halifax, 1932, pp. 31–2.
43 *Rules of the Huddersfield Co-operative Trading Friendly Society*, p. 6.

44 PRO, F.S.1/817/336, Rules of the Carr Green Co-operative Trading Friendly Society.
45 PRO, F.S.1/818/349, Rules of the Colne Bridge Friendly Society, PRO, F.S.1/1819b/423, Rules of the Kirkheaton Co-operative Trading Society.
46 *New Moral World*, 30 November 1839.
47 *Northern Star*, 9 May 1840.
48 ibid., 1 January 1838.
49 *Rules of the Huddersfield Co-operative Trading Friendly Society*, p. 3.
50 *Northern Star*, 7 July 1839.
51 ibid., 6 April 1839.
52 PRO, H.O.40/5/463, Huddersfield Magistrates to Russell.
53 *Northern Star*, 12 October 1839.
54 *Northern Liberator*, 7 September 1839.
55 ibid.
56 ibid., 21 September 1839.
57 *Northern Star*, 6 June 1840.
58 ibid., 14 March 1840.
59 ibid., 2 Mary 1840. Rushton was a handloom weaver by trade. He preached for the Methodist New Connexion for a period. He was actively involved in the anti poor law agitation, and, later, in the Chartist movement. See E. P. Thompson, *The Making of the English Working Class*, 1963, reprinted Harmondsworth, Penguin Books, 1968, pp. 437–40. F. Peel, *Spen Valley Past and Present*, Heckmondwike, 1893, pp. 317–19.
60 *Northern Star*, 2 May 1840.
61 ibid., 22 February 1840.
62 PRO, F.S.2/11, Index of West Riding Friendly Societies.

Chapter Four

GEORGE JACOB HOLYOAKE: SOCIALISM, ASSOCIATION, AND CO-OPERATION IN NINE-TEENTH-CENTURY ENGLAND

PETER GURNEY

Holyoake's long life (1817–1906) consisted of committed, critical engagement with many nineteenth-century creeds. One of the most important of these was Secularism, not touched upon here: E. Royle's work is invaluable on this, for instance in *The Infidel Tradition*, London, Macmillan, 1976. Holyoake's views on three of these creeds, Owenism, Co-operation, and Liberalism, are the subject of this chapter.

In recent years social historians have tended to portray Holyoake as the archetypal labour aristocrat, motivated by the desire for respectability. T. R. Tholfsen, for instance, has contended that his 'unexceptional radicalism' was 'well adapted to cultural patterns that tended to assimilate and deradicalise the principles of the early-Victorian Left' (*Working-class Radicalism in Mid-Victorian England*, London, Croom Helm, 1976). In this schema, Holyoake becomes an agent of working-class 'incorporation' into the dominant bourgeois culture. He has been labelled 'a good bourgeois democrat' by a labour historian (Royden Harrison, *Before the Socialists*, London, Routledge & Kegan Paul, 1965). His most recent American biographer, L. Grugel, *George Jacob Holyoake: A Study in the Evolution of a Victorian Radical*, Philadelphia, Porcupine Press, 1976, has rehearsed such views uncritically, reading the intentions of middle-class patrons of Co-operation as if they were the reality of the working-class movement itself.

This chapter challenges such interpretation. It begins a disinterment of Holyoake and the co-operative movement from the 'labour aristocracy' debate which will be carried further in Peter Gurney's Sussex Doctoral thesis, forthcoming in 1989. It sees Holyoake's life and thought as a continuous attempt to theorize and to mobilize working-class self-activity, advising the people, in William Thompson's phrase, to 'become, as you may be, the fabricators of your own destiny'. Social reform from above, for Holyoake, was *in principle* different from collective self-help, and it was worth fighting for the distinction in movements and with words. This meant that the state was a problem for his project, rather than an opportunity: so much so that late in his life he was prepared to ally with 'individualists', because they were statists and not managerial collectivists. Communism, Association, Co-operation, were key words for someone who, as his first biographer, McCabe, suggested, 'kept all the breadth of the Owenite ideal in his mind' all his life. He was a good bourgeois democrat only in the sense that he was always trying to push democratic forms beyond the limits currently acceptable to the bourgeoisie, of whom he was not one. Whether he had Robert Owen, Ferdinand Lassalle, Karl Marx, or Sidney Webb in his sights, he struggled against the intentions and the effects of those who 'ridicule the dwarfish efforts of the slaves of wages to transform capitalist society'. Holyoake never accepted dominant forms of capitalism, and was never at ease in what he called a 'rascal system': as a 'deliberate liberal', there was no reason why he should be. Liberalism was more serious than that. 'We live in a society of thieves', he wrote in a pamphlet on *The Logic of Co-operation* in the 1870s, 'who competition licences to plunder; and he who does it most adroitly is said to have "great business capacity".' The continuity in his thought was the theory and practice – against this – of 'association', a notion which united all the radical creeds Holyoake espoused and for which he drew on Mazzini and Blanc as well as on English culture.

For nineteenth-century co-operators, Holyoake was a figure to respect and to love – the Grand Old Man of the movement who devoted much of his life to emancipate the class he had sprung from, and in ways directly related to his earliest Radical Owenism. After he died in 1906 the very large sum of £25,000 was collected by local co-operative societies to erect a monument to his memory. In 1911 Holyoake House, a centre for federated administration and learning and the headquarters of the Co-operative Union, was opened in his memory.

I

In 1848, the year of the European revolutions and the great Chartist demonstration, George Jacob Holyoake was editing the *Reasoner* from London and helping William Lovett set up the society of 'Friends of All Nations League' at the John Street Institution. The uprisings in Italy, Poland, Austria, and most of all France, had a profound effect on him and exposed him to new ideas and strategies: 'He began to realise that England was part of the map of Europe, and that the dream of revolution as a short-cut to the golden age was not quite ended.'[1] Inspired by these events, Robert Buchanan and Lloyd Jones started a weekly paper called *The Spirit of the Age* in the summer of 1848. Thoroughly Owenite in tone, it gave space to the ideas and practices of continental, and especially French, socialism. Holyoake edited it from November until its demise in March 1849.

It was at this critical juncture that he encountered the ideas of Fourier, Proudhon, but more importantly, Louis Blanc and Giuseppe Mazzini. Blanc headed the provisional government in France after the 1848 revolution and was involved in the establishment of national workshops in Paris in that year. He was known chiefly for his work entitled the *Organisation of Labour*, published in Paris in 1848 and translated immediately into English. *The Spirit of the Age* recommended it enthusiastically.[2] Blanc advised the provisional government to set up 'social factories' ('ateliers') and provide workers with the instruments of their labour. These factories, after a period of about a year, would pass into the hands of the workers, to be run on democratic lines, after they had understood the usefulness of the principle of 'association'.[3] Blanc advised the social and democratic party to take subscriptions in support of the enfranchisement of working men, and place this fund at the disposal of associations of workmen, so they themselves could establish 'ateliers' if the government failed to act.

The concept of 'association' was crucial in Blanc's work. In French the word had a more ominous ring than in English, as it described not only the action of combining together for a common purpose or cause, or a group of people so combined, but was also specifically located within Fourier's socialist critique of society.[4] Although Holyoake supported the European revolutions enthusiastically, he was aware of the dangers of their dependence on violence rather than reasoned argument. He recognized that in a despotic country, where even the most basic civil liberties had not been secured, there was little alternative.[5]

In England, the principle of voluntary association could triumph peacefully. In the spring of 1849 he wrote a series of articles in the *Reasoner*, using the pseudonym 'Ion', on the subject of association, in which the direct influence of Blanc on Holyoake's intellectual development was evident. He commenced the series by pointing out that owing to the failure of Owenism in England and the degeneration of the Parisian republic, 'communism' in both its senses had been discredited: in the Owenite sense referring to the idea of 'community' and the establishment of 'communities'; in the

French sense originating in the secret societies that sprang up under the July monarchy of Louis Philippe (1830–48), and implying secret, conspiratorial, and violent overthrow of the state.[6] Although the prospect looked gloomy, friends of communism could 'work for Association'. Holyoake emphasized that the ultimate goal, communism – the holding of all goods and land in common, full equality – had not been forgotten. It was the context that had changed: 'The statement of the "Communistic Question" upon reflection, I prefer to attempt under the head of "First steps of Association", commencing with the desirability of co-operative and fraternal action.'[7] 'Association' was to be a transitional phase, replacing the word 'socialism': 'Socialism is not despised by the poor – who are well-informed enough to recognise their old friend with its new face, "Association" '.[8] Leading eventually to 'communism': 'Communism only differs from the Association beginning to be recognised in the press . . . in this, that it is a more enlarged and comprehensive form of co-operative life.'[9]

This theory of the transition was later articulated by another old Owenite, Dr John Watts, who became an important influence on J. T. V. Mitchell and the CWS, in a series of articles in the *Co-operative News* in 1871. Watts contrasted the selfish and existing 'competitive state' of society with that 'perfect state of society' described by the term communism. He went on to explain that 'between these two extremes of society, retaining the individualism of the first, while rendering possible some of the advantages of the second, stands the new phase introduced by co-operation'.[10]

II

Who was Holyoake and why did he find 'association' so attractive? Born in Birmingham in 1817, his father, George Holyoake, worked in the Eagle Foundry; his mother, Catherine Groves, was a very independent woman who ran a domestic button-making business. He attended a dame school at the age of seven, and later went regularly to a Wesleyan Sunday School until he was fifteen. Starting work with his father at the foundry at the age of nine, he became a skilled whitesmith and the foreman of a shop. From 1834 to 1840 he attended classes at the Mechanics' Institute where some of the best teachers were staunch Owenites. A contemplative and intelligent young man, he worked hard to educate himself within the educational culture of voluntary association.

In October 1840 Holyoake became a 'stationary-lecturer' in Worcester; the following year the Owenite Congress assigned him 'Social Missionary' to the diocese of Sheffield on a salary of 30s per week. Owenism appealed to Holyoake because it looked forward to the replacement of the competitive system with the new 'social system' of co-operative communities, where goodwill and harmony would replace struggle and self-interest. The social system organized on alternative principles of political economy, or 'social science' as the Owenites called it, would be remodelled, becoming truly 'social'. It has been suggested that Holyoake's experience of the Birmingham workshops was that of a close, fairly harmonious relationship between masters and men, and that this coloured his later political attitudes.[11] The opposite was in fact the case. It was in the small workshops that proliferated around Birmingham that Holyoake first made contact with the harsh world of industrial capitalism. Looking back fifty years later this experience was still very clearly in focus:

> The employer, by finding the men work, thought them under obligation to him; sympathy for them was little in his way. He indeed kept the wolf from the door, but like the wolf-dog, he bit them if they turned aside. Over the whole plain of labour and trade you saw society in conflict: Neither giant nor feudal lord were any longer there; a new tyrant reigned in their stead, more omnipresent and pitiless than they – whose name was Capital.[12]

Holyoake was also attracted, by personal temperament and political judgement, to the Owenites' commitment to non-violent social change:

> Persons favourable to the organisation of the social state, whom Robert Owen had incited to action, came to be called 'Socialists' . . . . Continental Socialists meditated rearranging society by force. There never were in England any philanthropists of the musket or the knife. English Socialists expected to improve society by showing the superior reasonableness of the changes they sought.[13]

As Holyoake stated throughout his life, he was himself a socialist in the Owenite sense, and he never rejected or tried to obscure this heritage.

If the Owenites eschewed violence as a method of changing society, how was this to be effected? The answer lay in education. Holyoake continued to be an 'educator' in the widest sense until his death; lecturing, writing, editing newspapers. Some of his earliest published works were intended to help working people in their efforts at self education.[14] The Rochdale Pioneers, of whom many were Owenites, were lauded by Holyoake particularly because they assigned a portion of their profits (2½ per cent) to the education of co-operators even when it was illegal to do so.[15] One of his last works was concerned solely with co-operative education.[16]

The Owenite critique of women's oppression also left its mark. Holyoake was critical of the Chartist demand for universal male suffrage, and although he supported it, as he later supported other limited political demands, he saw it for what it was – a compromise. Years after his Owenite 'phase', when standing as a parliamentary candidate for Tower Hamlets in March 1857, he advocated married women's independent property rights, not achieved in law until 1881.[17] In the summer of the same year he published a series of articles in the *Reasoner* on the 'Civil Freedom of Women', which consisted of lectures delivered previously to the women of Glasgow. They reveal a very keen sense of female oppression couched in uncompromising language:

> A wife is a negro – she may be shut up and flogged. She cannot even run away. As there is a Fugitive Slave Law in America, so there is a Fugitive Wife Law in England – which compels the wife to be given up to her husband, however brutal he may be: she is his 'property'. The husband is the policeman of his wife.[18]

He exposed the hollowness of an encroaching anti-associationist domestic ideology, when applied to working-class women:

> Do not believe a word about the reserve and ease of 'women's duties', and the romantic luxuries of 'women's sphere'! This may be all very well with the rich, but it is not so with the poor. Women are addressed as angels before marriage, and are made drudges afterwards.[19]

57

In the early 1840s Holyoake was often in conflict with Owen and the Central Board. Between December 1843 and December 1844 Holyoake was editing *The Movement* with the London engraver and member of the Lambeth branch of the Rational Society, M. Q. Ryall. In this paper he pointed out that in attempting to appeal to all classes the new Owenite Executive had committed a serious blunder. He recommended the establishment of a 'working man's community'.[20] The Owenites could not achieve everything at once, he continued, and must concentrate their efforts on those members of society most in need of help. The problem was that the 'community' at Queenwood was constructed and imposed all at once, from above. In the autumn of 1844 Holyoake visited Harmony Hall and published his observations in a series of articles in *The Movement*:

> Even Mr Owen, the last thing he said was, 'I doubt the power of the working classes (from their necessarily contracted knowledge of things) to manage beneficially their own affairs, or to carry on the Harmony experiment successfully.' Now it will be to libel the working classes to ascribe the failure of Harmony to them. If fail it should, it will not be through the 'contracted knowledge of the working classes', so much as through the distracted condition in which the capitalists have left it, who not only expended, in a nearly useless manner, all the money the working classes subscribed, but mortgaged all they can now raise in the shape of debts, they, the capitalists left unpaid.[21]

He railed against the Executive – a 'paternal despotism' – and hoped his pamphlet would quicken a necessary principle in the Rational Society: 'I desired to awake the Society from the sleep of paternal despotism, and open the Argus eyes of democracy.'[22] Two years later he was still driving the lesson home; comparing Owen's obsession with upper-class patronage and change from above, with his own predilection for working-class self-activity, a preference reinforced no doubt by his own roots in a vigorous artisan culture. These two approaches had been confused within Owenism, and 'the error was that they ever met'. He summarized the differences thus:

> The desire of self-government and the independent control of common means, and the reduction to practice of absolute

equality on the one part, and the class control and class distinctions on the other, were the respective badges of the differing parties.[23]

Such convictions were deeply rooted in Holyoake's mind prior to his contact with continental ideas concerning association.

III

When Blanc and Mazzini were exiles in London in the 1850s, Holyoake became the good friend of both, and helped them with financial appeals in the pages of the *Reasoner*. In 1853 he published a pamphlet entitled *Organisation; Not of Arms but of Ideas*, which incorporated some of the notions he had become acquainted with over the preceding five years. This work was chiefly concerned with the creation of political organizations, parties, but was also tentatively directed to the problem of building any voluntary association. Mazzini's theory of the party which stressed the importance of principles, aims, and instruments was approved, and Holyoake cited the Secularists as evidence. Proceeding, he argued that the associative life changed the individual member for the better: 'As the soldier is always known by his bearing, so should he who is in association. The mark should not be an air put on, but a result coming out of special purpose.' The 'associate' should be disciplined in speech, manner, and dress, concerned with self-improvement. The associative life had to be learnt and practised like military discipline, and took time. He went on to detail the nature of the associative relationship, and he was referring not merely to individual improvement but to the improvement (in the sense of elevation and liberation) of a whole class, through a restructuring of social relations:

> Let him who takes an associate, at the same time understand that he takes a master. It is equally true of marriage, of friendship, as of confederation. Companionship implies the intention of mutual service, service includes mutual submission. . . . Organisation is a vow; it involves a plan of life.[24]

A few years later Holyoake praised the Rochdale Pioneers because 'they had discovered the art of holding together, and of managing their own affairs'.[25] Gradually during the 1850s Holyoake became more and more interested in this particular branch of associational endeavour, which was expanding rapidly. As 'Co-operation' became increasingly widespread and popular amongst working-class people, so Holyoake took up its standard, and spent much of the remainder of his life theorizing Co-operation as association.

'Co-operation' was often used in Owenite discourse, regularly coupled with 'community'. In 1817 Owen used the term 'Mutual Co-operation' in a letter to the *London Newspaper*, and in 1824 William Thompson, a major theorist of Owenite 'social science', contrasted 'Labour by co-operation opposed to labour by individual competition'.[26] 'Mutual Co-operation', the combination of a number of persons for purposes of economic production and/or distribution, entailed fellowship, support and equality – it was *mutual*. It would make the greatest number happy, solve the problem of wretchedness and pauperism, and offer a truly 'social' education. 'Individual Competition', on the other hand, isolated individuals, fractured 'society' into competing groups thus denying humanity's social nature, depended on 'force and fraud', engendered oppression. In 1827 Thompson advised the 'industrious classes' to build 'Communities of Mutual Co-operation', in order to 'remove some of the evils of isolated exertion and Individual Competition'.[27]

In 1851 Holyoake advertised the Central Co-operative Agency on his lecture tours. He concentrated most of his energies on Secularism during this decade, but newspapers he edited gradually paid more and more attention to Co-operation. Towards the end of 1858, and especially during 1859, Co-operation began to figure prominently in the pages of the *Reasoner*. A weekly feature entitled 'Co-operative News' appeared, which presented details concerning the growth of Co-operation throughout the country. A weekly supplement was published in 1860 called the *Reasoner Gazette of Co-operative and Secular News*. In 1858 Holyoake published his first study of Co-operation, *Self Help by the People: History of Co-operation in Rochdale*. This book rapidly became a best-seller and key-text for the movement, was translated into Spanish, French, Italian, German, and Hungarian, and according to McCabe it took : 'Co-operative inspiration all over the civilised world'. It was reprinted thirteen times between 1858 and 1907. Henceforth, until his death in 1906, Holyoake worked tirelessly to promote the cause.

Co-operation directly addressed the crucial problem faced by the working class as Holyoake saw it; the necessity of securing their own capital. It is here that his own debt to William Thompson becomes most apparent. Thompson had argued that in order to achieve emancipation from 'individual competition', the 'industrious classes' must accumulate their own capital and use it for their own purposes – to buy land and machinery in order to employ them-selves, in communities. The fundamental division of capitalist society, that between capital and labour, would thereby be transcended, the labourers now becoming 'capitalist-labourers'. Thompson ex-pressed this in a memorable passage:

> It has been shown to you that the fatal disseverance of capital from labour and skill, and the consequent ignorance of the industrious, have led to the monstrous systems of force, fraud and competition, (when free, the worst species of exertion), engendering enormous inequalities of wealth, the parents of almost all the crimes and vices that desolate society; and that it is necessary for human welfare to reunite capital and labour, to render all the industrious 'capitalist-labourers', labourers possessing all the materials and implements necessary to render their labour productive.[28]

Holyoake had studied Thompson's text in the winter of 1841 and voiced his appreciation of this work more than thirty years later:

> Where every step was new and every combination unknown, Thompson wrote a book like a steam engine, marvellous in the scientific adjustments of its parts. His *Distribution of Wealth* is the best exposition to which reference can be made of the pacific and practical nature of English Communism.[29]

Holyoake's commitment to the idea of creating 'capitalist-labourers' coloured all his activities in the co-operative movement. It implied that the working class must do things for themselves, that self-help, not in an individualist, Smilesian sense, but as a method of elevating a whole class, should be practised. There was no need to wait for the millennium, the egalitarian society of the future could be built and assume prefigurative form in working-class associations, most importantly in the co-operative societies. Working-class capital had to be used wisely, and this principle underpinned Holyoake's attitude to the trade union movement. He argued consistently, in classic Owenite fashion, that trade unions were beneficial in many respects, but that they did not challenge capitalism fundamentally because they misused their capital, wasting funds on strikes. In 1869 he read a paper at the Trades Council Congress in Birmingham on 'Industrial Partnerships', in which he advocated profit-sharing in capitalist enterprises in order to reduce conflict and increase profits. When Thompson's notion of the 'capitalist-labourer' is borne in mind this becomes intelligible as something other than bourgeois incorporation. Profit-sharing entailed a recognition of the fact that all profit should not go to capital and its owners, that labour also deserved its share – that the wage-system was essentially fraudulent. The extra bonus labour would receive could be accumulated in a central fund and eventually used to set up co-operative workshops and manufactories.[30] Convinced that wage-labour was a transient and historically specific form, limited to the epoch of competition, profit-sharing and co-operative production would point the way towards a new mode of economic organization: 'When profit-sharing workshops come to prevail as stores do now, co-operation will sensibly determine the future of the working-class by superseding hired labour, and terminating the precariousness of competitive renumeration.'[31]

The importance he placed on working-class independence was always central in his co-operative ideology. It was to lead him into antagonism to state socialism from the 1880s onwards. What men like Ferdinand Lassalle, Karl Marx, and Sydney Webb had in common, in Holyoake's opinion, was a desire to change society from above, by capturing the state machine and driving it down the socialist track. Not only that; 'they ridicule the dwarfish efforts of the slaves of wages to transform capitalist society'.[32] For Holyoake, socialism had to be voluntary. He attacked the state socialists in the same spirit as he had criticized Owen in the 1840s:

> the ambition of co-operators is to reach that condition in
> which they shall be under no obligation to charity, to
> philanthropy, to patronage, to the capitalist or the State, nor
> need the dubious aim of revolution. Their ambition was not
> to be taken care of by the rich, but to command the means of
> taking care of themselves.[33]

Owenites had never countenanced the violent overthrow of the state, and Holyoake pointed this out repeatedly in his later life:

> The State is ponderous, unsympathetic and slow to move,
> except on behalf of property. Sometimes Socialists talk of

accelerating the pace of the State by force; but that is the language of despair which ceases to have meaning in the face of hope.[34]

This suspicion, which Holyoake never lost and which was shared by many other co-operators, helps explain his misgivings concerning direct involvement by the co-operative movement in parliamentary politics, aired at the 1890 Congress.[35] Legislative change through the state was not enough for him. To Holyoake, very sensitive to the changing meanings of words, 'Co-operation' in the last quarter of the nineteenth century bore more relation to the Owenite socialism of the 1820s–1840s, because of its voluntary nature, than did the state socialism developing in the 1880s and 1890s. In fact over a period of about half a century, 'co-operation' had replaced 'socialism' in its original English sense:

> the co-operative scheme is no recent invention in opposition
> to the new Socialism – for 'new' Socialism it is since
> Co-operation was known as 'Socialism' sixty years ago. . . .
> The policy of co-operation now was its policy then.[36]

Holyoake was insistent on this point, and his remarks make the division of his career into an early Owenite phase and a later co-operative, reformist phase, misleading. The project remained the same, the emancipation of the working class through their own efforts. What had now changed was the historical context – this cause was now progressing under the banner of Co-operation. 'We have had many religions in England, but only one religion of industry, whose name is Communism – the first article of whose creed is Co-operation. This creed does not want priests but it wants preachers'.[37] As 'association' had been a transition phase, so Co-operation, as the most successful example of the associative principle, came to be equated with this phase. Holyoake maintained that communism was re-born in Rochdale, through the efforts of the Pioneers:

> The Rochdale Pioneers founded a new form of Co-operation;
> their inspiration was Communistic. . . . Their intention was to
> raise funds for community purposes. It was because they had
> these aims that they provided for education. They carried
> participation into the workshop, as their object was the
> emancipation of labour from capitalist exploitation. They had
> no idea of founding a race of grocers but a race of men.

Communism suffered incarnation in their hands, and the new birth was the co-operative store; still that was much.[38]

Co-operation was an attempt to build 'community' although plans for 'communities' were now subordinated to the creation of stores, libraries, workshops, farms, newspapers. An oppositional and emergent culture which enshrined the concept of 'community' was being actively and imaginatively constructed, and Holyoake maintained this faith in 'community' all his life. Writing in 1893 he stated:

> An English community, as the followers of Robert Owen understood it, was a self-supporting industrial city, distinguished by common labour, common property, and common means of intelligence and recreation. These communal cities were to be examples of industrialism freed from competition. In the communal life an ethical character was to be formed in the young and impressed upon adults, and all assured education, leisure and ultimate competence . . . this was the first systematized social conception in which I believed, and believe no less in it still.[39]

IV

Holyoake chose the title of his autobiography, published in 1893 when he was seventy-six years old, very carefully. He had originally intended to call it 'Adventures of a Propagandist',[40] but decided finally in favour of *Sixty Years of an Agitator's Life*. The self-description 'agitator' is important. The word means an agent who acts for others, usually to keep up a political agitation, and was first used during the English Revolution.[41] 'Agitators' were elected by the rank-and-file of the New Model Army in 1647 to protect their interests from the authority of the generals. They represented, along with the Levellers, the most radical-democratic force within the Army.[42] The word still carried subversive overtones in the late nineteenth century. According to *The Times* it had been 'agitators' who had caused the disturbances on 'Bloody Sunday' in 1887.[43] The term fitted Holyoake. The obituary which appeared in *The Daily News* noted this characteristic:

> He was a born agitator, but everything about the man's life shows he was an agitator not from mere turbulence of nature

or a vulgar hankering for notoriety. He travelled over the country a good deal, and became widely known as one of those agitators who are bent on turning the world upside down.[44]

Holyoake's involvement with co-operation from the late 1850s did not cause him to ignore parliamentary politics, or the necessity of political reform. He had been an active Chartist and was voted on to the Executive in 1852. In 1857 he stood unsuccessfully as parliamentary candidate, against a 'stationary Liberal', for Tower Hamlets, supporting residential suffrage, the ballot, triennial parliaments, equal electoral districts, married women's independent property rights, and the foundation of Home Colonies, a scheme for settling the poor and unemployed on waste lands.[45] He took part in the agitation preceding the Second Reform Act of 1867, and in 1865 was voted vice-president of the Reform League, a predominately working-class organization. He stood for Parliament again in 1868 as an independent labour candidate, against both Liberals and Tories in Birmingham, but failed to be elected. His third and final unsuccessful election attempt was in Leicester in 1884, when he stood as a Gladstonian Liberal.

Holyoake's political trajectory has usually been seen as complementary to his interest in co-operation – yet another area of incorporated compromise. In 1908 McCabe wrote: 'To a modern mind, with a vague knowledge of political history, it seems to be a swift and long stride from Chartism to Liberalism. Yet the transition was an easy one'.[46] He has been labelled a 'good bourgeois democrat' by a modern labour historian.[47] This label raises more problems than it solves. Holyoake did believe that political change could be achieved through parliament, but such an opinion can hardly be understood as essentially bourgeois. Here I can only attempt, very schematically, to pinpoint some of the tensions between Holyoake's variety of liberalism and that of the party politicians. The path from Chartism to Liberalism was not an easy one, but rather fraught with dilemmas, disappointments, and conflicts. In each movement he was in, Holyoake stood his own ground.

The middle-class composition of Parliament was clear to Holyoake, and he was well aware of the inequalities of power and wealth this Parliament sanctioned and upheld: 'The fact is we have

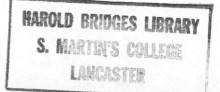

a middle-class Parliament, and not a Parliament of the people at all. The tone, the talk, the interests consulted in the House of Commons are essentially middle-class',[48] he wrote in a pamphlet in 1865. Parliamentary politics was the reserve of a single class which legislated 'class laws' in its own interests. The unenfranchised working-class men and women needed their own voice if Parliament was to become 'a Parliament of the people'. The passage continued: 'Now and then some piece of legislation is executed for the benefit of the people, but it is the act of "patrons" and not of "delegates".' The problem was that members of Parliament were 'not the servants of the people'. This was the kernel of Holyoake's political ideology; the resolution that working-class independence and self-provision was as crucial in politics as it was in the areas of production, distribution, and education. 'Capitalist-labourers' would, ideally, produce, distribute, and consume their own goods, knowledge, and politics. 'Patrons' would not be tolerated.

In the same pamphlet he strongly attacked the notion that working-class interests could be represented by middle-class members. The middle-class, he pointed out, did not accept political patronage in 1832 and that was why they achieved power – 'the people' must not accept it now. Partial enfranchisement would solve little, and the 'old Cartwright doctrine' must be stressed: 'I adhere to Major Cartwright's dictum, a non-elector is a slave, and I hate to see a slave beside me.' He analysed various schemes which would open up the franchise to the working class: Earl Grey's plan to establish guilds to enable a certain number of working-class MPs to be elected; Buxton's plan for a plurality of votes so that the working class would not 'swamp' Parliament; J. S. Mill's suggestion of graduated votes. Holyoake added to these the idea of an intelligence franchise, which he had been propagating since 1859. Every person able to demonstrate a knowledge of certain works of political economy and constitutional history would be given the vote through this scheme. This was not an attempt to cream off the self-educated 'labour aristocracy' and annex it to the electorate. It was to be in addition to reform based on property and contained, in germ at least, the idea of universality. Anyone, no matter how poor, could in principle become a voter. In the same breath he emphasized the vital necessity of independent action; merely waiting for reform would be fruitless: 'Nothing remains now but for the people to take their own affairs into their own hands, with singleness of purpose and fixed resolution to carry their own ends themselves'.[49] He went on to recommend the use of violence to effect political change, in a quite untypical way. The pamphlet had been an exercise in careful political manœvring. It closed with a threat:

> There must be advocacy and organisation. If it can be shown that violence can carry their objects it would be perfectly right to employ it. Those who are refused political recognition in a state, own no allegiance to it.

A few years later, in his election manifesto to the people of Birmingham, he compared working-class dependence in the political sphere, even after the passage of the Second Reform Act in 1867, with the self-reliance shown by co-operators. The lesson to be learnt from this contrast was important: 'This quality of independence must be shown in politics, or your representatives will be regarded by the House of Commons but as the nominees of the middle class.'[50] As co-operators understood only too well, independence required capital, therefore the working class should establish a 'great Political Fund' and not rely on money provided by rich Liberals. They must depend only on themselves.

Holyoake often lamented the decline in working-class political activity from the mid-century, but unlike, say, Thomas Cooper, this did not provoke him to retire disillusioned from the struggle. He recognized that 'apathy', though indeed serving the interests of capital, could be materially explained. In the mid-1860s he argued that working-class involvement had decreased because there was so little difference between political parties; 'the people do not know which is which'.[51] Other factors reinforcing this state of mind were disappointment with the 1832 Reform Act and the diversions offered by communists and co-operators, who 'preached material comfort as a substitute for political rights'.[52] Although he fully supported Co-operation by this time he did not hesitate to criticize any movement. More importantly, 'apathy' had become in some senses institutionalized from above, Holyoake thought. The right of meeting in the open air had been restricted, and 'Agitation has become so costly that only rich men can employ it.' It was not strange then, 'that men turn away in apathy and quiet hate'.[53] This notion, that 'apathy' was structured and imposed by the powerful, helping to undermine working-class self-activity, was a recurrent theme and helps to explain Holyoake's sensitivity to the details of democratic practice and political form.

In 1868 he wrote; 'A free and intelligent Democracy is a great spectacle, but it is a great trouble. Everybody has to be consulted.'[54] Democracy was something that had to be worked at and refined. People needed to be educated and free if it was to operate successfully, all forms of coercion and domination had to be swept away. Bribery and corruption must cease, as the cost of electioneering made it very difficult for the working class to promote their own representatives. In the same vein, the Chartist demand for the payment of MPs and the abolition of the property qualification continued to have relevance: 'The House of Commons is a rich man's club, and at present it is meant to be so'.[55] The ballot was an absolute necessity if patronage was to be eradicated, and Holyoake disagreed violently with J. S. Mill over this issue, the latter condemning the ballot as 'secret suffrage'.[56] These reforms would allow working people to take part, to make politics, and restrictions on participation imposed by the state through legislation must be lifted:

> Every impediment over which the State has control should be removed out of his [the citizen's] way. To put any obstacle in his way, to impose a penalty upon him, or to make the discharge of a citizen's duty a difficulty or peril, is the act of those who distrust the people. Our policy is to reverse all this.[57]

The largest obstacle blocking involvement, poverty, should be made a thing of the past.

In 1886 Holyoake advocated *Deliberate Liberalism*, and the pamphlet that bore this title was chiefly concerned with democratic practices. The Liberal Party, he argued, underestimated these problems, and failed to take democracy seriously enough. When the franchise had been extended in 1867 electors had been excluded from the lobby of the House of Commons. Only a few persons were now admitted and these by appointment only. This was an old right and Holyoake was very indignant about its loss; it was 'an affront put upon the people'. He regarded this as a dangerous trend illustrative of the increasing distance and isolation of politicians from the people, which enable Liberal MPs to forget their duties and responsibilities: 'No sooner do men of the people attain position they join the caste which slams the door, or do nothing when it is slammed, on those below them.'[58] Holyoake's ambition was to open the door of democracy to everyone, to eliminate political 'castes'. Further, there was no enforcement of the theory of the ballot.

Canvassers, who had a great deal more influence than now, continued to pressure and intimidate electors. They should, he argued, be abolished and replaced by 'advocates' whose function would be to provide political information rather than to cajole. This would safeguard the electors from the 'surreptitious intimidations of property and privilege'. Finally, members must be constantly reminded that they were merely delegates, or 'servants', their role to communicate the views of their constituents. The independence of members in practice meant only the freedom to betray their working-class supporters; 'The representative must be either delegate or dictator.'[59]

A wide gulf separated the interests and concerns of a working-class activist like Holyoake from those of the Liberal Party politicians and the local party managers. Democracy within the party was not conceded by the Liberal association of the 1860s and 1870s, but what did occur, as Vincent has pointed out, was a 'broadening of participation by the many, in decisions necessarily taken as before, by the few'. The upper echelon of the party in the localities was dominated by the leading families in the area, and campaigns were led invariably by large businessmen: 'For rank within the party corresponded very closely to rank on the Exchange and in society'.[60] Members unlimited and the notion of universal suffrage for both men and women were not serious considerations for the Parliamentary Liberal Party. In contrast Holyoake's idea of democracy was inclusive and active. It was about maximum participation not effective manipulation and control. He disliked these in Liberalism as much as he had disliked them in Owenism.

NOTES

1 J. McCabe, *Life and Letters of George Jacob Holyoake*, London, Watts, 1908, vol. I, p. 127. This is the first and by far the best biography.

2 *The Spirit of the Age*, no. 1, 1 July 1848, p. 13. For a detailed treatment of Holyoake's relationship with Mazzini, see P. Onnis, *Battaglie Democratiche e Risorgimento in un Carteggio Inedito di Giuseppe Mazzini e George Jacob Holyoake*, n.d., in Birmingham Public Library.

3 L. Blanc, *Organisation of Labour*, London, 1848, pp. 78–9.

4 See A. E. Bestor, 'The evolution of the socialist vocabulary', *Journal of the History of Ideas*, 1948, pp. 266–7. Fourier's major work was entitled, *Traité de l'Association Domestique-Agricole*, 1822.

5 See his comments in *The Spirit of the Age*, 13 January 1849, p. 40.

6 Bestor, op. cit., pp. 279–83. The term 'communist' was first intro-duced into England from France by J. G. Barnby in 1841.

7 *The Reasoner*, vol. VI, no. 150, 1849, p. 225 (pagination continuous).

8 ibid., no. 152, p. 258.

9 ibid., no. 151, p. 242.

10 *The Co-operative News*, 2 September 1871, pp. 1–2 and following issues.

11 By L. Grugel in his *George Jacob Holyoake: A Study in the Evolution of a Victorian Radical*, Philadelphia, Porcupine Press, 1976, pp. 1, 3. For a more plausible view see C. Behagg, 'Custom, class and change: the trade societies of nineteenth-century Birmingham', in *Social History*, vol. 4, no. 3, October 1979.

12 G. J. Holyoake, *Inaugural Address, delivered to the 19th Annual Co-oper-ative Congress*, Manchester, Central Co-operative Board, 1887, p. 4.

13 G. J. Holyoake, *Sixty Years of an Agitator's Life*, London, T. Fisher Unwin, 1893, vol. 1, p. 133.

14 *Practical Grammar; or Composition Divested of Difficulties*, London, J. Watson, 1844; *Handbook of Grammar*, London, J. Watson, 1846; *Mathematics no Mystery*, London, J. Watson, 1847. Between 1852 and 1854 he published four English language pamphlets for children.

15 *The History of Co-operation in England: its Literature and its Advocates*, London, Trubner, vol. 1, 1875, vol. 2, 1879. Complete edition referred to here, 1906, p. 288.

16 *The Essentials of Co-operative Education*, London, Labour Association Central Office, 1898.

17 McCabe, op. cit., vol. I, pp. 283–4.

18 *The Reasoner*, vol. XXII, p. 85.

19 ibid., p. 97.

20 *The Movement*, no. 36, p. 286.

21 *A Visit to Harmony Hall*, London, Hetherington, 1844, p.16.

22 ibid., p. 24.

23 *The Reasoner and Herald of Progress*, no. 2, 10 June 1846, pp. 26–7.

24 *Organisation: Not of Arms but of Ideas*, London, J. Watson, 1853, pp. 5, 13.

25 *The Reasoner*, vol. XXII, no. 576, 7 June 1857, p. 90.

26 *Oxford English Dictionary*, p. 964.

27 W. Thompson, *Labour Rewarded*, London, 1827, reprinted New York, Kelley 1969, p. 94.

28 Thompson, op. cit., p. 115. Note also his major treatise, *An Inquiry Into the Principles of the Distribution of Wealth, Most Conducive to Human Happiness*, London, 1824, reprinted New York, Kelley 1963, pp. 593–5.

29 Grugel, op. cit., p. 16 and Holyoake's *History of Co-operation*, p. 16.

30 Published in *The Social Economist, Industrial Partnership's Record and Co-operative Review*, edited with E. O. Greening from London, vol. III, no. 31, 1 September 1869.

31 G. J. Holyoake, *The Growth of Co-operation in England*, Manchester, Central Co-operative Board, 1887, pp. 19–20.

32 *History of Co-operation*, vol. II, p. 591.

33 *Inaugural Address*, p. 12.
34 'Co-operation and socialism', from *Subjects of the Day*, August 1890, p. 101.
35 See *Co-operative Congress report*, 1890, p. 12.
36 'Co-operation and socialism', p. 96. Note also his comment in 'Higher co-operation: its inner history', *The Fortnightly Review*, vol. 71, 1902, p. 96: 'Co-operation is Socialism with the madness left out.'
37 *The Social Economist*, vol. III, no. 28, 1 June 1869, p. 53.
38 Holyoake, *History of Co-operation*, vol. II, p. 616. See also his comments in *The History of Co-operation in Halifax*, London Book Store, 1867, p. 5: 'Co-operation, by raising the low and increasing the means of the common people, and giving them a common interest in the success of their trading and manufacturing societies, imparts to them Communistic habits and introduces features of that mode of life.'
39 *Sixty Years of an Agitator's Life*, vol. I, p. 196.
40 Plan of contents, MS, n.d., in the Bishopsgate Institute, London.
41 See the *Oxford English Dictionary*, p. 184.
42 See C. Hill, *The World Turned Upside Down*, London, 1972, reprinted Harmondsworth, Penguin Books, 1975, p. 63. All of Chapter 4 is relevant.
43 *The Times*, 14 November 1887, p. 7. This report condemned the 'agitators' as the chief culprits, who had fomented disorder by manipulating the 'roughs' who made up the majority of the 'mob'.
44 *The Daily News*, 23 January 1906, in the Holyoake Papers, Birmingham Public Library, reel 9, section 7,c.
45 *The Reasoner*, vol. XXII, no. 566, 29 March 1857, pp. 49–50, and no. 567, p.53.
46 McCabe, op. cit., vol. I, p. 144.
47 R. Harrison, *Before the Socialists*, London, Routledge & Kegan Paul, 1965, p. 319.
48 *The Liberal Situation: Necessity for a Qualified Franchise*, London Book Store, 1865, p. 17.
49 ibid., p. 35.
50 *Working-class Representation: Its Conditions and Consequences*, London Book Store, 1868, pp. 8–9.
51 *The Liberal Situation*, p. 16.
52 ibid., p. 21.
53 ibid., p. 25.
54 *Working-class Representation*, p. 6.
55 ibid., p. 8.
56 See Holyoake's pamphlet, *A New Defence of the Ballot, in Consequence of Mr. Mill's objections to it*, London Book Store, 1868.
57 *Working-class Representation*, p. 12.
58 *Deliberate Liberalism: Four Instances of It*, London and Leicester, J. Heywood, 1886, p. 4.
59 ibid., pp. 12, 13.
60 J. Vincent, *The Formation of the Liberal Party, 1857–1868*, London,

Routledge & Kegan Paul 1966, pp. 92, 94–5. The domination of the local Liberal caucus by local employers and tradesmen helped to fuel working-class radicals' dissatisfaction with Liberalism towards the end of the century. For the importance of these organizational frustrations see D. Howell, *British Workers and the Independent Labour Party, 1888–1906*, Manchester, Manchester University Press, 1983, pp. 263–4.

Chapter Five

'THE LORD DOES COMBINATION LOVE': RELIGION AND CO-OPERATION AMONGST A PECULIAR PEOPLE

MICK REED

From the point of view of working people, co-operation is often not an organization available for joining (as in The Co-operative Movement with capital letters) or even a self-consciously chosen idea, so much as a convenience, even a necessity. Co-operation with a small 'c', or combination as the Cokelers had it, is daily practice for those 'who only have their labour force to depend on' or who are in a subordinate position of any kind (religious, political, economic, or whatever). The horizontal links of co-operation, solidarity, are one of the first things any authoritarian regime tries to break. Co-operatives and combinations of many kinds, trading under many names, have come into being through the emergencies of subalternity, in strikes, sackings, minority political work, dissidence of all kinds. Forms-for-labour are always being reinvented. 'For combination is so sweet, then combine,/it makes us all in one complete, then combine', in the words of the Cokeler hymn quoted by Mick Reed in this chapter. As well as visions, there are practical needs to be met, such as, in the case of the Cokelers, getting to be able to worship in the way you want, in a situation where your work and your employers make it impossible: 'this was the starting of our Stores'. The problem for early Cokelers was that work interfered with worship. Women in particular, often servants, could not easily attend meetings for worship. Hence the practicality of setting up a co-op.

Sectarian affiliation (in the strongest, most positive sense of sectarian) has been a powerful source of recruitment for the Co-operative Movement in its capital letter sense too. Bill Lancaster's work on Leicester (*Radicalism, Co-operation and Socialism: Leicester Working-class Politics 1860–1906*, Leicester, Leicester University Press, 1987) shows how important adherents of the Church of Christ were amongst the personnel of the Co-op in that town during the second half of the nineteenth century. J.T.W. Mitchell's membership of the Milton Congregational Church in Rochdale was fundamental to him, as was the Congregationalism of his friend J. C. Becket in Darwen. The history of federalism in working-class associations (CWS advocates, against the Anglican Christian Socialists, were sometimes known as 'feder-alists') has much to do with the history of nonconformity, as well as being a resource now for those interested in realizing the necessary contradiction between autonomy and coherence (the locality and the centre). Sectarian forms were crucial carriers of what Logie Barrow in his work on spiritual-ism (*Independent Spirits*, London, History Workshop, Routledge & Kegan Paul, 1986) has called a 'democratic epistemology', in social circumstances increasingly hostile to such democracy from the 1870s onwards. There may be many links which historians have not traced yet, between the associational creativity (closely connected with ideological/theological creativity) of seventeenth-century protestantism and nineteenth-century plebeian radicalism.

> Christ's combination stores for me
> Where I can be so well supplied,
> Where I can one with brethen be
> Where competition is defied.[1]

This chapter will look at a form of co-operation and communal living practised by the Society of Dependents which was articulated in religious terms, apparently without reference to socialism.

The story of the Dependents, better known to outsiders by their nickname 'Cokelers', has been outlined on several occasions, usually with much error and uninformed assertion about their beliefs.[2] Only a beginning has been made at studying their history.[3] Their founder, John Sirgood, was born into a weaver's family at Avening, Gloucestershire in 1821. In the 1840s he came to London, settling in Kennington where he became a disciple of William Bridges, founder of the Plumstead Peculiars and later described by Sirgood as his 'father in the Gospel'.[4] Sirgood, a shoemaker by trade, preached a good deal around south London, but in 1850, apparently disillusioned by the response to his efforts, he moved with his wife, Harriett, to Loxwood in north-west Sussex, where he soon built up a following amongst the agricultural workers. Eventually the 'Society of Dependents' was formed, so-called because its members were dependent upon God for everything.

Material published by the Dependents is extremely limited. Sirgood himself published two pamphlets of correspondence in the 1860s, revealing persecution by the authorities, and in this century a collection of hymns, almost all written by Dependents and used in the chapels, was printed. This would seem to be the sum total of published material from within the group. However, in addition to a strong oral tradition, Dependents have made multiple manuscript copies of testimonies, letters, and other material, all of which are circulated among the brethren for devotional purposes. These documents exist in great numbers and provide the historian with a major primary source.[5]

A key aspect of Dependent doctrine is their concept of 'combination', of which co-operation is a part. Before discussing this, a brief outline of their system of belief may be useful, if only to rebut some commonly held misconceptions about them. The formal 'tenets of the Dependent People' are fairly typical of several nonconformist churches. They believe that the divinely inspired Scriptures are entirely sufficient as a guide to faith and practice. Believers in original sin, they accept that Christ's atonement is sufficient for salvation, which is open to all human beings who live their lives in accordance to the laws of God.

Most of these ideas are readily acceptable to most non-Calvinist Christians, but it is the less formal aspects of Dependent faith that have aroused most interest and misunderstanding. A central aspect of their doctrine is said to be Antinomianism. The 'Coglers' (sic), according to a nineteenth-century observer, were 'a sect of teetotallers . . . its members considering themselves (but not being so considered by their neighbours) to be incapable of committing sin'.[6] Surviving Dependents reject this totally, though as Roger Homan points out, 'they consider themselves capable, once reborn, of not committing sin'.[7] Even this very different emphasis would doubtless bring charges of heresy from 'orthodox' Christians. One of my Dependent informants preferred to express it thus: 'With God's help, we can conquer sin.' Dependents have always tried to live humbly and abstemiously. Asceticism has often been misunderstood by outsiders. Generally teetotal, Dependents are said to have taboos against flowers in their homes, ornaments, literature other than the Bible, and photographs.[8] This last seems most unlikely, since Dependents treasure large numbers of posed photographs of their early brethren, including John and Harriett Sirgood. The other taboos mentioned cannot be found in primary sources, while pictures, ornaments, flowers, and occasional light reading, are prominent in the homes of Dependents that I have visited.[9] One informant thought it extremely unlikely that there had ever been taboos of this kind, and although changes may have occurred over time, most living Dependents grew up amongst people who had been in the movement from the beginning, and are probably in a position to know.

One aspect of Dependent life that has attracted much interest, and in the past, even hostility, has been their preference for celibacy. The sexual practices or non-practices of sects are always the subject of fantasy among outsiders. Ben Piper has described how his father Henry began to believe 'what a deal more liberty and freedom himself and dear Mother would have for Christ's sake if they remained as they were and not bring souls into the world, which if not born again is very sad'. At about the same time, John Sirgood began to preach 'the very same that how much more useful we could be for Christ's sake by keeping free from entanglements, which by the grace of God could be avoided'. Ever since, most Dependents have chosen 'to keep free for Christ's sake'.[10] Marriage though, it must be stressed, is not taboo. Some Dependents have married and have not been considered as failing. Deriving their position from Pauline authority, they note that 'He that giveth her in marriage doeth well; but he that giveth her not in marriage doeth better.'[11] Marriage can interfere with an individual's relationship with God, and it may also be 'that marriage does not fit very well with their somewhat communal way of life',[12] but it is not a sin.

Dependents are, however, very firm on one point. They are avowed pacifists, and were all conscientious objectors in both world wars. 'Whilst being ready to serve the State in any civil work of national importance they declined to do anything connected with the Army', and with one exception were exempted from military service, conditional upon their finding approved employment.[13]

Dependent lifestyle is, then, relatively abstemious, usually celibate, but comfortable. Asceticism and austerity seem inappropriate words to describe people who clearly enjoy life, laugh easily, and gain strength from their collectivity. This collectivity will be the focus of the rest of this chapter.

The doctrines preached by Sirgood and adhered to by his early converts cannot be completely established from the available evidence. It is clear he attracted large numbers of followers in several areas, nearly all of them farmworkers, with some small farmers and tradespeople.[14] Meetings and then chapels were established at Loxwood, Northchapel, Plaistow, and Warnham in Sussex; Lord's

Hill near Shamley Green in Surrey, as well as later, South Norwood, Chichester, and Hove. There were house meetings in many other places, including, in the early twentieth century, as far away as Marden in Kent. At the time of Sirgood's death in 1885, there were reputed to be around 2000 Dependents, though by 1904 it was estimated that only about 900 adherents remained. This numerical decline has continued until today, when only a handful of people worship at the two surviving chapels at Loxwood and Northchapel.[15]

Like many nonconformist groups, Dependents were persecuted with frequent evictions and sackings. Ben Piper recalled how 'my Father and Mother and us as a family were turned out of House and Father from his work because He had religious Meetings held in his House', while Sirgood himself was threatened with legal action for holding meetings in his house, and both he and his followers were subjected to 'rough music' and physical violence.[16]

Whether it was in direct reaction to persecution as well as the poverty of the farmworker that the most distinctive aspect of Dependent doctrine – 'combination' – was developed, we cannot be sure. Nor can the precise timing of its emergence as a central feature of Dependent life be discovered. But by the late 1870s, and perhaps earlier, 'combination' was a dominant part of Dependent thought and hymnody.

> All you who combination love, Now combine,
> All you who seek those things above, Now combine,
> All who will gladly now combine
> Like fruitful branches in the vine,
> To show your fruitfulness is mine, Now combine.
>
> For combination is so sweet, then combine,
> It makes us all in one complete, then combine.
> We by it to the world can show
> How sweetly we in Christ do grow,
> While we are living here below, then combine.[17]

Combination is defined by Dependents as 'spiritual oneness'. In the words of Paul:

> I beseech you brethren . . . that ye all speak the same thing, and that there be no division among you; but that ye be

perfectly joined together in one mind and in the same judgement.[18]

This was part of the process by which the faithful became members of but a single body – the body of Christ. Oneness in Christ is the ultimate destiny of the faithful with the coming of the millennium. Millenarianism is very much a feature of Dependent belief. While my informants believe in the millennium and Christ's second coming as certain, there is no sense of imminence, and they believe no one can foresee when it will occur and in what form. They insist that human beings will destroy the world rather than God.

There is some evidence that earlier, some sense of imminence may have been present. Many hymns express this idea.

> Be patient, my brethren, His coming is near,
> And we shall behold Him, so be of good cheer

Sirgood commented that 'even the professors [sic] will acknowledge that this is the last time or the latter days'.[19] Although the millennium will bring complete oneness, it is necessary to prepare for this while on earth, by trying to create the kingdom of Heaven on earth. Combination has this aim – to build the new.

> No twoness we among them see
> But all in one they will agree,
> Though they are yet but very few
> Who thus combine and build the new.[20]

Oneness – combination – is achieved through spiritual devotions, prayer, scriptural awareness, and frequent collective worship. The problem for early Dependents was that work interfered with worship. In particular, women, who were often in service, could not easily attend the meetings.

> There was a good number of Sisters in service who were serving worldly Masters and Mistresses, therefore they had . . . no liberty to be at the Meetings. There was such a desire in Br. John Sirgood, for the Sisters Souls welfare that he wanted them to have their liberty to be at the house of God to all be able to worship together so he began to work on their behalf . . . God also worked . . . and many brethren also. This was the starting of our Stores.[21]

The stores were the distinctive economic characteristic of the Dependent movement, and with their associated farms and other undertakings,were the physical manifestation of 'oneness' or combination. Stores were set up during the 1870s at Loxwood, Warnham, Northchapel, Lord's Hill, South Norwood, and perhaps elsewhere. At Northchapel

> the beginnings were very inauspicious . . . one of the first attempts to commerce was when someone baked six lard rolls with much trepidation in case they did not sell and precious food should be wasted. In fact they did sell and very quickly and soon the Dependents were baking hundreds. It was from such humble beginnings that the Dependents' stores grew.[22]

And grow they did. By 1885, the Loxwood store, known as the 'Combination Stores', was a flourishing enterprise with several departments. In the late 1870s the Warnham store employed three women and two men, but by 1904 it employed thirty-one of both sexes. In Northchapel, 'a small village . . . with a parish population of only 700', the store had 'three departments . . . employing thirteen saleswomen and assistants, besides delivery carts and their drivers'. The Loxwood stores in 1904 'in addition to selling provisions, haberdashery, china, clothes, &c. . . . even deal in bicycles, gramophones, and motor accessories. Indeed a motor is let out for hire, and . . . one could buy a motor through the store'.[23] In Warnham 'they sold practically everything. They were grocers, bakers, drapers, and hardware and furniture stores. Besides selling their own brand of china, they made their own furniture and restored antiques.'[24] By 1920 in Loxwood there was 'a whole street of shops, with a large garage and a great steam bakery'.[25] In each place where there were stores a similar wide range of activities was undertaken. Most branches remained under Dependent control until well after the Second World War, and the last to be sold was the 'Combination Stores' at Loxwood during the early 1970s. So successful had they been, that they had practically cornered all trading activities in their respective villages.

Except during the latter years of the stores, when age and declining numbers required the employment of non-Dependents, they were run and worked almost entirely from within the movement. Dependents had pooled their meagre resources to set up the first trading enterprise, and they continued to invest what they could in the stores. Any member of the group could be a shareholder and in 1904 'a very large number . . . invest their savings in the store, which explains the reason why the labouring class among the Cokelers are so much better off comparatively than those of other denominations'.[26] The stores at this time were reputed to pay big dividends, but 'it must not be imagined . . . that . . . they have given themselves up to money-making, for they close their shops for certain hours of the day for prayer'.[27]

In a single generation farm labourers and their families had dragged themselves from poverty to a reasonably secure comfort. What little wealth accrued to individuals seems to have remained within the movement after their death. Shares in the stores were bequeathed to other Dependents, while in the seventeen wills I have been able to examine, the entire estate was left to brethren, often mainly to the contemporary leaders, to be used for the benefit of the movement. Jane Overington, in 1916, left £50 to the deacons of the Loxwood chapel 'to be used by them solely for the aged needy brethren that are worshipping at the said chapel'.[28] Surviving Dependents may have acquired their shares in this way. None of my informants ever bought any, receiving all of theirs through legacies. As one commented, 'I never had any money to buy any.' Neither did the members necessarily take their dividend, often leaving it in the business to accrue for the benefit of the movement. Trade acquired a spiritual significance, but not trade for individual benefit.

But let us to each other prove
All by each other aiding,
'Tis love that do each brother move
For all to gain by trading.[29]

The near monopoly of trade in their respective villages did not result in Dependents taking advantage by charging high prices. Informants from outside the movement are unanimous that prices were invariably lower than elsewhere, even in towns. The poor were never left to go without basic necessities. One informant recalls that during the 1920s and 1930s, the unemployed were *given* groceries by the Dependent store-keepers, even when they had no religious sympathies. Outsiders are agreed that the Dependents were 'good people'. As one farmer remembered, 'I liked the Dependents: they were reliable and they were straight. Their word was as good as their signature I always said.'[30]

The stores were not the sole economic activity. Dependents took over the tenancy of several farms from the 1880s onwards, soon gaining the admiration of politicians of all colours. A Tory MP argued for the connection between the Dependents and agricultural co-operation:

> It is a matter of common knowledge that for years successive Ministers of Agriculture and others have endeavoured to improve the position of the British farmer by encouraging co-operation and a system by which British produce could reach the consumer directly without the medium of the middleman. In a small way certainly, but nevertheless success-fully, the Cokelers have solved this great question. . . . The Cokeler farmers sell their butter, milk, bacon, eggs &c., at their local stores, a state of affairs which one may call 'Free Trade within the Empire', since not only do the Cokelers themselves supply the stores, with provisions to sell, but they obtain nearly all their necessaries of life from the same source, while all the time the outside public is buying largely from them and selling nothing in return . . . there is no doubt that if this system of stores could be instituted in England generally . . . the position of the farming interest would be immensely improved.[31]

The Labour candidate for Chichester in the 1918 general election was equally impressed that the Dependents had been 'practising agricultural co-operation long in advance of the rest of England'.[32]

Like the stores, farms were worked by the Dependents until after the Second World War. These enterprises though, successful as they were in providing a good income and degree of security for all Dependents, were not in themselves the physical manifestation of oneness. It was the way in which they were worked and organized that embodied the ideals of combination, and which demonstrated the integral relationship between economic activity and Dependent doctrine.

Brethren lived – and still live – as far as possible, communally, with the majority of the staff of each store or farm living under the same roof. For example, in the late 1940s, some sixteen men and women lived above the store at Northchapel,[33] while twenty years earlier there had been about twenty-six. When Plaistow Place Farm was worked by the Dependents in 1881, ten members of the group lived in the farmhouse, and others in the ancillary cottages. On this farm of 600 acres, only one man and a boy were said to be employed at this time; resident Dependents provided the bulk of the labour.[34] Every enterprise was characterized by group residence. Of course some members, particularly married couples, lived in their own homes, but communal living probably provided the framework for most Dependents. Work seems to have been organized along fairly conventional lines. Women were the majority of shopkeepers and very often they managed the stores. Miss Hempstead, who was secretary of the Combination Stores at Loxwood in the 1940s, became its managing director. Men did the usual male farm jobs and craft activities. In Warnham 'the men ran the furniture business and a Bakery, the women the two shops'.[35] Decision-making, at least on major issues, was collective, following discussion of the problems, though it is probable that consensus was easily reached since the goals and motivations of each individual were so closely attuned. This comes across when talking to a group of Dependents. Their ideal of 'oneness' seems to have been achieved.

In 1947 the manageress of the grocery section of the Loxwood stores, and a resident there for over fifty years, described their lives:

> The workers get up at 6 a.m., have a light meal and bring a cup of tea upstairs to the four eldest. Then breakfast at 8 a.m. for those who are able, open shop at 9 a.m. The members usually have secret prayer in the morning before business, to ask God for help and guidance through the day. At 12 o'clock we have our mid-day meal, close shops for one hour. Tea at 5 o'clock when shops are closed for the day. After the various duties are finished, the members again retire for prayer, or reading the Scriptures, or visiting the sick.

Chapel services were held on Tuesday and Thursday evenings from 7 p.m. until 9 p.m.; while on Sundays, services were from 10.30 a.m. to 1 p.m.; 2.30 p.m. to 4 p.m.; and 6 p.m. to 8 p.m. Dependents attended *all* of these services whenever possible. Leisure was simple.

> We have a nice lawn where we can relax from business. . . .

We enjoy the peace and quietness and communion with God. We also have a boat and sometimes have a nice row on the river and enjoy the beauties of nature, the wonderful creation of God, sometimes a motor ride to the sea where we again behold the majesty of God in his beautiful handiwork.[36]

Meals were taken communally, with men and women eating together. Brethren received a small money wage, out of which they had only to buy clothes, from the stores of course. All else was found. Work was mainly collective, as were leisure and of course worship, where the emphasis was, and is, upon sharing personal spiritual experiences by public testimony. Prayers and hymns were almost all written by Dependents and are exclusive to them. In short, every aspect of the individual Dependent's life is organized within the framework of the group.

Another positive feature of Dependent belief was the emphasis on equality of the sexes. The stores were formed, at least partly, to liberate women from the constraints of domestic service, and women were prominent in managerial roles. Within the chapels, women can become elders of the church.[37] For a long time women seem to have been a majority within the group,[38] and are prominent as writers of hymns, some of which are expressly addressed to them.

> Come on my sisters, let us see
> How strong and valiant we can be,
> The will of God to do . . .
>
> As we are weak we may be strong
> For we to the right race belong,
> For of such God makes choice . . .[39]

One is reminded of John Harrison's discussion of the Shakers.

> A new and radical role for women was here proclaimed. To refuse to be married, to bear children, to have sexual relations; to be treated as the equal of men in status and authority was a reversal of the role of women in contemporary society.[40]

How then are the Dependents to be viewed within the wider context of socialism and co-operation? Commentators of all political views had no doubt that John Sirgood had 'socialistic tendencies', and Dependents have been dubbed 'communist',[41] but no evidence has been found which shows any articulation of their aims and ideas in these terms. It has been claimed, apparently with Dependent approval, that 'Sirgood seems in no way to have been interested in class division – his eyes were fixed firmly on another world.' Despite the early attacks on him by the clerical and lay establishment, 'it does not appear that he saw himself as in any way attacking their position and privileges'.[42] Perhaps this was true – and yet there are hints that it was not. Like many nonconformists, Sirgood was sure 'that all parsons are wicked men', who 'are worse than Highwaymen, because . . . they can enforce the payment of money from those to whom they render no manner of service, nor make any kind of return'; in support he cited the case of 'a poor man in Sussex that acted in his opinion right in refusing to pay the parson's tithe because he felt he stood . . . more in need of the money than the parson'. In reply to his landlord, a magistrate and member of Parliament, who asked him to stop holding religious meetings in his cottage, he commented, 'I think you must see the fewer [cottages] you have the more you will be free from care, anxiety and responsibility.'[43]

Whatever their views on these kinds of issues, Dependents lived, in practice, within a context of community and co-operation. Effectively, there was common ownership of property through the system of shareholding, and collective decision-making. Dependents provided almost all the labour in their enterprises, and shared equally in the benefits accruing from their labour. The enterprises were not capitalist, with the shareholders creaming off the surplus created by a hired labour force with no other stake in the firm.[44] Dependents really did live by the principle, 'from each according to their ability, to each according to their needs'. One must hope that in the future much wider access to Dependent sources will be possible, to give a fuller picture of a fine group of people, whose beliefs and practice enabled many working people to reach a level of security and well-being of which their contemporaries could only dream.

NOTES

I want to thank a number of people for their help with the research for this chapter. Roger Homan provided me with documents and ideas at the outset, while Eric Smith, Anthony Fanshawe, Jim Nash, Arthur Nobes, and Norman Manners, all provided me with information and hospitality. Peter Jerome sent me copies of the bulletin of The Petworth Society. Mrs Young of the Loxwood Women's Institute has kindly allowed me to copy documents in the possession of the W. I.: Most of all, I must thank those members of the Society of Dependents, who I feel would prefer to remain anonymous, who gave me access to documents and patiently explained the basis of their faith and their way of life. Any errors and misrepresentations remain my own.

1 *The Dependents Hymnbook* (hereafter *DHB*), Loxwood, n.d., hymn 64.
2 Viscount Turnour, 'The Cokelers', *The National Review*, 1904, pp. 106–11, reprinted as Earl Winterton, 'The Cokelers: a Sussex sect', *Sussex County Magazine* (hereafter *SCM*), vol. 5, 1931, pp. 717–22; F. E. Green, 'In Unknown Sussex', *The Nineteenth Century*, 1920, pp. 91–5; Donald MacAndrew, 'The Sussex Cokelers: a curious sect', *SCM*, vol. 16, 1942, pp. 346–50; Hardiman Scott, 'The Cokelers at Northchapel', in *Secret Sussex* London Batchworth Press 1949, pp. 81–8; John Montgomery, 'The Cokelers', in *Abodes of Love*, London, 1962; Peter Greenyer, 'The Cokelers: peculiar to Sussex', *Sussex Life*, vol. 16, 1980, pp. 52–3. This last item is perhaps the worst of all, repeating just about every error to be found in the earlier items. For a much better piece that also has the approval of at least some Dependents, see Peter Jerome, 'John Sirgood's way', *Bulletin of the Petworth Society*, no. 29, September 1982, pp. 27–32. The nickname 'Cokeler' is, popularly and dubiously, said to derive from Sirgood's liking for cocoa rather than beer.
3 Dennis Hardy in his book *Alternative Communities in Nineteenth Century Britain*, London, Longman 1979, pp. 139–42, repeats many of the erroneous claims of earlier writers, and wrongly asserts (p. 139) that the group assumed 'the locally-derived name of "Cokelers" '. In an altogether more qualitative piece of research, Roger Homan gives what is the first fairly authoritative, albeit brief, outline of Dependent doctrine and organization, as well as correcting some notions of earlier writers: 'The Society of Dependents: a case study in the rise and fall of rural Peculiars', *Sussex Archaeological Collections*, vol. 119, 1981, pp. 195–204.
4 Testimony of Br. Charles Holden, 23 November 1930, unpublished MS in possession of the Dependents. For the influence of Bridges on James Banyard, founder of the Peculiar People with whom the Dependents retain close links, see Mark Sorrell, *The Peculiar People*, Exeter, 1979, pp. 15–17. For a description, probably slightly lurid, of the Plumstead Peculiars a little later, see Reverend C. M. Davies, *Unorthodox London: or Phases of Religious Life in the Metropolis*, London, Tinsley, 1873, pp. 293–301.

5 Unrestricted access to them, and to whatever other documentation is possessed by the Dependents would be vital for a fuller theological and historical understanding of the group, but until such access is granted, the historian is limited to those documents that surviving brethren are prepared to show. I have been fortunate to have access to a number of these kinds of documents, which together with interviews with surviving Dependents, provide the basis of whatever understanding I have of their beliefs. For a fuller discussion of the problems of sources, see Homan, op. cit., pp. 198–9. Sirgood's pamphlets are: *Intolerance in the Rural Districts of West Sussex: A Lawyer's Notice to a Shoemaker to discontinue Religious Worship in his Dwelling House. The Shoemaker's reply: with a Few Incidents connected Therewith*, n.d. (1861?); *Religious Intolerance in the Rural Districts of Sussex: A Notice from a Magistrate to Discontinue Religious Worship in a House belonging to him, and a Working Man's Reply*, n.d. (1866?). I am grateful to Roger Homan for copies of these documents.

6 J. H. Blunt, *Dictionary of Sects, Heresies, Ecclesiastical Parties and Schools of Religious Thought*, London, Rivingtons, 1874, p. 110. See also Turnour, op. cit., p. 108; MacAndrew, op. cit., p. 347; Greenyer, op. cit.,
p. 52; Hardy, op. cit., p. 139.

7 Homan, op. cit., p. 197.

8 Turnour, op. cit., p. 109; MacAndrew, op. cit., p. 348; Green, op. cit., p. 94; Scott, op. cit., p. 82; Greenyer, op. cit., p. 52; Hardy, op. cit., p. 139.

9 Homan, op. cit., p. 197, makes much the same point.

10 West Sussex Records Office (hereafter WSRO), MP 1994, 'Testimony of Brother Benjamin Piper of Warnham (1868–1948) written 1936', unpublished typescript.

11 I Corinthians 7: 38. A clear exposition of Dependent position on marriage is in WSRO, MP 1994.

12 Jerome, op. cit., pp. 28–9.

13 *West Sussex County Times*, 8 July 1916. The exception was F. C. Greenfield, who, for reasons I have been unable to determine, was imprisoned for the duration of the Great War.

14 Homan, op. cit., p. 196; Turnour, op. cit., p. 106.

15 Turnour, op. cit., p. 110. Turnour claimed (p. 109) that the Dependents formed about one-third of the total population of Northchapel and Wisborough Green (Loxwood is in the latter parish). The visitation returns of 1898 suggest that around a quarter of the population were in fact of this faith. WSRO, EpI/22A/2.

16 WSRO, MP 1994; Sirgood, *Intolerance* and *Religious Intolerance*.

17 *DHB*, hymn 15.

18 I Corinthians 1:10.

19 *DHB*, hymn 317; John Sirgood to Tom and Anne Overington Warnham, 21 September 1884, unpublished MS in possession of the Dependents.

20 *DHB*, hymn 119.

21 WSRO, MP 1994.
22 Jerome, op. cit., p. 30.
23 Turnour, op. cit., pp. 110-11.
24 Typescript newsletter by the Vicar of Warnham, n.d.
25 Green, op. cit., p. 93.
26 Turnour, op. cit., p. 111.
27 Green, op. cit., p. 93.
28 WSRO, STM 31 f. 296.
29 *DHB*, hymn 22.
30 Interview by the author with Arthur Nobes of Plaistow. Tape in my possession. Interview by the author with Norman Manners of Plaistow.
31 Turnour, op. cit., p. 111.
32 Green, op. cit., p. 93.
33 Scott, op. cit., p. 88.
34 PRO, RG 11/111, 1881 census enumerators' schedules for Kirdford parish.
35 Warnham Historical Association, typescript report of visits to surviving Dependents, 23 February 1981.
36 Miss Sarah Woods, 'The Stores (Combination) Loxwood', typescript preserved in the scrapbook of the Loxwood Women's Institute.
37 Interview by the author with Jim Nash of Loxwood; interviews by the author with surviving Dependents. Female elders included, for example, Ann Overington of Loxwood, before the Great War, and Miss Hills, the last elder at Warnham.
38 Green, op. cit., pp. 93-5.
39 *DHB*, hymn 121.
40 J. F. C. Harrison, *The Second Coming: Popular Millenarianism 1780-1850*, London, Routledge & Kegan Paul, 1979, p. 169.
41 Turnour, op. cit., p. 107; Green, op. cit., p. 93; MacAndrew, op. cit., pp. 348-9.
42 Jerome, op. cit., p. 28.
43 Sirgood, *Intolerance*, p. 9; *Religious Intolerance*, pp. 3, 8, and 15. I have not positively identified the magistrate, but he was probably Sir Denzil Onslow, a leading supporter of the Tichbourne Claimant.
44 This last comment would not hold for the period following 1945, when, as Dependents became fewer and more elderly, hired labour *was* brought in increasingly, and the shareholders came to assume a position similar to that in any capitalist enterprise.

Chapter Six

THE 'CO-OPERATIVE COMMON-WEALTH': IRELAND, LARKIN, AND THE *DAILY HERALD*

KEITH HARDING

This chapter, like the last one, moves outside the Co-operative Movement as a set of dominant organizations, into co-operative ideas and associations with a smaller 'c'. One of the most salient of these has been the notion of the 'co-operative commonwealth', used as a name for their project more by socialists during the late nineteenth and early twentieth centuries than by co-operators.

A learned co-operator and historian, W. H. Brown, 'so far as I have been able to trace' (1937), thought that the first usage of the 'co-operative commonwealth' within the movement was in an address by Dr Garth Wilkinson to the members of the St John's Wood (London) Co-operative Society in 1866 (see *The Co-operative Manager*, National Co-operative Managers' Association, p. 60). In 1937 W. H. Brown referred to it as 'a term which has come into common parlance in recent years'. In its influential usage by the American socialist Laurence Gronlund, in *The Co-operative Commonwealth* (1886), the term referred to the post-revolutionary socialist state rather than to voluntary, specifically co-operative, means towards it. Gronlund disapproved of these, in a characteristically Marxist fashion. But the phrase was quickly taken up by activists of another kind. In the New Life (1883–96) period and beyond, into the 1920s, it was used a great deal by new union, syndicalist, and socialist agitators such as Tom Mann. Mann became quite committed to the co-operative movement during the early 1890s, doing at least one speaking tour on its behalf. There seemed to be an elective affinity between 'the co-operative commonwealth' and constructive organizers/agitators close-up to class struggle, such as Mann, John Maclean, and – described in this chapter – Jim Larkin. Pataud and Pouget's notable syndicalist work *Quand nous ferons la revolution* was translated into English as *Syndicalism and the Co-operative Commonwealth* (London, Oxford University Press, 1913).

Language is always important, constituting different political inflections rather than simply reflecting them. As Keith Harding describes here, W. P.

Ryan tried to get at 'the co-operative commonwealth' through the Gaelic 'Cumannacht', meaning not only an organization or society but also 'fellowship, affection, love'. 'In *Cumannacht* we have therefore not only the idea of an organisation but a heartening sense of social fellowship and co-operation, and we might even add of affectionate spiritual companionship and idealism' (lecture to the Socialist Party of Ireland, 1909). The 'co-operative commonwealth' may be a vision worth tracing historically, in order to see what it has done and can still do politically.

In early August 1913 the *Irish Worker*, a radical paper of the Irish Transport and General Workers' Union, produced a front-page article entitled 'the jovial revolution'.[1] 'Revolution' must have been an often-used word in Ireland in the summer of 1913. There were the rantings of Edward Carson and his paramilitary followers; the indignant pledges of leading Tory Unionists, declaring their willingness to resist Home Rule whether it came by revolutionary or constitutional methods. There was James Connolly honing down his Marxism to a degree of theoretical sharpness that is still the envy of the Irish and British left – and this despite the frustrating pressures of the north, which he was experiencing first-hand as the Belfast secretary of the ITGWU. There were the Sheehy Skeffingtons extolling in the streets and parks of Dublin their vision of a new Irish citizenship based on the emancipation of women. There were the Larkins, Jim and Delia, fighting a series of small-scale but persistent battles against the forces of capitalist exploitation rooted in the sweatshops, the laundries, the confectionery and biscuit factories, and the docks of industrial Dublin. There was the imminence of industrial conflict on a horrific scale in the form of the 'Dublin lock-out'. And there were the shockwaves of social unrest sent out by liberal England as it died its strange death.

The *Irish Worker*'s revolution referred directly to none of these, although it took elements from many of them. The 'jovial revolution' with which the *Irish Worker* was concerned was taking place there and then in the unlikely setting of the grounds of a large manor house in the outskirts of Dublin, called Croydon Park. It involved fêtes and fairs, concerts and dancing lessons, boxing tournaments and football matches, basic instruction in gardening techniques and advice on how to milk a cow. Above all, it involved working-class families, men, women and children, and provided them with physical and mental relief from the oppression of sweated labour and tenement slum. It was small-scale – as indeed everything in Dublin was, except the enormity of its poverty – but it was a practical representation of a grand and far-reaching concept: the vision of a working-class 'co-operative commonwealth'.

Irish Co-operation in general had a long historical tradition but very few lasting forms. Connolly and others pointed to a primitive Celtic communism which had existed in early Gaelicism, and which later revivalist movements tried to recreate. The Ralahine experiment had also been one of the cardinal events of co-operative history.[2] Nineteenth-century British co-operators had often looked to Ireland in a romantic way, searching for the co-operative ideal expressed in rural forms or Gaelic culture. At the turn of the century the work of Plunkett and George Russell ('AE') and their bold attempts at agricultural co-operation on a grandscale fed into this tradition of unrealized potential. Rural creameries were perhaps the major achievement, but proved too fragile in the face of agricultural capitalism and the violence of the 'Black and Tans'. Above all, rural co-operation failed to link with urban forces in Dublin and Belfast.

The idea of the 'co-operative commonwealth' had a somewhat different aspect from this more conventional co-operative tradition. The ideology that fired it was more specifically socialist, containing the visionary idealism of socialism whilst at the same time being based on practical needs and urban realities, in particular the work of Larkin and the Dublin workers within the ITGWU. One definition of the co-operative commonwealth was provided by the Irishman W. P. Ryan, in a lecture to the Socialist Party of Ireland in 1909. He defined the co-operative commonwealth as

> that future Social Order – the natural heir of the present one – in which all important instruments of production shall be taken under collective control, in which the citizens shall be consciously public functionaries, and in which their labours shall be rewarded according to results.

More precisely he preferred to use the Irish word 'Cumannacht', rather than 'socialism', so as to stress the social and co-operative aspects:

It is apparently formed from *cumann* and *cumannac*. *Cumann* means not only a league or a society, but fellowship, affection, love. *Cumannac* as a noun means a friend, a companion, and as an adjective it means amiable, lovely. In *Cumannacht* we have therefore not only the idea of an organisation but a heartening sense of social fellowship and co-operation, and we might even add of affectionate spiritual companionship and idealism.[3]

The concept of 'Cumannacht', of 'the jovial revolution' at Croydon Park, of the militant struggle of Larkin fired by a co-operative vision, found links with British Co-operation. But they were with the phenomen of 'Heraldism' rather than with the institutional heirs of the co-operative tradition. The *Daily Herald* and the network of *Daily Herald* Leagues which it spawned were one of the most important features of the pre-First World War labour environment, and yet their isolation from the mainstream 'evolution' of the British labour movement and its ideology has ensured their historical neglect. The *Daily Herald*'s success was certainly not due to financial or organizational stability, but rather to the fact that it was firmly rooted in a working-class socialist tradition derived in part from the ethical socialist origins of the *Clarion* movement and the early ILP, and in part from industrialist attitudes that in the pre-war period were providing the context for British syndicalism.[4] Again 'co-operative commonwealth' was the label most readily applied.

The *Daily Herald* was a forum for socialist comment and debate as it related to the specifics of action, rather than to the censorship imposed by sectarian commitment. The essence of the *Daily Herald* was its 'rebel' spirit manifested by its immediate response to the attacks of 'boss-law' and the politics of capitalism wherever they revealed themselves, and in its unique identity and solidarity between readers.[5] A simple co-operative idealism underpinned this. George Lansbury explained it in 1914:

In our ranks are to be found Socialists and Anarchists, Syndicalists and Suffragists, Trade Unionists and others. We have been united by an idea and not by a programme, that idea being that our first step towards revolution – nay, even reform – is the awakening of the people. In this we have been most successful. Wherever there has been a strike, a lock-out, a

91

Labour fight or a Suffrage fight, the *Daily Herald* Leaguers
have rushed into the turmoil.[6]

The *Daily Herald* Leagues were the institutional expression of
this. They were formed in 1912 to promote sales and finances of
the paper, but soon took on a wider social and political importance. In pre-war years they were often the dominant local socialist
force, organizing supportive action for a variety of struggles.
Cultural and recreational activities, such as bands, concerts,
excursions, and sports became a vital part of League life, expressing
a microcosm of the co-operative commonwealth and its
communitarian ideals.[7] The transformation of the lives of the
working-class at a grass roots level, partly through such collective
activity and partly through the experience of day-to-day struggle
and militancy, would establish the basis of a new socialist polity, a
co-operative commonwealth.

A number of elements in the eclectic philosophy of the *Daily Herald*
made Ireland of particular importance. They can all be associated
with individuals: Connolly and W. P. Ryan in the first case, Francis
and Hannah Sheehy Skeffington in the second, and Jim and Delia
Larkin in the third.

Connolly wrote extensively on the historical and economic basis
of Irish nationalism, referring to an early Irish or Celtic communism which explained the existence and necessity of a socialist
dynamic to the Irish national struggle. In what Bernard Ransom
describes as Connolly's 'hibernicisation of Marxism' he drew heavily
on Gaelic traditions and practices and unpriestly contents in Irish
catholicism. In 1913 he wrote:

> Catholicism, which in most parts of Europe is synonymous
> with Toryism, lickspittle loyalty, servile worship of aristocracy
> and hatred of all that savours of genuine political
> independence on the part of the lower classes, in Ireland is
> almost synonymous with rebellious tendencies, zeal for
> democracy, and intense feeling of solidarity with all strivings
> upwards of those who toil.[8]

From the point of view of the *Daily Herald* this was an idea also being examined by W. P. Ryan. Ryan was a professional journalist
and had worked with the *Catholic Times*, the *Sun* and the *Weekly Sun*
(under T. P. O'Connor), the *Morning Leader* and the *Daily Chronicle*,

before returning to his native Ireland in 1905 to edit the *Irish Peasant* (later, *Irish Nation*).[9] The paper became notorious for its savage denunciations of the Catholic hierarchy, though never of catholicism itself, and in 1910, in the face of a crescendo of hostile criticism from Catholic bishops and dignitaries, Ryan was forced to close down and return to England.

In London Ryan had been one of the leading figures in the Gaelic League, and he continued to be active on his return. He had also been a member of the Socialist Party of Ireland from 1907, and this combination of Irish nationalism and socialism was expressed not only in his work for the *Daily Herald* but also in his book, *The Irish Labour Movement*, written in 1919, which remains one of the major works of Irish labour history. The book charts the growth and struggle of the Irish labour movement with particular emphasis on Gaelic roots, Co-operation and Larkinism. Ryan argued that the Irish struggle was social and co-operative in nature:

a fight for a wholly different civilisation, for the Gaelic system of clan or communal ownership of the land, and the features of life associated therewith, against the alien system of feudalism.[10]

Ireland's oppression by Britain was as much cultural as anything else – a 'war on the Irish language and distinctive Irish culture'.[11]

For evidence of 'democratic and co-operative' nationality in practice Ryan turned partly to the Gaelic League itself, which, admitting its many limitations, he described as potentially 'the most vivid and Socialistic fact and influence in the country'. The summer schools, scholarship schemes and other Gaelic League activities were 'practically all on an unconsciously socialistic basis . . . and things generally have worked out as in a Co-operative Commonwealth'.[12] Ryan also emphasized the achievements of the agricultural co-operative movement under the influence of Horace Plunkett and George Russell. Ryan also put particular emphasis on the necessity for the emancipation of women if the ideal of the co-operative commonwealth was to be achieved.[13]

W. P. Ryan's significance in Irish socialist thought and historiography has been reduced partly because from 1910 he lived and worked in London on a British paper, and partly because he became increasingly fascinated by theosophy and mysticism.[14] But his influence on the relationship between the British labour movement and the Irish issue via the *Daily Herald* was fundamental. Whilst editors came and went with alarming regularity in the early years of the *Daily Herald*, Ryan remained as assistant editor, night editor, and one of the main leader writers. He remained with the paper right through the war years and beyond.[15]

Co-operative socialism in Ireland and in the *Daily Herald* was given a greater intellectual coherence at this time through the work of Francis and Hannah Sheehy Skeffington. Francis was the *Daily Herald*'s Irish correspondent and one of the original shareholders and founder-members of the *Daily Herald* Printing and Publishing Society. He always used the Herald offices as his base when in London. Through their shared commitment to the cause of women's suffrage, Francis and Hannah Sheehy Skeffington remained close friends of George Lansbury, the Pethick Lawrences and other leading socialist-suffragists.[16]

The individual connection between Francis Sheehy Skeffington and the *Herald* was expressed, once more, in the label of the 'co-operative commonwealth'. Through his meetings in Dublin and articles in a variety of progressive European papers, Sheehy Skeffington developed his vision. For him the four causes of socialism, feminism, pacifism, and nationalism were intimately bound up – nationalism was not merely a question of constitutional or political adjustment, but a matter of profound internal social re-ordering. True nationalism involved the pursuit of immediate social freedoms. He frequently expressed this in relation to the sacrifices of suffragist prisoners: 'There is a stronger and purer Nationalism in Mountjoy Prison at this moment than any of Mr Redmond's followers can boast'.[17]

There was much in Francis Sheehy Skeffington's ideas that was akin to the ethical socialist tradition in British socialism, especially the confluence of individual freedom and enlightenment with communitarian practices and ideals. Eva Gore-Booth spoke of his 'unshakeable practical faith in some fundamental rightness in human nature', and referred to him as having 'that divine insight that is unfaltering and unshakeable – not because it cherishes illusions and dreams dreams, but because it feels itself in some strange way to be in touch with the ultimate truth of things'.[18]

Sheehy Skeffington's disapproval of the Easter Rising, which ironically claimed him as one of its greatest martyrs, has ensured his burial under the weight of the military-nationalist tradition in

Ireland. He has been dismissed as a cranky and rather irrelevant suffragist-pacifist. But at the time the writings of Sheehy Skeffington exerted a strong influence, and not only among *Daily Herald* readers. His death was mourned by eulogies in all the leading labour and socialist papers; these were larger and more discursive than those which greeted Connolly's death.[19]

But the force which gave the greatest practical credibility to the concept of the co-operative commonwealth in the *Daily Herald* and in Ireland was the phenomenon of 'Larkinism'. In most British labour history Jim Larkin has been presented as the epitome of radical trade unionism: a burly macho-militant rousing the rank and file in Britain and Ireland with his biting attacks on the evils of capitalism and the fudging of trade union leaders. This endeared him to much of the *Daily Herald* readership. But he was more than this, and it was the deeper elements in his philosophy which made him a hero and a mascot to the *Daily Herald* movement. He differed from the orthodox syndicalists in that he strove 'to articulate and promote an ethic of communal unity and brotherhood among the working-class based upon the notion that the groundwork for such an alternative community must be constructed now, not after some remote capitalist collapse'.[20] It is only recently that the idea of Larkinism as an 'alternative morality', attempting to create prefigurative forms of socialism as well as win specific industrial battles, is being accepted. For contemporaries like W. P. Ryan the visionary element of Larkin's work was clear. In 1913 Ryan wrote:

> We find a refreshing sanity, an enriching truth, a breath of divine fire in 'Larkinism'. Energising the lowliest sections, the despised 'dregs' of the nation, and enabling them to shed their degradation and feel their long-dormant power, it brings a new and unconsidered richness into the body politic.[21]

Larkin's commitment to the immediate creation of a new social order alongside industrial activity was derived in part from the socialism he had learnt in the *Clarion* movement and local ILP around Liverpool in the 1890s.[22] But it was given greater depth and poignancy by Irish factors, not least the alienation between Irish workers and British-based trade unions, which enabled Larkin to give physical form to his beliefs in the ITGWU. With the aid of Delia Larkin's Irish Women Workers' Union, the Union in Dublin became not only a formidable industrial union but also introduced a strong social orientation and communal consciousness among the working class.[23]

With the acquisition of Liberty Hall, the old Northumberland Hotel, early in 1912, the Dublin ITGWU was able to develop its social side fully. Workers and their families came regularly to evenings devoted either to drama practices, choir practices, concerts, social events, or to Irish language classes, and classes more directly geared to socialist teaching.[24] In the main these were the responsibility of Larkin's sister, Delia.[25] In 1913 the ITGWU acquired a mansion and grounds at Croydon Park in Clontarf, and the social aspects of the union were expanded with a new emphasis on gardening and basic farming (a cow and a calf were bought), and on sporting activities (boxing and football teams were formed). Weekly fêtes and fairs were held in the summer, at which Jim Larkin would occasionally give a rendering of 'The Rising of the Moon'.[26] The *Daily Herald* believed that the ideals of Dublin could help to end 'the whole sordid business of slave-labour',

> For the ultimate object of the Dublin pioneers is to abolish slave-classes and ensure a social state in which the workers will be co-operators and honoured individualities. As Larkin has said in regard to their schemes on their own ground at Croydon Park, they are going to show the toiler how we can get along without the capitalist.[27]

There was much similarity between the style of the *Daily Herald* and Larkin's *Irish Worker*, in their emphasis on daily battles fired by a vision of co-operative socialism and ignoring the bureaucratic practicalities of union organization. Larkin frequently used the term 'co-operative commonwealth'. While stressing the importance of co-operative idealism in a speech in Sheffield in 1914, for example, he used language and ideology identical to that of the *Daily Herald* 'rebels':

> Get in the co-operative movement. Make it a real co-operative movement. Build up round your trade union, as we do in Dublin, every social movement, every part of your material side of life. Make your centre of trade unionism a centre of all your life and activities. Get your own halls. Sheffield is big enough to have a hall forty times bigger and more glorious than this. If you haven't a hall to call your own you are a lot

of weak-kneed rebels. You want a great mansion. Nothing is too glorious in conception for you.[28]

'Heraldism', 'Larkinism', and the ideology and practice of the co-operative commonwealth in general, found their synthesis in the colossal struggle of the Dublin lock-out.[29] Through the long autumn and winter months the jovial revolution was put to a very serious test. Liberty Hall became the nerve-centre of resistance and the refuge for the cold and hungry. At Croydon Park concerts and drama were supplemented by the drilling of the Irish Citizen Army, formed by the ITGWU as a reaction to police activity against locked-out workers. Under the pressure of necessity working-class communal solidarity found institutional forms.

Across the water the *Daily Herald* was not slow to realize the issues that were involved and the need to put muscle into the ideal of the co-operative commonwealth. The Dublin lock-out became the paper's greatest concern. From the outset the *Daily Herald* tried to goad the official labour movement into action, condemning any signs of weakness on the part of labour and trade union officials in their dealings with Dublin ('fussy and faint-hearted Lib-Labs, runaways from the industrial battles of Britain'[30]), and responding with great enthusiasm to any evidence of sympathetic industrial action.[31] Such action was, however, short-lived and always retarded by the internal workings of the labour movement. The ideals of Co-operation involved more immediate assistance.

Material aid was in any case an essential prerequisite if the lock-out was to be resisted, for families were starving in Dublin. The early response of the British labour movement and the Co-operative Wholesale Society, which resulted in the sending of several foodships to Dublin, surprised many.[32] The *Daily Herald* believed that here was the way in which the solidarity of the working-class could be expressed, perhaps evolving into more industrial forms of action at a later date. Consequently it threw itself wholeheartedly into the task of raising money and clothing. Constant appeals appeared in the paper but the real activity took place in the local *Daily Herald* Leagues. The Leagues underwent a boom as a result of their work for the Dublin cause. Parades, concerts and collections were organized on a regular basis, as well as the arrangement of meetings and speakers. The *Daily Herald* Leagues were the main co-ordinators of local action, and it was the Leagues which were responsible for the organization of Jim Larkin's successful, vitriolic, 'fiery cross' campaign in November.[33] The organizers of the Food Fund at Liberty Hall, Patrick Lennon and Sean O'Casey, fully realized the role of the *Daily Herald* League, writing in the Glasgow *Forward*:

> owing to the kindness and generosity of the subscribers to the *Herald* League Fund, 1,335 children of the locked out workers have been fully dressed with serviceable warm clothing, and a second supply of underclothing during the period 12th November to 31st December. . . . A large quantity of the clothing has been sent direct from the *Herald* League branches in England, Scotland and Wales, the largest supplies being sent from London, Glasgow and Plymouth.[34]

Many years later the contribution which had been made to the Dublin fight had become part of the *Daily Herald*'s tradition. For a time it was even referred to in the formal list of the objects of the *Herald* League – the third way in which working-class emancipation would be achieved was 'by infusing into the Co-operative movement the spirit which animated its founders, so that it shall become, as it did during the historic Dublin strike, a powerful weapon in the hands of the workers'.[35]

One other effect of the *Daily Herald*'s response to the lock-out was the establishment of a successful if short-lived *Daily Herald* League in Dublin itself. Earlier attempts had been made to organize a League in Dublin, but it was not until the lock-out and the work of an English 'rebel' and NUR officer, Bob Wigzell, that the League was soundly formed. From Wigzell's articles in English labour and radical papers, and from his involvement with the Sheehy Skeffingtons and the Dublin Industrial Co-operative Society, it is clear that he was fired by a belief in Co-operation as a revolutionary ideal, with an emphasis on action and working-class communal solidarity.[36]

After only a month the membership of the Dublin League had grown to 410, and by the end of 1913 it was described as 'perhaps the strongest branch we have'.[37] Francis Sheehy Skeffington and Delia Larkin were both members, and it seems that a majority of members were women. The executive of the League contained seven women and three men, and Irish women were urged to buy the *Daily Herald* by suffragist organizations.[38] The League arranged a number of meetings in Dublin and played a part in the working-class resistance to the lock-out. On 26 January 1914 Tom Mann spoke in the Antient Concert Rooms under *Daily Herald* League auspices. Francis Sheehy Skeffington was in the audience and his notes of the meeting are preserved. His record of Wigzell's opening speech captures in its barest form the ideology of action and rebellion, at times ill-considered and emotional, which was the essence of the *Daily Herald*:

> D.H.L.: Permanent means of expression for all sections of working-class movement. Not attached to any party section. Any worker – rebel – . . . Murphy's police arrest Larkin: why haven't we enrolled our police? Try & sentence Murphy & build prisons & fill with the enemy.
> Armies & Navies: let us have ours.
> Get ready for fight. Don't fight guns with stones. Get a gun & pull the trigger at the right time. [sic].[39]

Meanwhile in Britain the *Daily Herald* had been continuing to campaign on behalf of the Dublin workers. Encouraged by a successful meeting in the London Memorial Hall in October, the *Daily Herald* organized two of the biggest and most important meetings to be held in the London Albert Hall. The first, on 1 November, was packed by thousands, with many more outside. The speakers included Connolly, Lansbury, Tillett, 'AE', Delia Larkin (Jim was in prison), Bernard Shaw, Sylvia Pankhurst, Charlotte Despard, and Mr Pethick Lawrence.[40] Suffragism provided an important bridge between the *Daily Herald* and Ireland. According to one commentator 'the meeting owed almost everything to women'.[41] 'London's magnificent rally to the Dublin rebels', as the *Daily Herald* described it, was an unqualified success; twelve years later George Lansbury wrote of 'the red-hot enthusiasm which prevailed throughout the meeting, which was more like a religious revival than anything else'.[42]

The rally coincided with a wave of genuine indignation throughout the British working class over the imprisonment of Jim Larkin. The *Daily Herald* campaigned vigorously for his release, and after two by-election setbacks the Liberal government freed him. Larkin immediately began a 'fiery cross' tour, speaking at *Daily Herald* League rallies throughout the country. In all nearly £1,300 was raised at these meetings; in several cases wealthy suffragist supporters of the *Daily Herald* paid for the hire of halls.[43] On 19 November

Larkin spoke at the second Albert Hall rally. Again the atmosphere was electric. Three hundred right-wing medical students had infiltrated the meeting and had to be ejected, largely through the intervention of a strong contingent of London taxi-drivers. Francis Meynell and Edgar Lansbury swung down from the balconies to join in the fray as the hall echoed to 'The Red Flag' and 'England Arise'. In Meynell's words 'the whole hall throbbed to the words and tunes and to Lansbury's thunder and Larkin's lightning'.[44]

In the vision of the co-operative commonwealth and its practical manifestations at Croydon Park and Liberty Hall, in Larkinism and Heraldism, the role and position of women was one of the key elements. Women were involved in the lock-out as workers (more exploited even than the men), strikers, demonstrators, and as the expected providers for the family. They were also its victims in a more literal sense when, for example, Alice Brady was shot dead by a strike-breaker on 1 January.[45]

Liberty Hall became the symbol for British and Irish women alike, and the *Daily Herald* highlighted the work being done there. Delia Larkin, the IWWU, and the Irish suffragist organizations had transformed Liberty Hall into a centre of communitarian resistance, dispensing food parcels and clothing to beleaguered families and providing breakfasts and dinners for children and mothers. Delia Larkin was helped at Liberty Hall by a variety of people including Louie Bennett, Constance Markiewicz, and members of the Dublin *Daily Herald* League. One of her main assistants was the English woman Grace Neal, who had come to Ireland after resigning from the Women's Council of the British Socialist Party because of ill-health. She was also a trade union organizer and active in the *Daily Herald* League.[46] Her involvement symbolizes the concern of many British women for what was happening in Dublin. The scenes in Liberty Hall were described in the *Daily Herald*:

> Miss Neal and her assistants are kept busy all day, sorting and altering clothes, and giving them out 'to those who come with tickets' from Union delegates. Beside the clothing store, another room has been converted into a sewing-room, and here a band of the locked out girls are cheerfully at work all day mending and altering the clothing that comes in.[47]

Later in the year Dora Montefiore described the scene:

The work has grown to such proportions that five rooms in Liberty Hall are set aside for the various activities of the Fund. Miss Larkin as organising secretary for the Irish Women Workers' Union, which during the strike has reached a membership of six thousand, holds naturally all the threads of the complicated administration; and under her work loyally Miss Grace Neal, the Hon. Mary Lawless and Miss Coyle. Employed in various capacities are the locked out and victimised girl Unionists; while a tramwayman cooks the daily dinners for the mothers and another transport worker prepares the 3,000 children's breakfasts.[48]

British women suffragists and socialists were active in many ways. Women were noticeable in large numbers at many of Larkin's meetings in Britain. Their interest was probably inspired by the same factors that induced Sylvia Pankhurst to attend the Albert Hall rally on 1 November:

> The Dublin lock-out was to me a poignant incident in our common struggle for a fairer and more humane society. I was glad to accept the invitation as an opportunity to show solidarity with the Dublin workers, and to keep the women's side of the struggle to the front.[49]

Women's organizations, like the Women's Freedom League and the Women's Labour League, were active on behalf of the Dublin workers, organizing meetings and collections.[50]

Perhaps the major contribution to relieving the plight of Dubliners – and certainly the contribution most akin to the ideas of the co-operative commonwealth – was the attempt to organize holidays for Dublin children by sending them to British families. This was the idea of Dora Montefiore, for many years an active campaigner against poverty in East London, a member of the SDF and BSP executive, and a leading figure in the *Clarion* movement and in the *Daily Herald* League. Her realization that 'it was the working woman who needed citizenship more than did her middle-class sister' made her an advocate of adult suffrage.[51]

It was at Larkin's meeting in the Memorial Hall on 10 October that Dora Montefiore first thought up the scheme – 'a great opportunity for workers in England to prove their solidarity with the locked-out men in Dublin, by taking into their homes some of the children who were suffering so severely from the effects of industrial strife'.[52] Looking back in 1927, she spoke of her ideals at the time:

> I felt, from what I had heard and read of the slums of Dublin, and the abysmal poverty of the sweated workers that if we could give the children a holiday from such surroundings and fill them with a vision of what life might hold in the way of a cleaner and more hopeful environment, my colleagues and I might be the means, not only of saving some of the children, who should be the hope of the race, but also of doing some constructive work for the future of organised industrialism.[53]

She got the immediate backing of Larkin, Charles Lapworth, and Lady Warwick, who agreed to act as treasurer for the 'Dublin Kiddies Fund', and the plan was put into action by the *Daily Herald* League. Within a week three hundred offers of homes had come in, as well as many donations of clothes and boots. Several trade unions and trade councils offered to finance the fares and expenses of children received by their members. Dora Montefiore wrote:

> This movement of the workers, small though it may be in its inception, will have among its by-products the implanting in the minds of the workers the sense that they are gradually evolving a workers' state within the capitalist State – a State of an efficient and co-operative administration of things, as opposed to a State for the government of persons.[54]

In spite of the hysterical opposition and accusations of 'kidnapping' which came from the Catholic Church, some children and their mothers did get to England. Merseyside socialists put up at least eighteen for three weeks.[55] In Battersea Charlotte Despard had formed a Catholic Women's Committee to provide holidays for the Dublin children, but it is not clear whether any actually arrived.[56] Emmeline Pethick Lawrence, whose political origins in the *Clarion* movement and in social philanthropy as well as her feminism made her favour the scheme, had six girls and one mother to stay in her country cottage in Surrey for three months.[57]

One other manifestation of the ideals of the co-operative commonwealth was provided by the various schemes for co-operative production, mainly involving women, which emerged towards the end of the lock-out. In 1914 Delia Larkin began to set up co-operative workshops making shirts, blouses, and children's clothing. She also had plans to establish a workers' restaurant, which like the workshops would employ victimized women workers. The *Daily Herald*, looking for something optimistic as the lock-out began to edge towards defeat, gave eager coverage to these plans.[58] For various reasons the plans did not achieve much material success, although a later co-operative society, next door to Liberty Hall, established by Constance Markiewicz and Helena Molony in 1915 to make and sell clothes, was to be more effective, until the work-room was smashed in Easter Week.[59] In the spring of 1914 the IWWU's Irish Workers' Dramatic Society, which had existed since June 1912 as part of the social and cultural programme for trade unionists at Liberty Hall, toured England in order to raise money for the co-operative proposals.[60]

The *Irish Worker* saw the tour as a 'safe inauguration of a new method of fighting moneybugs like Murphy in a saner and more effective manner than just sitting down and starving'; help was given by *Daily Herald* Leagues, Clarionettes, militant socialists, and 'the men and women connected with the fighting suffrage move-ment'.[61] The *Daily Herald* was especially keen on the tour, seeing it as the microcosm of artistic co-operative socialism.[62]

In the north of England, local *Daily Herald* Leagues, such as the Sheffield League where J. T. Murphy was the secretary, organized the tour arrangements.[63] The main London performance at the King's Hall Covent Garden on 9 May raised £125, and local *Daily Herald* Leagues helped organize smaller shows in Battersea, Walthamstow, Willesden, Penge, and Hackney.[64] In terms of raising enough money to begin full-scale co-operative production in Dublin the tour may well have been a failure. Nevertheless it was evidence of the willingness of many sympathetic organizations, such as the *Daily Herald* League, to demonstrate their support and solidarity despite the limitations imposed by sexual, institutional and class oppression.

In the end the Dublin lock-out did not see the triumph of the co-operative commonwealth. It was, after all, a defensive struggle to resist capitalist aggression. The forces and finances of capital were too strong for it, and the vision itself did not permeate far enough into the institutions of labour. The co-operative commonwealth was to be buffeted by the First World War, the rise of a new form of nationalism in Ireland, and a new form of labourism in both Britain

and Ireland. After a final attempt to encourage co-operative production and organization in 1914, Larkin went into exile.[65] He
returned much later to a very different Ireland. The *Daily Herald*
changed its form and eventually became an official labour paper.
The context of the co-operative vision was changed and its practical
roots eroded and replaced by more prosaic realities. The idealism
of 'Cumannacht' was far from the minds of William O'Brien,
Thomas Foran, and the other hard-headed trade unionists of post-
1918 Ireland who were creating a soundly-based solid labour
movement from the remnants of the previous decade. Croydon
Park, the location of Jim Larkin's 'jovial revolution', was now a
foolish extravagance:

> Verily, the Dublin men and women were starving. In the middle
> of it all Larkin could fiddle with hot-house gardening at
> Croydon Park and order from Liverpool – not from Ireland –
> 'seeds plants etc, up to the value of £20'! A veritable marvel
> of 'constructive leadership'![66]

Ten years earlier, however, the vision had been a noble and practical reality for many. When the Congress of British Co-operators
had met in Dublin in 1914 the *Daily Herald* was still able to enthuse:

> To the Ireland that has not been spoiled, enslaved or
> Anglicised the spirit of co-operation is entirely natural; we
> have seen it in being quite spontaneously and cheerily in the
> avowedly poorest parts of the country. This healthy and human
> order of things is a tradition of dateless age. It is one of the
> factors on which the comprehensive and scientific pioneers of
> co-operation in our own day have been able to count
> effectively. . . . The Co-operative, Labour, intellectual and
> other movements give gratifying promise that Ireland in due
> course will realise that precious thing, a human nation, a true
> community.[67]

NOTES

1 *Irish Worker*, 9 August 1913.
2 W. P. Ryan, *The Irish Labour Movement from the 'Twenties to Our Own
 Day*, Dublin, Talbot, 1919, ch. 3.
3 W. P. Ryan, 'Dr Socialism and the Irish Hypochondriac', lecture to
 the Socialist Party of Ireland, 17 October 1909, pp. 6–8, National

Library of Ireland, William O'Brien pamphlets.

4 For more on the *Daily Herald* see R J Holton, '*Daily Herald* versus *Daily Citizen*, 1912–1915: the struggle for a labour daily in relation to "the labour unrest" ', *International Review of Social History*, 1974; for another moment in socialist history when 'the co-operative commonwealth' was used, see Stephen Yeo, 'A new life: the religion of socialism in Britain, 1883–1896', *History Workshop Journal*, 4, Autumn 1977, pp. 5–56.

5 R. Postgate, *The Life of George Lansbury*, London, Longman, 1951, p. 144.

6 Circular to members of the *Daily Herald* League, 11 February 1914, National Library of Ireland, Sheehy Skeffington papers, uncatalogued MS.

7 *Daily Herald*, 10 June 1919, for George Belt's advocacy of the same style in 1919.

8 *Forward*, 3 May 1913. See also J. Connolly, *Labour, Nationality and Religion*, Dublin, Cumanacht Na Heireann, 1910. For a full analysis of this, see B. Ransom, *Connolly's Marxism*, London, 1980.

9 *Who's Who*, 1944.

10 Ryan, *The Irish Labour Movement*, pp. 150–1.

11 *Daily Herald*, 25 May 1914; see also 15 September 1913; 27 October 1913.

12 Ryan, 'Dr Socialism', pp. 10–11.

13 ibid., pp. 9–10. Also Ryan, *The Irish Labour Movement, passim.*

14 See especially W. P. Ryan, *The Celt and the Cosmos*, London, D. Nutt, 1914.

15 G. Lansbury, *The Miracle of Fleet Street: The Story of the Daily Herald*, London, Victoria House, 1925, p. 37.

16 National Library of Ireland, Sheehy Skeffington papers, uncatalogued MS.

17 *Irish Citizen*, 13 July 1912.

18 National Library of Ireland, MS. 22, 654.

19 e.g. *Daily Herald*, during May 1916; *Women's Dreadnought*, 13 May 1916.

20 R. J. Holton, 'Syndicalism and its impact in Britain with particular reference to Merseyside 1910–1914', unpublished D.Phil. thesis, University of Sussex, 1973, p. 283.

21 W. P. Ryan, *The Labour Revolt and Larkinism*, London, *Daily Herald*, 1913, p. 23.

22 E. Taplin, 'Jim Larkin, Liverpool and the N.U.D.L.', *Saothar*, 4.

23 The IWWU was formally created in September 1911. It was affiliated to the ITGWU.

24 *Irish Worker*, 27 May 1911 – 5 December 1914.

25 ibid., 2 May 1914.

26 S. O'Casey, *The Story of the Irish Citizen Army*, Dublin, 1919, pp. 36–40. New edition, London, Journeyman Press, 1980.

27 *Daily Herald*, 14 November 1913.

28 *Sheffield Independent*, 13 July 1914.

29 The best account of the Dublin lock-out is in C. D. Greaves, *The I.T.G.W.U.: The Formative Years*, Dublin, 1982, pp. 95–104.
30 *Daily Herald*, 9 September 1913.
31 For a full analysis of sympathetic industrial action see K. R. Harding, 'The Irish issue in the British Labour movement', unpublished D.Phil. thesis, University of Sussex, 1983, pp. 161–70.
32 Foodships sent jointly by the TUC and the CWS began arriving from mid-September.
33 Larkin was released from prison on 13 November and began his tour of British cities thereafter.
34 *Forward*, 17 January 1914.
35 *Daily Herald*, 6 May 1916.
36 National Library of Ireland, MSS 22,666 and 15,650. *Railway Review*, 5 September 1913, 24 October 1913 and 28 November 1913.
37 *Daily Herald*, 13 December and 31 December 1913.
38 ibid., 16 December 1913; *Irish Citizen*, 31 January 1914.
39 National Library of Ireland, MS 22,256(i).
40 *Daily Herald*, 3 November 1913.
41 Henry Harben, quoted in A. Raeburn, *The Militant Suffragettes*, Michael Joseph, London, 1973, p. 222.
42 Lansbury, op. cit., p. 53.
43 *Daily Herald*, 6 January 1914.
44 Lansbury, op. cit., pp. 56–7; F. Meynell, *My Lives*, London, Bodley Head, 1973, p. 81.
45 For a description of the role of women in the lock-out and in the relationship between British labour and Ireland in general, see Harding, op. cit., pp. 106–47.
46 *Socialist Record*, July 1913.
47 *Daily Herald*, 28 November 1913.
48 ibid., 24 December 1913.
49 S. Pankhurst, *The Suffragette Movement: An Intimate Account of Persons and Ideals*, London, Longman, 1931, p. 502.
50 *Labour Woman*, October 1913 and January 1914.
51 D. B. Montefiore, *From a Victorian to a Modern*, London, Archer, 1927.
52 ibid., pp. 156–78.
53 ibid., pp. 156–7.
54 ibid., p. 158.
55 Letter from R. J. Holton, *Bulletin of the Society for the Study of Labour History*, Autumn 1974.
56 A. Linklater, *An Unhusbanded Life: Charlotte Despard, Suffragette, Socialist and Sinn Feiner*, London, Hutchinson, 1980, p. 174.
57 E. Pethick Lawrence, *My Part in a Changing World*, London, Gollancz, 1938, pp. 301–2.
58 *Daily Herald*, 31 January 1914.
59 J. Van Voris, *Constance de Markiewicz: in the Cause of Ireland*, Amherst, University of Massachusetts Press, 1967, p. 157.
60 *Irish Worker*, 8 June 1912; *Daily Herald*, 23 April 1914.
61 *Irish Worker*, 14 March 1914.

62 *Daily Herald*, 24 April 1914.
63 J. T. Murphy, *New Horizons*, London, 1941, p. 39.
64 *Daily Herald*, 11 May 1914.
65 Workers' Union of Ireland, *1913, Jim Larkin and the Dublin Lockout*, Dublin, 1964.
66 Irish Transport and General Workers' Union, *The Attempt to Smash the I.T.G.W.U.*, Dublin, 1924, p. xiv.
67 *Daily Herald*, 3 March 1914.

Chapter Seven

'DOMESTIC DRUDGERY WILL BE A THING OF THE PAST': CO-OPERATIVE WOMEN AND THE REFORM OF HOUSEWORK

ALISTAIR THOMSON

'The fact of so many changes having occurred in domestic life, impels one to ask, Why should there not be others?'

Thus Ben Jones (1847–1942) whose mother had been a power-loom weaver and father a dyer's labourer, and who became the first manager of the CWS London branch. Ben Jones wrote the massive and still useful *Co-operative Production* (1894). The quotation comes from the Proceedings of the Industrial Remuneration Conference in 1885. His wife, who died early, was a leading activist in the Womens Co-operative Guild. In his *Working Men Co-operators*, written with Acland in 1884 (p. 106) Ben Jones also tried to theorize 'associated homes'. In 1885 he wrote,

> It is worth while expressing one's opinion in favour of these institutions, even at the expense of being taken for a visionary. Every man knows the immense benefit that has resulted from division of labour. The home has not been free from direct invasions. Cotton and wool used to be spun and woven at home; now it is not. Stockings used to be almost universally knitted at home; now the practice in England is rare. Most articles of underclothing used to be made at home, the practice is becoming less frequent, owing to the invention of sewing machines. The home has also been invaded by labour-saving machinery, such as these sewing machines and wringing machines. The fact of so many changes having occurred in domestic life, impels one to ask, why should there not be others? The work of women would be made much lighter by division of labour. In an associated home, one could cook, another could nurse, a third could act as chambermaid, a fourth could be the waitress, and so on. Those who wished to do nothing, and could afford the luxury, could pay their poorer or more energetic sisters to do the work for them.
> (*Proceedings of the Industrial Remuneration Conference*, 1885, p. 294)

This chapter follows through the limitations as well as the possibilities of such an outlook. First, however, it insists that there *was* vision, concerning association and home, however hard historians now have to dig for it. Majority silence from places where noise is difficult to make, let alone to federate in order to get heard (whether pre-enclosure villages, 1920s housing estates, or that most sealed place of all: HOME) does not mean assent. Historians are privileged to try to listen, like this chapter does, to rumours from such places: most domestic irritations and visions necessarily had no echo, but some got through. There were challenges to the division of labour *between* homes, even if the challenges to the division of labour *within* homes and between genders were (seem to historians?) far more rare.

But then this chapter also makes clear what obstacles there were to any kind of grand co-operation in the domestic sphere from within the co-operative movement itself. The movement *was* mainly male: women *were*, for the most part, seen 'with a basket': patriarchy was the rule (for which see the sympathetic autobiography by Linda McCullough Thew, *The Pit Village and the Store,* London, Pluto, 1985). But the movement *did* also nurture, or at least (see Chapter 8), *allow*, the most successful working-class womens' organization yet seen in Britain, the Women's Co-operative Guild. The visions, however partial, and the obstacles however sexist are each worth knowing. And the obstacles, while evidenced within the movement itself, were, of course, far more strongly based in the society outside.

Imagine a world in which housework is taken out of the house, and out of the hands of women! At the end of each block of houses there is a common kitchen, providing meals for householders who have not the time or energy to cook for themselves. A neighbourhood washing service collects washing once a week and returns it washed, ironed, and folded, and a house-cleaning service is available for those who need it. Perhaps these services are collectively owned and controlled by a neighbourhood co-operative, perhaps they are sponsored by local government. They are not privately owned, profit-making enterprises. The home has become a place for rest and relaxation. And women, just as much as men, are freed to enter their preferred employment and to enjoy their leisure time as they wish.

This bold domestic future was keenly debated within the Women's Co-operative Guild during the late nineteenth and early twentieth centuries. Guildswomen argued about domestic life and reform with pride, anger, and despair. Primarily 'married women belonging to the artisan class',[1] they had good reason for all three.

Many guildswomen were wary of communal or co-operative

alternatives to their individual burden of housework. As working-class women they feared for the independence and privacy that the home could, ideally, offer a working-class family. As women they perceived a threat to their self-respect and power as managers of the home and family. A woman's hard work was essential for the family's survival. More than that, she would slave so that her family could 'turn out' as well as possible. A rarely used front parlour would be kept scrupulously clean, collars and pinafores would be dutifully ironed, scrubbing the flagstones could become a ritual performance. A family's good name in the neighbourhood, 'respectability', was at stake. It was also a woman's dignity.

Working women were also forever conscious of the middle-class ideology of 'the angel in the house' which was urged upon them. For example, in 1890 'Narcissus' wrote to the Guild's 'Woman's Corner' in the *Co-operative News* of the 'sacred thoughts that cling around that little word "home" . . . we should make it our pride to do our work in that sphere so well that . . . it will always be a place that our fathers and brothers may think of with pleasure'.[2]

The hard-working women of the Guild were not easily taken in by such 'sacred thoughts'. 'Mary' responded to 'Narcissus' with a ferocious protest:

> Dear Madame, I am sure you and the other ladies mean well and kindly; but dear heart! how sick I am of being told that we ought to have a bright clear room ready for the menfolk when they come home, and a good supper, and be nicely dressed and so on! . . . . I ask you, when the blessed evening does come, who has the most right to be 'hungry and tired', I after my day of being cook, housemaid, laundress, nurse, governess, playmate, sewing-woman and mother . . . or my husband after his day of sawing planks and drawing plans in a workshop full of mates?[3]

Concluding with 'it's a comfort to have spoken my mind for once', 'Mary' opened a valve of feeling. A stream of letters admired and repeated her protest. 'Polly' thanked her for the truth – 'it has been white-washed long enough!' – and 'P.P.' knew 'full well the crowd of duties each day brings in domestic life.'[4]

Above all, these guildswomen agreed that housework was an exhausting, isolated and unhealthy drudgery. For example, here is the domestic routine of Mrs Bury, a Lancashire guildswoman at the turn of the century:

I arrange my housework each week, as follows: On Monday I clear up all rooms after Sunday, brush and put away all Sunday clothes, and then separate and put out to soak all soiled clothes for washing. On Tuesday, the washing is done, the clothes folded and mangled. After the washing, the scullery receives a thorough cleaning for the week. Wednesday is the day for starching and ironing, and stocking darning, as well as the usual week's mending. On Thursday I bake the bread and clean the bedrooms. On Friday I clean the parlour, lobby and staircase, as well as the living room. Saturday is left for all outside cleaning – windows and stonework – besides putting all the clean linen on the beds.[5]

More detailed descriptions of guildswomen's 'Characteristic Working Days' fill in the gaps of that weekly routine.[6] They add Sunday to the working week and make each day less ordered, rising before first light to start the fire, feed and send off husband to work and children to school, the all-day, every-day tasks of scrubbing and dusting and shopping and cooking, the nursing of a baby and worried watch over infants too young for school, the family trooping home for dinner and then again for the crowded turmoil of the evening, the working into the early hours while husband and children sleep, ironing, darning, sewing.

Working women usually struggled with inadequate household equipment to do this work. An Accrington woman described her washing facilities to a neighbouring guildswoman, Mrs Haworth, in 1900:

'I've got to heat every drop in kettle and pan, and carry it from the sink.' 'But', said I, 'there's a boiler in this range.' 'Won't hold a drop. It was cracked when I came to the house.' 'But haven't you told the landlord?' 'Yes. It's no use. He won't spend a penny. And the oven takes me hours to heat. Do you know, often I put to the fire and toil all morning to get a pie and pudding for dinner, and often I have to take potatoes out and cook in the pan. It takes hours to heat it to bake with, and I am poking and toiling all day. Well . . . I often sit down and cry.'[7]

A married woman could rely on at least some household help from her family, but most important was the help of other women. Mrs Scott was a felt-hat worker and described her life in the 1931

Guild publication, *Life As We Have Known It*: 'We had the nights to ourselves, though in those days there was housework to be done, baking at night and cleaning, but my auntie was very good and used to help me very much.'[8] She was also helped by 'that ministering angel, the good neighbour'. The basis of this assistance was reciprocity. You helped a neighbour because one day she would help you, and the survival of both families depended on this mutual aid. Most working women shared the grateful memory of activist Hannah Mitchell: 'If I had a genius I could write a book on the good neighbours who have helped me so much in life.'[9]

The informal communality of working women's lives could only help so much with the housework. Assistance was most readily available in emergencies, during childbirth or illness, or when a woman had to go out to work. The everyday tasks fell mainly on the woman by herself. Homes were not built for common housework and most neighbours were equally busy in their own kitchens. Guildswomen determined 'to lessen this constant drudgery and make life worth living'.[10]

One thing the Guild could do was help make working women 'better and more efficient housewives'. System and method in housework could reduce the drudgery and make time for another life. So guildswomen carefully studied recommended pamphlets and books about 'The Making of the Home', and at branch meetings regularly swapped household hints from their readings and from their own practical experience. In 1894 the Guild Annual Report noted that there had been ninety-seven courses of lectures in dressmaking, cookery and washing, sick-nursing and ambulance work, and that topics of domestic economy were among the most common on branch agendas.[11]

This domestic educative activity was particularly encouraged by the Guild's founding women. By the 1890s women with wider ambitions for the Guild questioned that emphasis. Household advice became a less frequent item in the 'Woman's Corner', and in the branches 'the study and practice of co-operation and other methods of social reform' became more important.[12] Yet domestic economy classes were always extremely popular among the working women of the Guild. They were not the condescending lectures of middle-class 'ladies' who blamed working-class wives and mothers for the appalling conditions of working-class life. Instead, working women were sharing their own skills, and gratefully received and offered household hints which suited the practicalities of their lives and saved time and money.

Domestic education did not challenge the conditions in which housework was done. Some guildswomen who approved 'the woman's mission in the home' argued that individual improvement was preferable to altering the conditions of housework. Most agreed that domestic education was a useful adjunct rather than an alternative to other change. At the Guild's Manchester Festival in 1892, Mary Spooner from London argued that the working woman's domestic burden was 'due to lack of method, but still more to the conditions under which we live'. She concluded that Guild lectures and classes should educate women to 'demand a change of conditions which will ensure more leisure and variety to the hard worked wife'.[13]

In her paper on 'Future Guild Work', Mary Spooner referred to this reform of the conditions of housework as 'a new subject for Guild consideration'. It had probably got onto the Guild agenda when the innovative and energetic Margaret Llewelyn Davies became General Secretary in 1889. In 1890 she first proposed to the Sheffield branch that the Guild was a means of 'liberating them from the drudgery of housework', and strongly advocated for that purpose public kitchens and bakeries, 'associated homes' and improved home design.[14] She and Mary Spooner agreed that working women needed to be 'educated up' to understand these reforms and then to demand them. A couple of months after the Manchester Festival an outline of 'Practical Work for Branches' was circulated by the Guild Central Committee. It was divided into four fields for Guild endeavour, which reveal the relative significance of housework as an issue for the Guild: 'The Home' was given equal priority with the store, trade unionism, and women's citizenship. For 'The Home', branches were advised to:

> Arrange lectures and classes on sick-nursing, dress-making, cooking, clean-starching, ambulance etc. Arrange debates on the education of children, care of babies etc. Make out lists of all kinds of labour-saving articles and forward to general secretary. Promote co-operative wash-houses, bakeries, kitchens, gardens.[15]

Attached to the circular was a list of 'Popular Papers' which could help guildswomen to understand these proposals and which would foster branch discussion. An extraordinary, eclectic set of papers about 'The Home' reveals the origins of the Guild's reforming ideas. At one extreme were papers on 'The Making of the Home', including one by Mrs H. O. Barnett, who believed that 'It is the woman's work to make the house into a home. It is a beautiful work.'[16] But the list went beyond making 'better and more efficient housewives'. A significant recommendation was a biography of the early-nineteenth century English radical, Robert Owen. Owen and the Owenites wanted to abolish private housework. They thought it an 'unproductive and repulsive drudgery' which enslaved women in 'an eternal prison house'.[17] Owenites planned and created model communities in which housework on modern scientific principles was to be a collective responsibility.

In England, the seven Owenite communities established between 1821 and 1845 were crisis-ridden and short-lived, but memories of the attempt and its possibilities survived with Owenites who moved into the new-founded co-operative movement around the middle of the century. Edward Vansittart Neale was a late-nineteenth-century co-operator who retained an interest in the ideas of Owen and his French contemporary, Charles Fourier. Neale was particularly impressed by a Fourierist experiment, M. Godin's 'Familistère' at Guise. In that community, Godin's factory employees and their families lived in a large block of apartments which opened onto a central hall. Each apartment included modern domestic conveniences, and the tenants had the use of a common washhouse and restaurant, infant nurseries, and schools. In the 1880s Neale promoted such 'associated houses' as a possibility for co-operative enterprise.[18] But few apart from the women of the Guild took his ideas seriously. Co-operators were usually more interested in gaining control of economic relations than in reforming the relations of domestic life.

Edward Greening was one other male co-operator who thought the domestic arrangements at Guise were 'splendid for the ladies'. His story of *The Co-operative Traveller Abroad* described Godin's 'Familistère' and was included in the Guild's list of readings about the home. Greening's daughter, who was an active guildswoman, supported such schemes which would 'see women relieved from their domestic drudgery'.[19] Other daughters also brought the ideas of veteran Owenites and co-operators into Guild discussion. Miss Bamford of Manchester gained from her father, Samuel Bamford, editor of the *Co-operative News*, an interest in co-operation which extended to domestic reform; in 1895 she was listed as a Guild lecturer on 'Associated Homes'.[20] Emilie Holyoake, daughter of the revered Owenite and co-operator, George Jacob Holyoake, was on the Guild's Central Committee in the 1880s and argued that guildswomen should fight for co-operative kitchens and washhouses.[21]

Owenites and their ideas also had a continuing influence in North America. Between the 1880s and 1920s a distinctive group of American women, recently rediscovered and labelled 'material feminists' by Dolores Hayden in a magnificent history of their 'Grand Domestic Revolution', developed and practised the old Owenite ideals.[22] For example, Charlotte Perkins Gilman campaigned for professional domestic services to end the primitive wastefulness of housework and to liberate women from the trap of the home. She was widely influential in British socialist and feminist circles. Working women read her haunting poems and revolutionary proposal in the labour and suffrage press, and her most powerful work, *Women And Economics*, was available in a 'popular library' circulated by the Women's Co-operative Guild.[23]

'Leisure for workmen's wives', an 1892 article by labour activist Tom Mann, was also on the Guild reading list. Mann was deeply involved with the co-operative movement during the early 1890s, in ways which labour historians have not yet indicated. In this article he urged working women to rebel against their wretched lives and to set up communal kitchens and washhouses.[24] In another book on the list, Stanton Coit argued that 'Neighbourhood Guilds' would be one way to fight for these and other community services.[25] Last on the list was a pamphlet on 'Co-operative Housekeeping'. This was an early draft of a paper delivered by Catharine Webb at the annual Guild conference in Leicester in 1893.[26] Catharine Webb was a member of the Battersea branch of the Guild. She was a single woman of independent means, and she was one of a number of influential guildswomen who had the money and thus the time for administrative work. There was some tension between the domestic ideals of middle-class guildswomen like Mary Spooner, Margaret Llewelyn Davies, and Catharine Webb, and the practical needs and desires of the bulk of working-women members; Catharine Webb confessed that for her the details of domestic life were 'more a matter of theory than of practice'. Yet there were working women like Sarah Reddish who fervently argued for radical domestic reform, and middle-class guildswomen were very keen to listen to working women and help them get the changes they wanted; Catharine Webb affirmed in her paper that she merely wanted to promote discussion of housework among more practically-minded guildswomen. Her ideas clearly benefited from those of the other recommended writers, though she reworked them to suit modern circumstances and the practical workings of Co-operation. Her arguments conveniently summarize the theoretical possibilities and limitations of the Guild's challenge to housework.

To understand those possibilities we need to ask what Catharine Webb wanted to free working women from, and what she hoped to free them to become. She wanted to free women from 'the unending burdensomeness' of housework, simply 'to make life worth living for working women', to give them more time for a life of their own. She also wanted them to have more time for public life. Perhaps the Guild's most impressive success was that it gave working women the confidence and skills to speak and fight for their needs. Mrs Layton of London concluded in her contribution to *Life As We Have Known It* that, in lectures and readings and campaigns:

> the Guild has been the means of making its members think more of themselves than ever they did before. The Guild training altered the whole course of my life. . . . From a shy, nervous woman, the Guild made me a fighter.[27]

But women needed time and energy for fighting, and guildswomen recognized that housework was a major obstacle. Catharine Webb agreed with Lancashire millworker Sarah Reddish that reform was needed so that housework could be done 'with the least possible expenditure of time and force . . . so as to leave time for the wider claims of citizenship'.[28]

Working women needed more time for themselves and for public life, but Catharine Webb contended that the Guild did not want to 'upset the relationships of domestic life', to draw women away from their obvious duties to husband and children:

> All that is good in domestic life – the sanctity of the home, the loving solicitude for the comforts of the husband, the increasing watchfulness and care for little children – these things we would not lessen, but rather encourage to a higher perfection.

Unlike their Owenite mentors, Catharine Webb and other guildswomen almost never challenged the different 'ideal' roles for men and women. With a few exceptions,[29] they were opposed to women entering the paid workforce, and argued instead for an improvement of women's nurturing role as mother and wife, as 'homemaker' (guildswomen rarely considered crèches as a co-operative possibility, and then usually with disapproval).[30] Indeed, their ideal woman would be both 'homemaker and citizen'. Conversely, though in private they may have pleaded or shouted at their husbands to give more of a hand, guildswomen almost never argued publicly that their husbands should share the work of the home and the family. But they did believe that they could abolish the hard work of the home and radically improve the quality of their lives.

Catharine Webb was quite convinced that domestic drudgery would become a thing of the past. She explained how women's domestic work of an earlier era, weaving, spinning, grinding corn, had been taken over by modern factory production, and that bakeries were ending the work of home-baking:

> We do but keep pace with the still onward march of civilization when we suggest that there are yet other tasks, equally laborious, pertaining to domestic life which could be performed by co-operation in place of individual effort.

Practically, she argued that the co-operative movement could make this revolution available to working women. Washhouses and laundries, kitchens and bakeries, connected to local co-operative stores and financed by the many small shares of working-class co-operators, could buy the best new domestic machinery. With this economy of scale, and without a private profit-making owner, working-class families could afford to use such co-operative domestic services. Co-operation would thus benefit the worker of the home as well as her husband in a factory.

Catharine Webb's proposals for 'Co-operation as Applied to Domestic Work' provoked enthusiastic debate at many Guild conferences and meetings. After she first read her paper at Leicester in 1893, delegates unanimously resolved:

> That it is desirable that the modern methods of production, namely, machinery and association, should be applied to

women's domestic work, and in this view, Co-operative
societies are urged to use a portion of their capital in the
establishment of co-operative washhouses, laundries, bakeries
and cookshops.[31]

Washhouses and laundries were most seriously considered. A focus
upon these co-operative alternatives to women's work of washing
will reveal arguments and tensions in Guild debates, the tactics
which the Guild used in its domestic campaigns, and the practical
possibilities of and obstacles to this new world for women.

When guildswomen looked for alternatives to the weekly work of
washday, the first issue was always whether or not washing should
be done out of the home, either in a laundry, or by the woman herself in a well-equipped common washhouse. They eagerly debated
this question. All women worried about the cost of putting the
washing out, and some complained that public washhouses or
laundries might lead to infection, or might mistreat clothes.[32]
Other guildswomen were proud of their washing work and the way
they did it, and objected to any change. Mrs Sibley of Willesden
Junction told an 1896 conference on 'The Home' that washing
'could be very well managed at home, and she told us how she did
it, and then made the beds and cooked the dinner too'.[33] Sometimes this was a regional pride: women in the North-West were less
enthusiastic about taking the washing out of the home than
guildswomen in the Midlands or the South. Sometimes it was a
question of status: common washhouses were fine in the poorer
districts, 'but the ladies of Leicester were too independent for that;
they liked to do their own washing and cooking'.[34]

Despite these objections, the majority of guildswomen agreed
that it would be better if washing could be done out of the home. It
was sometimes argued that the transformation was natural, almost
inevitable, for nothing was 'so silly as the present waste of time and
money of each household doing its own wash'; it was contrary to
the trend of a mass-produced, mechanical age.[35] The common provision of modern machinery was especially necessary for many
working-class families which simply did not have the room or the
equipment to do the wash properly at home. Guildswomen went
further than that and declared that all working-class families
needed such a reform, for Monday washday was 'an abomination
in every home'.[36]

The cheapest available alternative to washing at home was the municipal washhouse. There, for a couple of pence, a woman could use a compartment well-equipped with tubs for boiling, washing, and rinsing, a wringer and drying cupboards. Washhouses were few and far between, and working women in the Guild, and in the Social Democratic Federation and the Women's Labour League, urged local councils to build more of them.[37] Yet the main strategy of Guild domestic campaigns was to seek change through co-operative rather than municipal action, and to promote co-operative laundries rather than washhouses. Laundries were a more hopeful campaigning possibility than washhouses, which local co-operative societies scorned as a charitable service which could not possibly provide a safe return on invested capital. The steam laundry was a recent innovation, and it at least conformed to the usual model of co-operative enterprise, of shareholders paying for a service performed by co-operative employees and receiving a dividend at the point of service or purchase. It might even be a profitable investment and, for the women, it offered a complete relief from washing.[38]

From the early 1890s, guildswomen actively canvassed local co-operative societies to invest surplus share capital in a laundry. Quick off the mark were the women of the Dewsbury branch, who in 1894 urged their store committee to open a steam laundry as well as a bakery. Both would be profitable, they argued, and would be 'a boon to many overworked women. . . . Labour leaders agitate for better wages and a better distribution of wealth; we women ask for a better distribution of work'.[39]

At first, committees of men co-operators were wary of this pressure. They were not so enthusiastic about reducing women's work. One male co-operator advised guildswomen 'not to aspire too high' when he first heard Catharine Webb's domestic proposals (from across the Leicester hall: 'It is better to aim high.' ('Hear, hear').[40] They were even less keen if it would cost them. A laundry demanded a large investment for any society, and no one was sure that this most modern innovation could pay for itself.

But, in 1896, Glasgow co-operators led the way with a meeting to discuss 'the desirability of Co-operators entering on laundry work'. They concluded that a federation of local societies could best afford the full use of modern machinery, and a building project was begun.[41] Before the turn of the century, the Glasgow Co-operative Laundry

Association at Barrhead was proving that a federation of co-operative societies could successfully build and operate such a venture. For an investment of about £3,000 it could rely on a weekly trade of perhaps £100, which assured an adequate return on share capital and the dividend for users. Over the next few years other regional co-operative federations, prompted and supported by the Guild, followed Glasgow's example.[42]

Ironically, lessening the work of wearied wives was not high among the motives of men co-operators when they decided to invest in a laundry. Answers to the question, 'Shall we establish a co-operative laundry in our district?' were usually those of hard-headed businessmen co-operators. Would the investment of share capital pay? What sort of dividend could it provide? When a laundry was opened, speeches celebrated another co-operative triumph but neglected the hard-won relief for women. Sometimes women of the Guild were not even given a chance to use their practical experience in the planning or management of a laundry: in 1907 three guildswomen who asked to join a laundry committee were laughed at by a meeting of northern co-operators.[43] The Guild responded to these taunts and this neglect with an official policy to get members elected to Laundry Committees.[44] They wanted to work out a way of bringing the luxury of a laundry service to as many working women as possible. Mrs J. Green suggested in 1896 that those who could afford to put their washing out should share their dividend with the less well-off, and so also share the service.[45] But guildswomen could not resolve the problem of providing a cheap laundry service from limited co-operative resources. They were defeated by the politics of the economics, which deemed that the social needs of working women were not worth a 'non-economic' service. This was men's politics. As husbands and on co-operative committees, men were not willing to pay for a service which was usually provided for free. When guildswoman Mrs R. Nash lectured in 1907 about 'Married Women and Their Work – How Freedom May Be Gained', the editors of the *Co-operative News* were appalled by calls for co-operative laundries, for improved home-working conditions, and for the power of the vote. They feared that the speech foreshadowed a woman's domestic strike, and denounced the Guild as 'a militant trade union'![46]

Bread-baking was already a successful co-operative venture by the end of the century. If there was any resistance it was from women, especially in the North-West, who were proud of their home-made bread. But many more were glad of relief from baking day.[47] Certainly, the local store committees were eager to erect co-operative bakeries, which kept stores well-supplied with bread and profitably used share capital. But few, apart from the women of the Guild, promoted bakeries expressly to lessen housework.[48] Guildswomen sometimes hastened the establishment of a bakery, but the women were successful because bread-making was a task which could easily be capitalized, whether by co-operators or capitalists, at a price which working people could afford.

Co-operative kitchens did not get far beyond the imaginations of Guild idealists. In 1893 Catharine Webb produced detailed plans of how a kitchen attached to every co-operative store could provide cheap and nourishing cooked meals.[49] Other Guild domestic pioneers, Louisa Martindale in Brighton, Emilie Holyoake, and Margaret Llewelyn Davies,[50] agreed with her that well-equipped common kitchens with food and fuel economies of scale could provide cheaper meals than a woman cooking at home, possibly of a better quality. This was not an 'unnatural' alternative, for the well-to-do had no qualms about employing cooks. In association, working women could afford this luxury and end 'the tyranny of meals' and the most constant household labour of cooking, day in, day out.[51]

The Guild did have one opportunity for a practical experiment along these lines. In 1902 the Guild combined with the Sunderland Co-operative Society to establish a 'People's Store' in the poor East End of that city. It was hoped that, eventually, many such 'People's Stores', with low entrance fees and moderate prices and dividends, would allow the people of poor districts to benefit from Co-operation.[52] One of the many innovations in the Guild scheme was the 'Coffee and Cooked Meat Shop', which would provide cheap cooked food to be eaten on the premises or taken away.[53] A 'cookshop' was attached to the Sunderland store, and within a couple of weeks Margaret Llewelyn Davies reported it was 'perhaps the greatest success. . . . Its corner window, where the steaming food is in full view, is never without its admiring gazes.' Customers were two rows deep, queueing for soup, pease pudding, boiled pork and other meats, and one morning over 40 gallons of soup were sold.[54] The cookshop was so successful that another was opened at a second co-operative branch. Overworked wives and mothers, without the time, energy, or equipment to cook decent meals for their families, were glad to pay a little.

Guild hopes for 'Coffee and Cooked Meat Shops' were dashed when two years later the Sunderland Society decided that 'People's Stores' too radically departed from usual co-operative methods, and withdrew its special support. Once again, men co-operators refused to extend the benefits of Co-operation to the less well-off, or to women. Significantly, the Guild did not fight so hard for co-operative kitchens as it had for laundries and washhouses, and the cause lapsed. There was much more opposition within the Guild to the idea of common kitchens. Home-cooking was more important for a working woman's self-respect than laundering or bread-baking. It was also a crucial part of the image of 'true womanhood'. And public or even co-operative kitchens resembled the despised charity of soup kitchens, and seemed to threaten working-class indepen-dence.[55]

We need to look more closely at the uncertainty and opposition which crippled this and other similar experiments. For example, the 'cost price restaurants' and National Kitchens inspired by Sylvia Pankhurst during the Great War were extremely popular among working women. They welcomed a domestic alternative which did not undermine their self-respect, and which they could afford. Unfortunately, as soon as the war ended, councils decided that women should be back at their stoves and wash-tubs, and withdrew funding.[56] To realize their domestic dreams, women needed power as well as conviction.

The Guild waged other domestic campaigns. In 1898 it began a campaign to improve the quality of working-class houses, so they would be healthier and more comfortable, but also to reduce women's work. From intensive investigations and local discussions, guildswomen developed plans of well-equipped houses which would be easier to work in and to clean.[57] They tried to get elected to co-operative house-building committees to put these plans into effect. In association with the Women's Labour League (WLL), the Guild also tried to get its ideal working woman's house incorpo-rated into the post-war council-house building programme.[58] Other histories will need to look more closely at the ambitions and effectiveness of these campaigns. What is striking is that working women were fighting to improve the quality of their lives. As a WLL pamphlet concluded in 1919, 'the working woman of today is neither contented with the conditions of her home, nor apathetic with regard to its improvement'.[59]

Efforts to make the home a better workshop for women did not challenge the fact that housework was women's work. But Guild and Labour League campaigns went beyond mere home improvement, to develop the old Owenite idea of 'associated homes'. Surely modern housing estates could include common domestic services?[60] Guildswomen tentatively suggested that co-operative building societies could include common laundries and kitchens and bake-houses in their housing projects.[61] In conjunction with women in the Labour League, they argued that this 'co-operative house-management' should be an essential part of post-war council housing estates.[62] Again, the dreams and campaigns for twentieth-century associated homes need a history. A 1907 report in the Guild's 'Woman's Corner' of an International Housing Conference suggests that it will be a history of bold enthusiasm, but also of scorn and obstruction and failure:

> In spite of the community ideals of Owen, and the enthusiastic advocacy of E. V. Neale for 'associated homes', co-operators, we know, have not looked kindly upon these schemes. . . . Probably had working women a say earlier . . . we should be much nearer a true ideal of home-building than we are today. Even today, we women have a far smaller share of this work than ought to be the case.[63]

The dreams of these women recall forgotten possibilities for Co-operation. Guildswomen favoured co-operative solutions to domestic drudgery because they could not afford private domestic services, and because working through the state seemed too indirect.[64] Catharine Webb concluded her 1893 plea for 'Co-operation as Applied to Domestic Work' with typically ambitious fervour:

> The day of 'association and mutual helpfulness' in all stages and phases of life is slowly but surely dawning upon the world, to drive out the black night of individualism and competition, and shall we Co-operative women be last to awaken on the morning of the day? Rather, let us be the heralds of the dawn, rousing the world to take notice of the 'good time coming'.[65]

NOTES

Many thanks to Fi Black, Katie Holmes, Jill Norris, Melanie Raymond, Gill Scott, Judy Thomson, Eileen Yeo, Stephen Yeo, and Deb Zion for helping me to make this chapter.

1 M. L. Davies, *The Women's Co-operative Guild 1883–1904*, Westmorland, Women's Co-operative Guild, 1904, p. 148.
2 *Co-operative News*, 15 February 1890. (Unless otherwise noted, all *Co-operative News* references are to the Guild's 'Woman's Corner'.)
3 ibid., 22 February 1890.
4 ibid., 15 March 1890.
5 Davies, op. cit., pp. 152–3.
6 'Characteristic Working Days' by 'Agnes', *Co-operative News*, 10 June 1896; 'Betsy', 27 June 1896; 'Ever Onward', 11 July 1896; 'Hypatia', 25 July 1896. See also M. L. Davies (ed.), *Life As We Have Known It, By Co-operative Women*, London, Virago, 1977 (1931); G. Mitchell (ed.), *The Hard Way Up: The Autobiography of Hannah Mitchell, Suffragette and Rebel*, London, Virago, 1977 (1968); and D. Nield Chew, *Ada Nield Chew: The Life and Writings of a Working Woman*, London, Virago, 1982.
7 Mrs Haworth, 'House of the poor', *Co-operative News*, 10 November 1900.
8 Davies, *Life As We Have Known It*, p. 92.
9 Mitchell, op. cit., p. 203; see E. Ross, 'Survival networks: neighbourhood sharing in London before World War 1', *History Workshop Journal*, 15, Spring 1983.
10 J. Green, 'Characteristic working days, the home', *Co-operative News*, 7 November 1896.
11 *Co-operative News*, 7 July 1894.
12 C. Webb, *The Woman With the Basket: The Story of the Women's Co-operative Guild*, The Guild, 1927, p. 59; see also *Co-operative News*, 2 February 1895.
13 M. Spooner, 'Future Guild work', *Co-operative News*, 8 October 1892.
14 M. L. Davies, 'Guild work', *Co-operative News*, 22 November 1890; see also S. Reddish, 'Our Guild work', *Co-operative News*, 4 January 1890.
15 *Co-operative News*, 8 October 1892.
16 H. O. Barnett, *The Making of the Home*, London, Cassell, 1885, p. 1.
17 W. Thompson, 1856, quoted in B. Taylor, *Eve and the New Jerusalem: Socialism and Feminism in the Nineteenth Century*, London, Virago, 1983, pp. 50 and 246–52; see also quotations from W. Thompson and A. Wheeler, 1825, in D. Hayden, *The Grand Domestic Revolution: A History of Feminist Designs for American Homes, Neighbourhoods and Cities*, Cambridge, Mass., MIT Press, 1981, p. 35.
18 E. V. Neale, *'Associated Homes': A Lecture*, Manchester and London, MacMillan, 1880.

19 *Co-operative News*, 24 June 1893.
20 ibid., 28 December 1895.
21 E. Holyoake, 'Neighbourhood Guilds', *Co-operative News*, 30 October 1891 and 14 November 1891.
22 Hayden, op. cit.
23 C. P. Stetson (Gilman), 'Six hours a day', *The Clarion*, 5 January 1895; *Co-operative News*, 6 July 1901; C. P. Gilman, *Women and Economics*, New York, Harper & Row, 1966 (1898); see also C. P. Gilman, *The Home: Its Work and Influence*, London, McLure, Phillips, 1903.
24 T. Mann, 'Leisure for workmen's wives', *Co-operative News*, 12 March 1892, also published in *Labour Prophet*, February 1892; *Trade Unionist*, 6 February 1892; *Halfpenny Short Cuts*, 28 June 1890.
25 S. Coit, *Neighbourhood Guilds: An Instrument of Social Reform*, London, Swan Sonnenshein, 1891.
26 All uncited references to C. Webb are from *Cooperation as Applied to Domestic Work*, Women's Cooperative Guild, 1893.
27 Davies, *Life As We Have Known It*, pp. 48–9.
28 S. Reddish, 'Women and co-operation', Women's Co-operative Guild, n.d.
29 See the discussion of this issue in R. Nash, 'Married women and their work: how freedom may be gained', *Co-operative News*, 6 July 1907; and see generally D. Nield Chew, op. cit., for the radical arguments of Ada Nield Chew; contrast these with more typical Guild responses: I. Nicolson, *Co-operative News*, 6 September 1902; A. Haworth and Mrs Grocott, *Co-operative News*, 6 October 1894; Mrs Burrows, 'Does it pay for married women to work in the factories?', *Co-operative News*, 29 December 1900.
30 See I. Nicolson, *Co-operative News*, 6 February 1897 and 13 March 1897; Nash, op. cit., and M. L. Davies, 'The claims of mothers and children', in M. Phillips (ed.), *Women and the Labour Party*, London, Headey Bros, 1919. For more radical responses to the issue of childcare, see A. Nield Chew, 'Mother interest and child training', *The Freewoman*, 22 December 1912, and E. Brown, 'A Freewoman's attitude to motherhood', *The Freewoman*, 11 January 1912.
31 *Co-operative News*, 24 June 1893.
32 ibid., 24 June 1893.
33 ibid., 28 November 1896.
34 Mrs Clarke, *Co-operative News*, 24 June 1893.
35 'F.G.', *Co-operative News*, 21 November 1896.
36 C.M.M., 'A Yorkshire weshin' day', *Co-operative News*, 30 January 1897.
37 'Christabel', 'The use of the franchise for women: co-operative, municipal and parliamentary', *Co-operative News*, 8 August 1903; M. Bondfield, 'The Borough elections – the washtub', *The League Leaflet*, October 1912; E. Watson, 'Socialist women and the Borough councils', *The Link*, October 1912; E. Keeling, 'Our women's column', *The Clarion*, 9 March 1895.
38 C. Webb, op. cit., 1893.

39 *Dewsbury Pioneer*, May 1894, quoted in *Co-operative News*, 26 May 1894.
40 *Co-operative News*, 24 June 1893.
41 ibid., 7 November 1896 and 25 November 1899.
42 See Davies, *The Women's Co-operative Guild*, p. 155 (Bradford); *Co-operative News*, 11 May 1907 (North West Section); 29 July 1907 (Northern Section); 28 September 1907 (South Yorkshire); 19 July 1909 (Sheffield).
43 *Co-operative News*, 11 May 1907.
44 ibid., 29 July 1907.
45 Green, op. cit.
46 *Co-operative News*, 6 July 1907 and 29 July 1907; see also M. L. Davies, 'An appeal to co-operative men', *Co-operative News*, 29 June 1907.
47 *Co-operative News*, 21 November 1896; cf. Green, op. cit.
48 *Co-operative News*, 5 January 1901 (Kettering); 7 September 1901 (Dewsbury); 27 February 1897 (Bingley women unsuccessfully agitating for a bakery).
49 Webb, op. cit., 1893.
50 L. Martindale, 'Co-operative kitchens', *Co-operative News*, 6 January 1900; see also H. Martindale, *From One Generation to Another 1839–1944*, London, Allen & Unwin, 1944, p. 41; E. Holyoake, op. cit.; Davies, 'Guildwork'; see also 'People's kitchens', *Co-operative News*, 24 November 1894; ibid., 21 March 1896; 'Domestic services and distributive kitchens', ibid., 20 July 1901.
51 Mitchell, op. cit., pp. 112–13.
52 M. L. Davies, *Co-operation in Poor Neighbourhoods*, Westmorland, Women's Co-operative Guild, 1899; in 1895 'The People's Society' had been started in London by the CWS and the CU to adapt Co-operation to London conditions. But it only lasted till 1900; see C. Webb, *Industrial Co-operation*, Manchester, Co-operative Union, 8th edn, 1919, pp. 99–100.
53 Mrs Knight, 'Coffee and cooked meat shops', *Co-operative News*, 5 May 1900.
54 *Co-operative News*, 15 November 1902 and 14 February 1903.
55 See Mrs Sudall, I. Nicolson cf. Mrs Brown, *Co-operative News*, 21 April 1900.
56 E. S. Pankhurst, *The Home Front: A Mirror to Life in England During the World War*, London, Hutchinson, 1932, p. 43.
57 C. M. Mayo, *Co-operative House-building*, Women's Co-operative Guild, 1898; Mrs Haworth, 'Co-operative house-building', *Co-operative News*, 10 November 1900.
58 A. D. Sanderson Furniss and M. Phillips, *The Working Woman's House*, London, Swarthmore Press, 1920.
59 ibid., p. 22.
60 References to 'associated homes' in the 'Woman's Corner' of the *Co-operative News* include: Dr Nichols, 'Co-operative housekeeping', 31 May 1890; Holyoake, op. cit.; 'Co-operative housekeeping', 30 April 1892; Spooner, op. cit.; 'Winter circular', 20 October 1900. Re-

ported lectures and discussions include: 26 March 1892 (Oxford); 24 June 1893 (Leicester); Miss Bamford, 'Associated homes' (Bury); 'Co-operative homes', 12 September 1896 (Hull and Halifax); L. Martindale, 'Simplification of housework', 31 March 1900 (Brighton).

61 *Co-operative News*, 24 June 1893 (S. Reddish); Martindale, 'simplification of housework', 1900; Mayo, op. cit.

62 Sanderson Furniss and Phillips, op. cit.

63 *Co-operative News*, 17 August 1907. Another history might look at E. S. Pankhurst, 'The house and the housewife', *The Worker's Dreadnought*, 13 October 1917, for housing reforms advocated by the famous socialist feminist; *The Link*, October 1912, for E. Watson of the British Socialist Party on women fighting for municipal housing; C. Black, *A New Way of Housekeeping*, London, Collins, 1918, for this women's trade union activist's dreams for 'Domestic federations'; and E. Howard, *Garden Cities of Tomorrow*, London, Faber & Faber, 1944 (1902), for Howard's plans for co-operative quadrangles of houses with common kitchens and laundries as the basic residential unit of the ideal Garden City; see the discussion of Howard's plans in Hayden, op. cit., p. 232.

64 Sylvia Pankhurst argued in 1917 that for domestic reforms, 'The co-operative plan has the advantage of avoiding the necessity for moving the far-off personages who man Government departments.' Pankhurst, 'The house and the housewife'.

65 Webb, op. cit., 1893.

Chapter 8

'WORKING OUT THEIR OWN SALVATION': WOMEN'S AUTONOMY AND DIVORCE LAW REFORM IN THE CO-OPERATIVE MOVEMENT, 1910–1920

GILL SCOTT

The Women's Co-operative Guild developed in the late nineteenth and early twentieth centuries as the most significant democratic organization of working-class women in Britain. It has recently become the centre of considerable historical attention. Among the publications to mark its centenary in 1983 Jean Gaffin and David Thoms, *Caring and Sharing*, and Chrys Salt, *Of Whole Heart Cometh Hope: Centenary Memories of the Co-operative Women's Guild* were outstanding. Its General Secretary from 1889 to 1921, Margaret Llewelyn Davies, is now attracting the attention of a number of feminist historians. Her period of office saw an expansion of membership from 1,800 to 51,000, and an increase in the number of branches from 51 to 1,077. In the 1980s, with a new General Secretary, Diane Paskin, the Guild is making a determined attempt to adapt itself to new times, new women.

The Guild has been unique in the history of the women's movement which has generally found it difficult to reach home workers. In no small measure the Guild's strengths lay in its emphasis on self-government and control over its own policy. Until the inter-war period at least, it was unusually self-conscious about the threats to these from within the dominant structures of the co-operative movement itself as well as from outside pressures, including Labour (and later Communist) ones. As in the case of the Co-operative Party, there have been strong pressures to assimilate the Guild to dominant, orthodox political formations on the left, of which it could have remained a precious critique.

The Guild at its best had twin concerns, with citizenship issues (expertly mobilized, including pioneer women's writing) and with co-operative ('consumer') affairs as they could be changed through active organization by women. This chapter explores these strengths and the threats to them over divorce reform, and over proposals to rationalize the organization of the co-operative movement itself. It is part of wider work by Gill Scott, presented in her Doctoral thesis at Sussex during 1988.

A guildswoman argued with a male co-operator at Congress in 1915:

> Mr Fleming had said that the salvation of the workers
> depended on the workers taking their destiny in their own hands.
> Would he refuse to the women the same right of salvation? She
> believed the women would work out their own salvation, and if they
> did not agree with them, the men should leave them alone.

In October 1913, the Central Committee of the Women's Co-operative Guild received a letter from the general secretary of the Catholic Federation of the Diocese of Salford. A pamphlet on the subject of divorce law reform, circulated for the spring sectional conferences earlier in the year, had come to his attention and he wished 'to draw your attention to the disabilities that Catholic members of the Co-operative Movement are suffering in your persistent propaganda of the cause of divorce'. The Central Committee were reminded that the Guild was dependent on grants from the Co-operative Union, the Co-operative Wholesale Society, space in *Co-operative News*, and the subsidies of local societies; through these various channels Catholic co-operators were being 'mulcted of a portion of their dividends in order that your Guild may propagate divorce'. In this way, 'the power and the prestige of the Co-operative Movement' was being used for 'purposes alien to it and opposed to the religious convictions of its Catholic members' and of many non-Catholic members. The Central Committee was doubtless aware 'that any person who believes in the principles of Co-operation is eligible for membership of the Co-operative Movement, but you may not be aware that exploitation of legitimate membership for illegitimate purposes will ultimately disrupt the movement'.[1]

This was the opening shot in a battle that was to continue until 1918. When the Catholic Federation got short shrift from the Guild – the Central Committee stated in their reply that they considered 'the reform of divorce law one of the most important moral and social reforms which affect co-operative women, and therefore cannot alter their action in regard to it'[2] – it turned to the Co-operative Union, where it found a more sympathetic audience. A number of chords were struck in the minds of these officials: a desire not to offend their Catholic friends in the movement – especially given the approaching 1914 Dublin Congress – a belief that divorce was a religious question that had nothing to do with co-operation, and outright condemnation of any divorce law reform. But above all, the Central Board of the Co-operative Union were moved by a sense that the Women's Co-operative Guild had too much independence. It should be made to recognize the authority of the Board – and the Catholic Federation hit the right note here when they first appealed to the Board as 'trustee of the prestige of the Co-operative Movement'.[3] As one member of the Board, Mr Goodenough, put it: 'He had seen this problem coming for years, and he thought they should be thankful that it had come on a question on which they could be unanimous.' Personally, he did not think any subject too sacred to be discussed,

> he was only objecting to it being brought into the co-operative movement. Miss Davies [Women's Co-operative Guild general secretary] said it was a social problem; another person would say it was a religious question, or a sex question; but he would say it was a boundaries question.[4]

The intervention of the Catholic Federation over divorce law reform gave the Central Board a reason to take action against the Guild. But there were wider principles of autonomy at stake. The dispute threatened the Guild's identity as an autonomous women's organization. The Central Board saw it as an auxiliary body, subordinate to the executive power of the Central Board like the rest of the movement.[5]

The struggle between the Women's Co-operative Guild and the Co-operative Union was about whether or not politics should be brought into the movement, the need for a women's organization to determine its own political agenda and, crucially, how and by whom such decisions might be taken. It spanned the First World War – years which brought intense changes for society, for the Co-operative movement and for women. During the post-war years it appeared that the Co-operative Union had lost its argument with the Guild. In 1917 the Co-operative movement's entry into parliamentary politics and the government's decision to enfranchise women over thirty combined to underline the Guild's importance as a vehicle for organizing female support for the Co-operative Party. These developments considerably strengthened the Guild in its dealings with the Co-operative Union. In a wider sense the 1914–18 dispute brought the Guild to maturity, with a greater sense of its own strength. Yet the questions concerning women's autonomy and decision-making within the movement were not re-solved in 1918. They remained open. To its own detriment, the Guild never again pursued these issues with such clarity.

The Women's Co-operative Guild had emerged during the late nineteenth and early twentieth centuries as the largest and most successful of the co-operative auxiliary bodies. The Guild was also part of the women's movement. Through co-operation it was able to involve tens of thousands of working-class wives and mothers for whom 'the store' was part of daily life. This large-scale participation of women in the business of the 'great consumer movement' repre-sented a potential for the organization of women as a political force which far outstripped that of the workplace-based trade union movement, providing fertile soil in which a grouping addressing and mobilizing women around issues of interest and significance to them, as women as well as co-operators, might flourish.

In 1883 the Women's League for the Spread of Co-operation was formed, changing its name the next year to the Women's Co-operative Guild. The early guildswomen were motivated by the need for a forum in which women might read, learn, and discuss co-operative matters and not merely be asked to 'come and "buy" '.[6] But they were cautious about the ' ."much vexed" question of women's rights'.[7] Margaret Llewelyn Davies, however, who was appointed general secretary in 1889, had no such reservations – a feminist and a socialist herself,[8] she seems to have been acutely aware of the great opportunity the Guild held for the development of the women's movement. According to nineteenth-century con-ventions:

> a heavy curtain had, on marriage fallen on the woman's
> life. . . . Without money of her own, with no right even to her
> husband's savings, with no legal position as mother, with the
> conditions of maternity totally neglected, she had existed
> apart, voiceless and unseen.[9]

The Guild's achievement was to make this group visible and articu-late. Margaret Llewelyn Davies recognized that it was through Co-operation that 'the married woman living at home finds her work and place in the labour world',[10] and through the Women's Co-operative Guild that she acted most effectively for her sex and class. As she wrote of the Guild:

> Being composed of married women who are Co-operators . . . it has naturally become a sort of trade union for married women and it not only works for Co-operation helping to shape its policy and secure definite action, but it also takes in hand the reforms needed by wives and mothers.[11]

Under her leadership and with the administrative skills of her companion Lillian Harris, the Guild expanded and developed a coherence which bore out this view:

> Most people would have said that it was impossible to organize overworked and middle-aged mothers and housewives. But experience has shown that there is no class in the community who respond to organization and education more readily and effectively, and whose enthusiasm for public work is greater.[12]

The Guild's appeal may be measured by the speed of its growth – to ten thousand by 1897 and over thirty thousand at the outbreak of war – and by the impact of its educational and campaigning work on public opinion, successes which contrast strikingly with what Isabella Ford described in 1900 as the 'painful and disheartening' work of organizing female labour in trade unions.[13]

The Guild's commitment to radical politics were apparent in an 1896 pamphlet entitled 'How to Start and Work a Branch':

> Working women are beginning to find out, as men have done, that the means for improving their conditions and redressing their wrongs lie largely in their own hands. . . . Some privileges have belonged too exclusively to one sex; other privileges too exclusively to one class. It is high time that, as far as possible, all that makes a life most happy and fruitful should be brought within the reach of all.[14]

The Guild's strengths were especially marked in the struggle to have Maternity Benefit included in the 1911 National Insurance Act. As in its other single-issue campaigns, the Guild utilized what might be described as 'investigative agitation'. Careful study of an individual subject and a survey of the views of the membership yielded both powerful Guild support for a particular reform and detailed evidence from those women whose lives were most closely affected by the matter. When the National Insurance Bill was in the process of being drawn up, the Guild submitted 'a fully costed scheme of maternity benefit' which so impressed the Treasury that representatives of the Guild were invited for further discussion. This deputation brought the results of an extensive survey carried out among Guildswomen into health care during and after pregnancy. When the Bill was published the Guild opposed the proposal to pay maternity benefit to the father instead of directly to the mother. This question was debated by Margaret Llewelyn Davies and Lloyd George in *The Times* and great energy went into preparations for the amending bill which came up in 1913 – including petitions, lobbying of MPs, letters to the press, and the passing of resolutions. The amendment making the wife the recipient of benefit was carried by twenty-one votes in a free vote which won cross-party support.[15] 'Care of Maternity' work continued into the war with the publication of *Maternity: Letters from Working Women* in 1915, edited by Margaret Llewelyn Davies, which embodied her deep-seated belief that that section of the community which had traditionally been most silenced should be given its own voice. The letters and other pieces of autobiographical writing collected by the Guild are among the earliest examples of working-class women's writing.

The Guild's position as part of the co-operative movement was vital to its success; it could never have developed in a vacuum and its commitment to the movement was always as important as its citizenship work. Yet the fact that the Guild did have a dual purpose implicitly, at least, posed the possibility of there being a conflict between the two interests: co-operation and citizenship. In principle the movement supported the work of the Guild: its foundation was facilitated by the setting up of the 'Woman's Corner' in *Co-operative News* through the sympathetic editor Samuel Bamford; numerous societies gave assistance to Guild branches in the form of meeting places, other facilities and funds; in 1886 the first official recognition of the Guild's value to the movement came with a payment of £10 from the Co-operative Union which increased steadily to £400 in 1913, and from 1908 the CWS also made regular payments, money which together with membership subscriptions financed the work of the Guild head office. Despite this support, however, organizational autonomy within the Co-operative movement was crucial in enabling the Guild to make policy decisions untrammelled by the priorities of those insensitive to the needs of guildswomen. The logic of the Guild's existence required that should this autonomy be threatened in any way, loyalty to the movement would have to take second place to the imperative of guildswomen determining their own agenda.

While there were substantial sections of the movement behind the initiatives taken by the Guild in co-operative and citizenship work, it was also the case that from the 1890s onwards guildswomen were taking up controversial questions which went against the grain of convention inside as well as outside the movement. The controversy over divorce law reform was not totally unprecedented: the Guild's left-wing politics and feminist orientation periodically provoked opposition, especially from officials, within the movement. The 1902 Sunderland experiment in 'the extension of co-operation to the poor' was ended in 1904 when the society directors won the support of the quarterly meeting in moving that the Coronation Street settlement or 'People's Store' become an ordinary trading centre: 'In practice, the community aspect of the Coronation Street branch was incompatible with the views held by a large section of Co-operative members . . . the project not only collapsed in Sunderland, but also failed to take root elsewhere.'[16] The Guild's campaign for a minimum wage for co-operative employees, although ultimately successful, met with deep-seated resistance from its launch in the late 1890s. It was eventually accepted in principle by the Co-operative Union congress in 1907 but it was not until 1912 that continued pressure, petitions, and resolutions forced its adoption by the CWS. For many years the suffrage question was deemed unsuitable for the Co-operative movement – in 1907 the united board refused to accept a resolution calling for support of the vote for women on the congress agenda 'on the ground that it was political', but two years later the ground had shifted sufficiently for a similar motion to be presented and carried.[17] Education Committees refused to include the issue of Maternity in Guild course programmes and, as Margaret Llewelyn Davies confided in a letter to Leonard Woolf at the time of the divorce law reform dispute, the Co-operative Union had disliked the Guild's taking up suffrage and indeed all political work.[18]

Divorce law reform was among the most sensitive social issues to enter the realm of public debate prior to the First World War and it aroused strong feelings on both sides. When the Guild Central Committee was invited to give evidence to the Royal Commission on Divorce and Matrimonial Causes, appointed by Asquith's government in 1909, the leadership set out to discover as fully as possible the opinions of the membership on the subject; 431 branches were asked to discuss whether the grounds for divorce should be the same for men and women[19] and proceedings cheapened to be within reach of the poor. At Guild Congress in 1910 the same two questions were raised:

> The Central Committee member for the Midlands moved a resolution, in a weighty and restrained speech, with a grave sense of the difficulty and responsibility of her task. The seconder was a midwife from the south who spoke from intimate personal knowledge of the lives of women. The audience listened with great attention and a discussion was fully anticipated. Instead, not a single delegate rose to speak. They were prepared to vote instantly. The motion was put, and a forest of hands showed itself immediately and silently.[20]

Of the 431 branches surveyed 40 were opposed to divorce, mainly on religious grounds, but 413 branches, including some opposed to the principle of divorce, felt that if divorce was available it should be equal between men and women. As Margaret Llewelyn Davies put it: 'It is impossible to exaggerate the strength of the feeling that there should be an equal moral standard for men and women.' The great majority – 364 branches – wanted to see divorce proceedings made cheaper. In addition, 124 Guild officials were sent lengthy questionnaires, the results of which demonstrated widespread support for an extension of the grounds for divorce, even to include mutual consent, and for reforms such as the introduction of female legal assessors to act in divorce cases.

Margaret Llewelyn Davies admitted to the Commissioners that she could 'recall no other subject in the life of the guild which has aroused such immediate response, and elicited such strength and earnestness of feeling'.[21] The various returns were accompanied by letters 'often many pages long, laboriously written after thought and consultation' telling of the suffering experienced in unhappy marriages by guildswomen or women known to them. Through these the Royal Commission was able to hear personal accounts which showed 'the nature and causes of the suffering that goes on, and . . . how widespread it is especially among women. . . . No woman could inflict on a man the amount of degradation that a man may force on a woman.'[22] Thus cases appeared

> Where a woman, ill used and kicked, has taken her husband back five times; of a diseased husband compelling co-habitation, resulting in deficient children; of excessive co-habitation regardless of the wife's health; of a man frightening his wife during pregnancy in order to bring on miscarriage.[23]

One guildswoman wrote 'We want to get rid of the idea that a man owns his wife just as he does a piece of furniture'; another asked: 'Is it not more degrading for these women to be living what is, after all, legalised prostitution, than for them to be divorced?'[24]

The evidence of the Women's Co-operative Guild proved conclusively the 'overwhelming demand amongst married women belonging to the artisan class for drastic reform in the divorce laws'; both in representing this group and in the comprehensive way in which information and opinions were collected it made a unique contribution to the work of the Commission. At one point in her evidence, as she began to present lengthy detailed material, Margaret Llewelyn Davies asked 'Shall I continue with all this?', and was immediately told 'Yes I think this is so valuable we ought to have it all.'[25] The completed Majority Report after three years, 'a model of relevance, clarity and the thorough analysis of evidence . . . the last in the great Victorian tradition of investigating commissions',[26] recommended that divorce be made equal between men and women, cheaper, and that the grounds be extended. These proposals met with great hostility, but in any case the progress of a modified form of the recommendations through Parliament was interrupted by the outbreak of war in 1914 and no legislation was passed until 1923.

The Co-operative Union's first formal response to the Catholic Federation was to disassociate itself from the work of the Guild. The general secretary, Mr Whitehead, assured the Federation's agent, Mr Burns, that 'the Union did not and probably would not take any action in such matters as divorce law reform'.[27] The Guild leadership were equally clear:

> The Guild acts independently, and even in our strictly Co-operative campaigns on behalf of Anti-Credit, Extension of Co-operation to the Poor, Minimum Wage, it has seemed often as if the official movement preferred us to work apart. It is only when we have received support by resolutions from the Co-operative Parliamentary Committee or other bodies (e.g. on Women's Suffrage or on our present Maternity Scheme) that we are able to use publicly the valuable backing of the movement.[28]

A statement of organizational separation, however, was not enough; for the Catholic Federation the connections between the Women's Co-operative Guild and the wider movement were self-evident and the stain of divorce law reform must inevitably colour Co-operation as a whole. They 'took a very serious view of the matter . . . unless something was done it was quite possible Catholics would withdraw from Societies in large numbers'.[29] This not so veiled threat prompted the United Board (a committee of 14 drawn from the 72 members of the Central Board) to write to the Guild stating that 'whilst not identifying themselves with the opinions put forward by the Federation' they were of the opinion that the Guild should consider giving up Divorce Law Reform or 'it is bound to lead to disruption in the movement'.[30] The Guild's carefully reasoned refusal to comply was put before the Central Board at their pre-Congress meeting in Dublin where the decision was taken:

> That the application of the English Women's Co-operative Guild for a renewal of the grant of £400 be agreed to on condition that they cease the agitation in favour of Divorce Law Reform, and that in future the Women's Co-operative Guild should take up no work disapproved of by the United Board.[31]

Whilst the Board claimed not to share the views of the Federation unduly, there is no doubt that Catholic opinion weighed very heavily with officials. At the outset Mr Bisset attempted to warn his colleagues on the Board of the dangers of 'allowing a minority section of the movement to dictate the policy of the Co-operative Union in regard to the Women's Guild'. He pointed out that Roman Catholics were free to leave the movement but this would be against their own interests 'and he did not think they would be so foolish as to do that'.[32] This line of reasoning, however, was silenced by the retort which it drew from Mr McCreary, who deeply resented the inference that if 'the Catholics did not like what the Women's Guild had done they could withdraw from the Movement'. He reminded the Central Board that in certain areas up to 80 per cent of society's members were Catholics: 'If they attacked them [the Catholics] through the reform of the divorce laws, they would have no alternative to fighting the co-operative movement.'[33] Statements such as these struck fear into the hearts of co-operative officials. Mr Gregory, not himself a Catholic, was well able to imagine circumstances which would lead to 'ten thousand resignations from the local co-operative society on the following day'.[34] Anxieties such as these were exacerbated by the fact that Congress was taking place in Dublin and many officials displayed a keen concern to placate Catholic opinion. Mr Charter (Southern Section) spoke of the 'strong feeling running in Dublin. . . . They wanted to reduce to a minimum any friction which might arise.' Mr Fairbrother (North Western Section) emphasized that 'in an organization entirely opposed to religious conflict they should at least give the Catholics the same liberty and freedom of action which they all claimed for themselves'.

Board members also expressed strong criticism of the Guild for creating such a conflict within the movement. Mr Greening (honorary member of the board) spoke with scorn of the 'innocence' with which the Women's Co-operative Guild could be drawn into 'contentious matters. The women had an idea that it was not a religious subject; but political matters were woven with religious matters. They would find that out in Ireland.' He hoped that this controversy would be a lesson to the guildswomen and wanted to see the grant made conditional that outside questions not directly co-operative should not be taken up. In principle he claimed to share the Guild view that divorce law reform was a 'national humanitarian question' and not a religious one but none the less he objected to its inclusion in the co-operative movement.[35] In contrast Mr Redfearn believed very strongly that divorce was a religious matter and that the Catholics were not alone in finding it offensive – 'a great number of Anglican Church members were opposed to the recommendations in the report of the Divorce Commission'. He felt that it would be a 'mistake to allow the women to go on agitating, not only on that question but on other questions' and also held that the grant should be made conditional on the vetting of subjects.[36]

Board members with different personal opinions on divorce were thus united in the view that the Guild should not be involved in propaganda for reform and that the Board should have greater control over its activities. Mr Johnson was clearly in a minority when he stressed that the Guild had long carried out excellent work on subjects not strictly co-operative – minimum wage, maternity benefit, etc. – 'were the Board going to stop that?' ('No, no'), and that divorce law reform was badly needed.[37] The dominant position put succinctly by Mr Millington (Midland Section) was that 'If the board had to pay the piper, they should be able to call the tune.'[38]

The Central Board's decision at Dublin opened up a fundamental struggle with the Guild over the issue of self-government; it also exposed the Board to criticism on two other counts, both of which the Guild drew attention to in the campaign to reverse the decision of the Board: it had acted without reference to Congress and in response to the pressure of an outside sectarian body. The Guild leadership immediately put the question to its own Congress in June in an emergency resolution submitted by the Central Committee:

> Seeing that the position of the Guild has been attained through its power to act independently and to develop on its own lines, this Congress declares that it cannot accept the conditions laid down by the Central Co-operative Board as regards its grant to the Guild, believing that the future progress of the Guild and of the co-operative movement depends on the Guild policy being democratically controlled as in the past by the members themselves.[39]

As one speaker pointed out, the board

> had taken a very backward step in this action, but they [the Guild] were not going to be led into the trap. They were determined not to sacrifice principles for money. (Applause) She knew what the proposed reforms meant for downtrodden women, and she could not help but raise her voice in protest of the action taken by the Co-operative Union. . . . It was to be regretted that there were such men in the co-operative

movement, but she hoped they would repent of their ways and apologise. (Laughter and loud applause.)

The resolution was carried overwhelmingly to 'loud and prolonged cheering'.[40]

Thus strengthened the Guild Central Committee were able to concentrate on getting the decision of the Central Board over-turned at the 1915 Co-operative Union Congress. As the Guild had no official representation on the Co-operative Union Executive or at Congress it had to work through the societies, putting forward the motion:

That this Congress endorses the principle of the self-govern-ment of the Women's Guild; further, it directs that the grant of £400 for 1914 be paid to the Guild, and approves of grants being made in the future on the same lines as formerly.[41]

During this period the Catholics continued to oppose the Guild:

It cannot be too clearly or strongly stated that the opposition to our Divorce Law Reform work has been engineered by the Salford Catholic Federation. Week by week the Catholic Press has publicised long statements, speeches and directions by the Secretary of the Salford Catholic Federation, bishops and others. Leaflets have been distributed at Church doors, and priests have given instructions to Guildswomen and Co-operators. Societies have been asked to refuse grants to our local branches.[42]

A resolution which the Guild claimed originated with the Feder-ation was distributed for submission to the Co-operative Union Congress, endorsing the Central Board's withdrawal of the grant and the view that the Guild should abandon divorce reform propa-ganda as it was a religious question 'alien to the Co-operative Movement'.[43]

Catholic activity within the movement was increasingly a source of embarrassment for the Board. Eleanor Barton reported that she had 'heard it said by members of the Central Board that the de-cision was come to hurriedly at Dublin, and if Congress had not been meeting in a great Catholic city like Dublin, that decision would not have been arrived at'.[44] Yet as Margaret Llewelyn Davies commented, despite their feeling that they had 'behaved unfairly to us in submitting to the Catholics', the Board couldn't get rid of the 'piper as tune-caller idea'.[45]

At the 1915 Congress the Central Board's concern was to shift the terrain of the controversy with the Guild away from Divorce Law Reform and towards the issue of executive control within the movement. Its own motion to Congress appealed for affirmation 'as the administrative authority of Congress' fully entitled to 'withhold grants from any organisation which, in its opinion is pursuing a policy detrimental to the best interest of the Co-operative Movement'.[46] In the ensuing debate divorce law reform continued to be condemned, but more emphasis was placed on the offence caused to the movement rather than to its 'Catholic friends'. Mr Fleming (Irish Section) described divorce law reform as

> Objectionable to others besides Catholics. Churchmen, Non-Conformists, and, should he say, all who desired a clean bill of national moral health objected to pay for this agitation in favour of making divorce cheap and easy.[47]

Taking a similar view, the Reverend Hudson (Warsop Vale) stated: 'this agitation had been blamed on their Roman Catholic brethren, but 95 per cent of the Church of England people stood shoulder to shoulder with them'.[48] The strongest condemnation of divorce came from Mr Evans (Eccles), moving the resolution which the Guild claimed originated with the Catholic Federation. He claimed that divorce was offensive to many co-operators because it was 'tearing asunder – disruption of the home life of the individual'.[49]

This belief that the domestic sphere was essentially private and should remain beyond the intervention of the state or other bodies constituted an absolute refusal to question the existing balance of power between men and women. As such it accorded with the deeply patriarchal assumptions of the male labour movement – embodied, for example, in the emphasis on the family wage in collective bargaining, negotiated on the assumption that all men were providers and all women dependants. In the longer term, a reluctance to investigate and challenge the nature of power relations in social contexts – between men and women, but also between leaders and rank-and-file – has proved to be an obstacle in the way of profound social transformation and a great weakness of social democracy.

The view that dealings between husband and wife should not be interfered with informed both explicit opposition to divorce law reform and the conviction that it was too controversial to be brought into the movement. The general consensus here, and a reluctance to be seen to be dictated to by the Catholic Federation, created an opportunity for the Central Board to focus on its own executive power. As Mr Goodenough put it, divorce law reform was not the point, the question was 'whether there should be an authority to decide about these questions'.[50] The discussions about the proper place of divorce law reform at the 1915 Co-operation Union Congress proved to be inconclusive: Margaret Llewelyn Davies insisted that to make it a religious question 'was an interference with civil liberty. . . . It would mean the triumph of this narrow sectarian body.'[51] Other guildswomen and delegates protested at the interference of the Catholic Federation and pointed out that there had been no opposition to the Guild's divorce law reform work before they had intervened; undemocratic methods had been used against the Guild – the board had capitulated to blind unreason and Congress was appealed to 'to help the Board to repair its initial mistake by letting in an outside body.'[52] Yet in response it was argued that the Central Board was now putting the matter to Congress democratically.

Accordingly, in 1915 the debate turned around the Guild's relationship with the wider movement and the Central Board's right to define co-operative work. Before Congress the Central Committee of the Guild offered the Board a compromise: they would ensure that Co-operative Union funds were not spent on work disapproved of by the Board and meetings would be held to determine productive areas for joint activity. The Board was unimpressed. It seemed to them that the Guild and its executive would be the sole arbiters on policy and continue to campaign for divorce law reform through a book-keeping arrangement – would the Guild accept the final decision of Congress and give up divorce law reform in the best interests of the movement? Margaret Llewelyn Davies pointed out that the Guild had no formal representation at Co-operative Union Congress and their own Congress was the final decision-making body. Why, she asked, should the Co-operative Union attempt to control funds other than those provided by the Board?[53] But to claim absolute economic independence for the Guild was to venture onto thin ice. There was the question of the Guild's reliance on assistance from societies and education committees, which according to the Central Board's perspective should also be under centralized executive control. Then there was the fact that an assertion of autonomy could be neatly turned on its head: 'when the ladies themselves were saying they were an alien organisation, Congress ought to impeach the Central Board for subscribing to an alien organisation'.[54] Another delegate at Congress asked bluntly 'what was the position of the Guild in the movement?' He maintained that it was 'a body taking the Co-operative name . . . claiming to take part in joint funds, and to claim representation on official co-operative committees'. The Guild must therefore, he contended, accept 'corresponding responsibilities' and chief among these was to accept 'the decisions of the representative co-operative body as to what was and what was not to be publicly advocated in the name and with the influence of co-operation'.[55]

The Women's Co-operative Guild had no intention of severing its connections with the movement, but it fought hard for the self-government which had played such an important part in its development. In appeals to societies prior to Congress, Guild literature pointed out that

> Before the advent of the Guild, married working women were without an organisation, and their sufferings and grievances remained hidden. It is not only our work on their behalf which might entirely be stopped, but past experience shows that our co-operative work, the work where we fight for co-operative principles and for greatly needed co-operative developments, has met with so little sympathy from the official bodies of the movement that there is grave danger our active co-operative policy might be checked.[56]

The events of 1914–15 highlighted the extent to which, from its base in the co-operative movement, the Guild had developed as a widely respected women's organization with its own special identity in a way that had become threatening to the Central Board. In effect the Guild was the only other body in the movement with the organization and clarity to articulate a coherent and alternative political line which challenged the Central Board's definitions of what the movement should be about. Through the divorce law reform dispute the Guild focused the movement on a debate about co-operative democracy; although it was not able to defeat the Central Board at the 1915 Congress – which was largely fought on the Board's own ground – it attracted significant support for its position. The Women's Co-operative Guild resolution was defeated by 1,430 to 796, but as a Guild pamphlet commented afterwards:

> to have stirred Congress in the way it was stirred, and to have concentrated the interest of delegates on a subject involving matters of principle is a tribute to the force of the Guild, and a reward to all those who have worked so well for our resolution in their local societies.[57]

The Women's Co-operative Guild was unable to sway the Board's determination to withhold the grant but equally the Central Board had no further direct means of putting pressure on the Guild to win control of its policy. The Guild continued to campaign around democracy in the movement, arguing that the Central Board had no right

> to use its power of withholding grants in order to sap the self-government and initiative of co-operative organisations and . . . to stifle the freedom of speech and action on questions of social reform particularly important to an organisation of women. Nothing in our opinion could be more detrimental to the movement than a misuse of the Central Board's power in this way and we cannot ignore the fact that to a large extent the object was not to prevent something detrimental to Co-operation, but to assume the final control of the Guild subjects by the Board.

The assertion that divorce law reform was damaging to the movement was based on a 'vague fear' and threats of disruption; no evidence had been produced of real disruption or resignations of members. The Board's readiness to yield on divorce only served to underline its inability to act in the best interests of women co-operators:

> our experience is that a body practically composed of men, does not understand or give due consideration to the views of women, and that therefore it is most undesirable that the Guild's freedom should be limited by such a body.[58]

To define divorce law reform as an outside question not relevant to Co-operation was to ignore the strength of feeling on the subject within the Guild and its general commitment to citizenship work. This attack on a long-established aspect of Guild activity which was widely recognized as one of its great strengths, created anger and resentment among guildswomen: 'the guild taught its members not only to be co-operators, it taught them to be citizens as well. Social reform consisted of things that merged together; it could not be chopped up into sections.' Co-operative officials used a rhetoric of social progress but denied women the chance to improve their position. As one woman pointed out at the 1915 Congress:

> Mr Fleming had said that the salvation of the workers depended on the workers taking their destiny in their own hands. Would he refuse to the women the same right of salvation? She believed the women would work out their own salvation, and if they did not agree with them, the men should leave them alone.[59]

The determination of guildswomen to stand up to the Central Board created a deep impression on Margaret Llewelyn Davies. She wrote that she had

> no idea the strength and unity of feeling would be so great and that the determination to keep our Independence should be connected with Divorce was all the more remarkable . . . a very significant thing from the women's movement standpoint. The fact that they will work out their own salvation and not be driven, and just take on men's views – is so immensely important.

This realization of the significance of self-government marked a new stage in the growth of the Guild; it had developed successfully on principles of women's autonomy and rank-and-file democracy – now the Board's challenge to these premises was creating a profound consciousness of their importance and a new identity: 'I feel the women have now "arrived" – and they will never go back.'[60]

The Central Board's treatment of the Women's Co-operative Guild in 1914–15 was a rehearsal of the more precisely defined constitutional control over the movement which it sought to acquire through the mechanism of the General Survey Committee set up at the 1914 Congress. Historically the relationship between the Co-operative Union and other parts of the movement was nebulous and more dependent on good will and association than formalized procedure. The Survey Committee set out to make a comprehensive and representative investigation of this and other co-operative affairs affecting the whole movement. When the dispute began in 1914 the Guild Central Committee stated to the Board that

> the time for the Guild to put its case before the movement will come when the newly appointed Joint Committee of Inquiry makes its report, for the whole question of freedom for educational development will then have to be considered.[61]

Despite contrary intentions, the Survey Committee never achieved the desired broad-based composition which would reflect the diverse groups within the movement, but instead was dominated by the Co-operative Union, and this fact contributed to its failure to have any real impact on the movement. The Co-operative Wholesale Society refused to take part 'on the ground of the inadequate representation offered to it' and the outside experts originally intended to participate never materialized. The Committee, which sat for five years from 1914 to 1919, 'consisted principally of members of the Central Board'.[62] The Women's Co-operative Guild was involved in the sub-committees considering education and the constitution, arguing strongly that 'rank and file organisations should remain outside the control of official parts of the movement'. But the first concrete proposals to emerge from the committee set out the registration of all auxiliary bodies as members of the Co-operative Union, which meant in effect 'complete subordination'. The Guild's criticisms and a minority note from Margaret Llewelyn Davies were excluded from the first Interim Report of the Survey Committee and accordingly the Guild disassociated itself in protest in 1916.[63]

The conclusions of the Survey Committee, including wide-ranging recommendations for trading and economic growth, continued to appear from 1917 to 1919. Its 'outstanding recommendation . . . was that the central machinery of the movement should be greatly strengthened', with the Central Board playing a greater role as the main administrative and governing body, whose power should extend 'to the expulsion of any society deemed to be guilty of unco-operative conduct or refusing to accept arbitration'. The similarity between these proposals and the Central Board's attitude to the Guild during the divorce law reform dispute is very clear, and the connections between the two moves underlined by the Survey Committee's expressed disapproval of funds being 'frittered away on unsatisfactory forms of propaganda and on functions of no great educational value'. It was soon made plain, however, that 'the local societies were not prepared to accept the stronger central discipline advocated by the Survey Committee.' An amended version of the recommendations of the Survey Report which retained provision for greater control over the auxiliary bodies was passed at Co-operative Union Congress in 1920, 'but no great zeal was shown in putting them into effect'.[64] The Survey Committee had failed to do more than express the views of a section of the Central Board and was unlikely therefore to have any real impact on the movement; perhaps more importantly it failed to take note of the changes which meant that: 'The British Co-operative Movement to which the Survey Committee reported in 1919, was in many respects a different movement from that which appointed it in 1914.'[65] The war had transformed British society and created new issues outside the scope of the Survey Committee and its preoccupation with internal affairs. Accordingly its proposals proved to be largely irrelevant to the new developments taking place in the movement at the end of the war.

The most significant initiative taken by the movement was the founding of the Co-operative Representation Committee in 1917, re-named the Co-operative Party two years later, a product of 'acute grievance and a disbelief that Co-operation could ever look for fair treatment from Governments unless it took matters actively into its own hands',[66] and what Sidney Pollard described as 'the general swing to the left of all sections of the labour movement in 1917'.[67] For the first time the movement was explicitly committed to a strategy for change which went beyond the business of co-operative trading methods and engaged directly with politics. This shift was very much in line with the Women's Co-operative Guild's long-established emphasis on citizenship work and social reform as necessarily complementary to trading matters. At the same time it undermined the arguments used by the Central Board in 1914–15 that co-operators should keep politics and social questions out of the movement. The Guild's position was further strengthened by the enfranchisement of women over 30, announced in November 1917 and effected in 1918. As Margaret Llewelyn Davies commented in her pamphlet The Vote at Last. More Power to Co-operation:

This is a tremendous new fact, and Guildswomen must seize hold of it and consider what it means. They will find that they have suddenly become much more important, and that their views and actions will receive far greater consideration.[68]

The great value of the Women's Guild to the co-operative political cause was manifest from the beginning as it worked closely with the Co-operative Representation Committee at the national and local level. In Sheffield, for example, four out of the twelve members of its first executive were guildswomen. Eleanor Barton, a leading Sheffield guildswoman, was chosen to stand for municipal and parliamentary elections, and local Guild branches were among the first organizations to receive co-operative political speakers.[69] The potential of a broad-based working-women's organization was widely apparent and the Guild received overtures from a number of groups anxious to secure the women's vote. This fact increased the Central Committee's determination to proceed systematically with the political education of co-operative women. Speakers, meetings, and training sessions, essential to this purpose, would all need extra funds and this requirement became the basis for a new approach to the Co-operative Union for the restoration of the annual grant. The suggestion that the Guild and the Central Board might arrange meetings to find ways in which the two bodies 'might work harmoniously together' brought a curt refusal, however, followed by plans for a joint political committee to mobilize men and women that would completely by-pass the Guild. At the same time the insistence of the United Board on executive control over all aspects of the movement was leading to 'serious differences' with the Co-operative Parliamentary Representation Committee, in which the Guild supported its right to orchestrate 'all work connected with political action'.[70]

The United Board's intransigence could not continue indefinitely – political work went on and the skills of the Women's Co-operative Guild were inevitably drawn into its momentum. In 1918 Co-operative Union Congress discussions on the grant to the Guild demonstrated a new sense of political priorities within the movement, and an appreciation of the great potential which the Guild represented. Mr Whitely (Manchester and Salford) described how he had

had the opportunity of speaking to women's guilds in various parts of the country with respect to the work of co-operative organisation, and in every part the women's guilds are ready and willing to work, but they do not get the support of the men.

Mr Carding (Leek and Moorlands) discussed the Guild's 'magnificent record of accomplished work' and asked:

> Must all this now become subservient to the will and supreme control of the Central Board, which, with two exceptions, is composed of men? The recognition at last of their claims by granting votes to six million women is an important factor in the history of this movement. . . . Is it reasonable to ask these guildswomen to give up control of their guild just as they have got political freedom?

Another speaker dismissed the tired rhetoric of

> control of the women's guild; what we forget is the women are in advance of the movement. If the Central Board is going to restrict the guild's powers it will be a bad thing for the co-operative movement.

Quoting J. S. Mill, Mr Goodenough continued to argue that restrictions on the Guild were necessary for the good of the movement, but added that a meeting would take place between the Guild Central Committee and the Central Board 'to see if they could persuade them [the women] as to the error of their ways in this particular case'.[71]

In August 1918, the subcommittee that was subsequently set up to meet with the Guild Central Committee to discuss the grant, reported a feeling of new confidence in 'the renewal of cordial relations between the two bodies' and a desire to ensure that 'all the energy of the women's guild and of themselves should be used to further the propaganda and educational work in the movement'. The renewal of the grant was proposed on the basis of the last year's work with joint meetings to determine productive areas of co-operation between the Guild and the Central Board. But certain officials persisted in their demand for greater control. Mr Rae put forward an amendment to the effect that the Guild would not take up any position in opposition to the Union's policy. 'He did not want to tie their hands to prevent their fighting but to prevent any similar trouble to that which he hoped was now at the end.' Mr Agnew, doubtless aware that the Guild would not accept any such measure, pointed out that Mr Rae's clause would have the effect of undermining the agreement already arrived at, and a general anxiety to close the 'misunderstanding' as soon as possible was expressed by the Chair, so Mr Rae withdrew.[72]

The Guild Annual Report for 1918/9 announced the 'happy ter-
mination of the four "lean" years', a great renewal of Guild activity
with the end of the war, the women's vote and the unity of labour
and a marked membership increase. In case it was supposed that in
this reconciliation the Women's Co-operative Guild had wavered
in its original purpose, the work for divorce law reform was firmly
renewed – albeit in something of a vacuum as no legislation was introduced until 1923 – with a 1918 reprint of the earlier Guild publication on the subject.[73] The disquieting proposals of the Survey
Committee in relation to auxiliary bodies still hung over the Guild,
but it gradually became clear that 'no change of rules affecting the
Guild's position is to be submitted on this matter . . . therefore it
has been unnecessary to take any steps to maintain our Self
Government'.[74] The goodwill and encouragement of the co-operative
Union was sustained with the increase of the annual grant to
£500, as the General Secretary Mr Whitehead explained in his letter:
'the Board appreciate the work which is being done by the Guild
and quite recognise the reasonableness of your request'.[75] Between
1918 and 1921 membership increased by twenty thousand and in
all respects the Guild appeared to be strengthened – as a self-
governing women's organization, in its standing within the movement and its reputation at the national level. Yet for the Guild, also,
the war years signalled the end of the early phase of its development. While it survived the divorce law reform dispute without losing
its integrity, it did not survive unchanged. The Guild took its part of
the agreement with the Central Board very seriously and its work in
the years following the renewal of the grant increasingly featured
'Push the Sales' campaigns and the promotion of single products
like 'Lutona'. The retirement of Margaret Llewelyn Davies in 1921,
and the different political climate of Britain in the 1920s, brought
an end to the pre-war single-issue campaigns. The rapid expansion
in numbers and a new generation of leaders brought greater di-
versity to the issues taken up by the Guild and a tendency to spread
its energies so widely that the former distinctive identity was lost.
The Guild's political direction was dominated by the Co-operative
Party and in 1926 Guild Congress 'agreed to the inclusion of support to the Co-operative Party in the aims and objects of the
Guild'.[76] Despite the fact that this effectively anchored the Guild to
policies which were compatible with the male-dominated Co-
operative Party, there was no discussion about the implications of

such a decision for self-government. It was not until 1938 that the issue of Pacifism breached the alliance, necessitating a Guild addendum 'providing the Party policy was not inconsistent with declared Guild policy'.[77] The explicit commitment to self-government and the logic underpinning it – the need for guildswomen to determine their own political agenda – had ceased to be a priority for the Guild.

NOTES

1 22 October 1913, Monks House Papers, Sussex MS18.
2 *Co-operative News*, 28 March 1914.
3 ibid.
4 *Co-operative Union Annual Congress Report* (hereafter *CUAR*), Manchester, 1915, p. 27.
5 ibid., p. 522.
6 C. Webb, *The Woman with the Basket: the Story of the Women's Co-operative Guild*, Manchester, The Guild, 1927, p. 18.
7 J. Gaffin and D. Thoms, *Caring and Sharing. The Centenary History of the Co-operative Women's Guild*, Manchester, Co-operative Union, 1983, p. 13.
8 Margaret Llewelyn Davies (1861–1944), the daughter of the Reverend John Llewelyn Davies, Christian Socialist, and the niece of Emily Davies, founder of Girton College, Cambridge. In 1890 she gave a paper at the Co-operative Union Congress entitled *The Relations between Co-operation and Socialistic Aspirations*, Manchester, 1890.
9 M. Llewelyn Davies, draft foreword to C. Webb, *The Woman with the Basket*, in Lillian Harris papers, LSE, vol. I, 36.
10 Material illustrating the work of the Guild and kindred interests, manuscript, typed and printed papers, photographs, erstwhile property of M. Llewelyn Davies presented to the LSE after her death by L. Harris, 1890–?1944, 11 vols, vol. 1, item 25.
11 M. Llewelyn Davies, draft article 'Cooperation at the Fountainhead', in Lillian Harris papers, LSE, vol. I, 25.
12 ibid.
13 B. Drake, *Women in Trade Unions*, London, Labour Research Department, 1920, p. 4.
14 Women's Co-operative Guild, *How to Start and Work a Branch*, Kirkby Lonsdale, 1896.
15 Gaffin and Thoms, op. cit., p. 69.
16 ibid., p. 67.
17 Webb, op. cit., p. 98.
18 Margaret Llewelyn Davies to Leonard Woolf, undated, Sussex MS18.
19 The Matrimonial Causes Act of 1857 laid down that a man could divorce his wife for a single act of adultery; a woman was obliged to prove some form of cruelty *in addition* to adultery.

20 *Royal Commission on Divorce and Matrimonial Causes*, 1912, Cd. 6478, *Evidence*, 4 vols, vol. 3, Cd. 6481, xx. I, p. 150.

21 ibid., p. 149.

22 ibid., pp. 150–1.

23 Women's Co-operative Guild, *Divorce Law Reform, Majority Report of the Divorce Commission*, London, Heinemann, 1913, p. 12.

24 ibid., pp. 151 and 156.

25 ibid., p. 152.

26 O. R. McGregor, *Divorce in England, A Centenary Study*, London, Heinemann, 1957, p. 26.

27 *Co-operative News*, 28 March 1914.

28 *Women's Co-operative Guild, Annual Report* (hereafter *WCGAR*), 1913–14.

29 *Co-operative News*, 28 March 1914.

30 *CUAR*, 1915, p. 515.

31 ibid., 1914, p. 575.

32 *Co-operative News*, 28 March 1914.

33 *CUAR*, 1914, p. 13.

34 *Co-operative News*, 28 March 1914.

35 *CUAR*, 1914, p. 13.

36 ibid., pp. 13–14.

37 ibid., p. 16

38 ibid., p. 14.

39 *Co-operative News*, 20 June 1914.

40 ibid.

41 Women's Co-operative Guild, *The Self-government of the Guild*, London, 1915.

42 *WCGAR*, 1914–15.

43 Women's Co-operative Guild, *Self-government*.

44 *CUAR*, 1915, p. 23.

45 Margaret Llewelyn Davies to Leonard Woolf, undated, Sussex MS 18.

46 *CUAR*, 1915, p. 596.

47 ibid., p. 514.

48 ibid., p. 523.

49 ibid., p. 518.

50 ibid., p. 27.

51 ibid., p. 22.

52 ibid., Mrs Found, p. 517; Mrs Cooper, p. 520; Miss Webb, p. 525.

53 ibid., p. 25.

54 ibid., p. 516. The speaker was Mr Goodenough once again.

55 ibid., p. 526.

56 *Co-operative News*, 20 June 1914.

57 Women's Co-operative Guild, *Self-government*.

58 ibid.

59 *CUAR*, 1915, p. 523.

60 Margaret Llewelyn Davies to Leonard Woolf, undated, Sussex MS 18.

61 *WCGAR*, 1914–15.

62 G. D. H. Cole, *A Century of Co-operation*, Manchester, Co-operative

Union, 1944, p. 264; F. Hall and W. P. Watkins, *Co-operation. A Survey of the History, Principles and Organisation of the Co-operative Movement in Great Britain and Ireland*, Manchester, Co-operative Union, 1937, p. 226.

63 Women's Co-operative Guild, Central Committee Minutes, MS University of Hull, 8 and 9 December 1915; 26 June 1916.

64 Cole, op. cit., pp. 293–7.

65 Hall and Watkins, op. cit., p. 228.

66 Cole, op. cit., p. 269.

67 S. Pollard, 'The foundation of the Co-operative Party', in A. Briggs and J. Saville (Eds), *Essays in Labour History*, London, Macmillan, 1971, p. 186.

68 Margaret Llewelyn Davies, *The Vote at Last. More Power to Co-operation*, Manchester, Co-operative Union, 1918, p. 1.

69 Sheffield Co-operative Party Records, Minute Book of the Political Council 1918–21, MS, Sheffield Local Studies, Sheffield Central Library.

70 *WCGAR*, 1917–18; Central Committee Minutes, 24 January 1918 and 11 and 12 March 1918.

71 *CUAR*, 1918, pp. 636–8.

72 *Co-operative News*, 27 July 1918.

73 Women's Co-operative Guild, *Divorce Law Reform*, London, 1918.

74 *WCGAR*, 1920–1.

75 Central Committee Minutes, letter from General Secretary, Co-operative Union, 15 June 1920.

76 *Co-operative News*, 19 June 1926.

77 ibid., 25 June 1938.

Chapter 9

LET ME DREAM: JOHN WALL, BRISTOL SHOEMAKER POET, 1855–1915

SALLY MULLEN

This chapter could be about anywhere – or Nowhere in William Morris's sense. It brings news about a new life which was, in aspiration and with many defeats, already being lived in the 1880s and 1890s.

A new age does not begin all of a sudden.
My grandfather was already living in the new age.
My grandson will probably still be living in the old one.
The new meat is eaten with the old forks.

(Brecht, 'New Ages')

Between the mid-1880s and mid-1890s there was a remarkable flowering of working-class culture and politics in Bristol. One of the driving forces behind this moment was a rediscovery of the power of Co-operation. It meant a quite different form of production, economic and cultural. Poetry, song, reading and writing, together with political activism, were important features of this time. These initiatives were later absorbed in a limited way by the educational wing of the expanding retail co-operative movement in the city, as well as giving a particular quality to Bristol socialism.

The chapter happens to be about Bristol because that is where Sally Mullen has done the work. And it is also about one man, John Wall, in a place where there were others like him. In this book, one (largely 'unsuccessful') man in one place will have to stand in for many other people and places where the density and creativity of 'local' (a horribly subtracting word when used with reference to politics and culture) working-class, socialistic and co-operative, relations during the late nineteenth and early twentieth centuries has not yet been researched.

We need – and with sufficient digging could probably obtain – similar news from Bolton, Croydon, Reading, Glasgow . . . and from many different decades too. Bristol is, perhaps, easier for the historian in so far as Edward Jackson's *A Study in Democracy: Being an Account of the Rise and Progress of Industrial Co-operation in Bristol*, Manchester, CWS (1911) and Samson

Bryher's *An Account of the Labour and Socialist Movement in Bristol*, British Labour Weekly (1929) are rich 'local' stories, from within. But, as Sally Mullen relates, the recovery work is still difficult, full of accident and loss. In *The Industrial Muse*, London, Croom Helm (1974), Martha Vicinus showed that it was not uncharacteristic during the nineteenth century for artisans to have written, and published, poetry. In the main, her study could only recover writers who achieved 'success'. It is the huge amount of unpublished and largely lost work – and the large number of working people who wrote and write – with which one has, somehow, to conjure. Otherwise notions of the paucity of working-class culture will continue to ratify large-scale capitalist culture with its projected subordination of 'the masses'.

It was as part of Bristol Broadsides, *Bristol's Other History* (1983), itself a part of the Federation of Worker Writers and Community Publishers' project to contest that subordination, that Sally Mullen's work first appeared. It shows how much there is to be done on the culture of Co-operation, with a big 'C' and a small one, at all periods of its history.

This chapter will focus on the life and work of a Bristol shoemaker poet, John Wall (1855–1915). His experience vividly illustrates the origins of the ideals of the Bristol pioneer co-operators, and his writings clearly show the new moral world to which they aspired.

This study began several years ago with the chance discovery of a few long forgotten volumes of poetry written by John Gregory (1831–1922), another Bristol shoemaker poet and socialist activist, in the Avon County Reference Library. Further investigations revealed that others who were involved in the city's co-operative and socialist movement around the turn of the century, such as Rose Sharland and E. J. Watson, had verse published. These discoveries led me into some original research into the co-operative and socialist movement in Bristol in the late nineteenth and early twentieth centuries. It became clear that poetry represented one facet of a flourishing alternative culture amongst a small section of the local working class during this period. The culture appeared to 'peak' between the mid-1880s and the mid-1890s.

In view of the stress placed on expressive activities it occurred to me that more unknown and unpublished verse might be held privately in Bristol. In the course of research I was interviewing an 82-year-old daughter of a boiler-stoker, and she informed me that had

I called a month earlier I could have seen her father's large collection of books, poetry, and writing which, having occupied the front room since her childhood, had recently been removed by the corporation dustman. Appeals for information in the local press and local radio led to a remarkable discovery. Dorothy Young (née Wall), the 85-year-old daughter of a long-dead Bristol co-operator and socialist, John Wall, had lovingly preserved in her front room three suitcases full of the unpublished poetry, novels and correspondence of her father. What follows is the story that emerged out of those dusty old suitcases.

John William Henry Wall was born, as he used to say, 'in the shadow of the castle' (site of Bristol Castle), near Mary-le-Port Street, in a small row of terraced cottages.[1] He was, during his lifetime, an active supporter of the co-operative movement, instigating one of the first 'Co-op' stores; General Secretary of the Boot Cutters Union; Secretary of the Bristol Trades Council; founder of the Bristol Pioneers Boot and Shoe Productive Society; and an ardent promoter of education for the working man and woman, organizing free evening class scholarships for working people.[2]

Besides these duties and commitments, which frequently took place outside his daily work as a clicker[3], John Wall wrote novels, romances, short stories, songs, and poems. Frequently his writings focused upon class inequality, particularly the 'ogres' of unemployment and poverty. He wrote short articles for publication in magazines and newspapers[4] and also had some poems printed in the *Bristol Observer*. His writing reflects his deep love of history – both fact and legend – especially relating to the City of Bristol, and of medievalism, in which his extensive reading of Scott and the Romantics like Byron, Shelley, and Keats powerfully influenced him.

In addition to the writing, Wall conscientiously preserved record accounts, reports, press cuttings, and correspondence relating to his social, political, and literary activities. For example, he made copies of letters he sent, kept letters he received and even wrote short historical accounts of the two societies he pioneered.[5] In fact, Wall's history of the Bristol and District Co-operative Society was used by Edward Jackson in his book *A Study in Democracy: An Account of the Rise and Progress of Industrial Co-operation in Bristol*. The 'history' was also posthumously published in the co-operative magazine *Counterpoint*. Some of Wall's life's work (the bulk of which remains unknown) has survived to enrich our knowledge of class struggles in Bristol in the late nineteenth and early twentieth centuries.

As a working man of very modest means, bringing up a family of six, Wall would use any available scrap of paper upon which he drafted his poems and novels. Letters, envelopes, posters, advertisements, propaganda sheets and leaflets of meetings, discussions, debates both political and recreational, formed the bulk of Wall's writing paper. Even thread cards and boot lace packets advertising his trade were used, each card displaying one stanza of a poem. By using each scrap, as an essential piece in constructing the jig-saw puzzle of this man's life, I was able to build up pockets of information relating both to the personal and public life of John Wall and the more general class nature of life in Bristol. In Wall's life, socialism, co-operation, and the church to some extent, overlapped, and he conceived socialism as a 'practical form of Christianity'. Consequently, Wall's increasing disaffection with the Baptist faith, in which he was brought up, and his embracing of Unitarianism, led him to write some interesting theological expositions.

John Wall left Castle Green Day School at the age of 13 and was apprenticed to become a clicker in the boot and shoe trade. A clicker cut the 'uppers' or leather top part of the boot and shoe, which were composed of six distinct pieces. To cut these out with the minimum waste of leather was a skilful task and the clicker was often considered the 'aristocrat' of the various processes involved. The term 'clicker' was possibly derived either from the noise of the sharp knife used to cut around the zinc patterns or was a derivative of the French word *claquer*, to snap or smack.

The boot and shoe trade in Bristol, although one of the 'newer industries' which experienced a revitalization in the late nineteenth century, was comparatively late in experiencing mechanization. Whilst many factories existed in the central parts of the city they were technologically backward and operated a 'putting out' and sweated labour system in which employers were under no obligation to provide a week's work, or indeed any work at all. In fact Wall's friend, fellow socialist poet and shoemaker John Gregory, well known locally, earned less than three shillings and sevenpence per week. Like others at that time he had a 'hard job to make a living' and it is on record at one meeting of the Bristol Trades Council that he had made a computation of his wage. Over a period of many weeks 'his earnings had not reached an average of 3/7d.

per week and he had to be at his shop waiting for work like a fisher at a stream waiting for a bite'.[6] The boot and shoe industry was one of the most insecure and irregular forms of employment in Bristol during the late nineteenth and early twentieth centuries, subject to fluctuations in supply and demand. Kingswood, for example, was an area which specialized in the production of hobnail boots and when trade was brisk 100 tons were produced weekly. However, the Kingswood trade supplied boots to the South Wales tinplate industry, and when slumps occurred there the bootmakers found themselves temporarily out of work or on three-quarters time.

In the 1892 lockout, resulting from a long-standing pay award which was disputed by the employers, 30,000 workers in the industry were affected. The lock-out tactic was enforced to starve the workers into submission. The bootmakers' eventual victory, however, undermined the employers to the extent that one Kingswood manufacturer, Jay Bros., in a dispute later that year, dismissed all union men and refused to employ unionists. Another manufacturer opposed the pay award and threatened to move his factory out of Bristol. In the winters of 1895 and 1898, three to four thousand operatives connected with the industry in East Bristol were unemployed for several weeks and relief funds were set up to prevent starvation of families without food or fire. It was conditions such as these which led Wall to search for alternative, more humanitarian forms of production and distribution. Clearly his short stories and novels, which are probably semi-autobiographical, reveal his hatred of the tyranny of the factory system. Petty rules and regulations, piece-work, excessive hours of work and the despicable situation of competition between fellow men and women to secure and retain employment, were some of the evils he described in 'The Murder of Ada Collins: True Stories of the People'. In this short story Wall interweaves a tragic romance with incisive social comment on the tyrannies of a late-nineteenth-century boot and shoe factory.

> Under the old regime the foremen were 'jolly good fellows everyone', who did not kick, if they heard that a hand was going into the office to beg a favour of the 'guv'nor'. On the contrary, if the case was a deserving one they helped it forward: When there was a doubt about it – well! Even then they never cut mean. But now! all this was changed. . . . Saxton's

entrance into the cutting room was the signal for talking to
cease. There was a time when this was not so. In the days of
yore the men had been accustomed to chat a little over their
work. It helped the time away without interfering with the
work. . . . The late foreman thought so too; for he never inter-
posed unless it were to check irregularity or objectionable
language. Sometimes he would join in the discussion. But the
new man quickly altered all this. . . . 'Talking interferes with
the despatch and finish of the work. . . . And so do singing
and whistling'. . . . Thus it was that in Saxton's presence the
clicking room became as silent as a mortuary.

I must first explain the economy of a clicking room. . . . To
those who know, the whole system is comprehended in two
intelligent words – 'Grinding' and 'Costing'. 'Grinding' is
getting the greatest amount of work done for the lowest
amount of wage. 'Costing' is ascertaining how much work has
been cut out of a given piece of material or skin. Uppers are
cut in pairs. 'How many this week?' and 'Does your costing
pay?' are two questions which are periodically, if
surreptitiously, asked in the cutting shops of Bristol and the
district. The man who can cut the largest number of pairs per
week is known as a 'slogger': he who can get the most out of a
skin is considered the best or most clever workman. Every
employer has a laudable desire to place his goods in the market
as cheaply as possible commensurate with quality – How is he
to do this? Here is one way – By curtailing the wage-sheet.
This is the justification – the only justification, for overseers.
They are paid to regulate and organise, to keep the
workpeople at their tasks and reduce the expenses of the
departments over which they have charge. To accomplish
these points the foremen of some clicking-rooms summon to
their aid the labours of two men, the 'slogger' and the clever
workman. When they have ascertained what the one can cut
per week, and the other per skin, they expect the rest to produce
the same. If they cannot, they are told either that they have
not earned their money, or that their costings do not pay.
These are the effectual weapons to weed them out or reduce
their wages. But there is another weapon open to the over-
seer. He may set up an imaginary standard to which even the
quickest and the most skilled cannot attain. This is

incontrovertibly proved by the dual fact, that although clickers have been at no time more quick and skilled than at the present, yet wages all round are lower, now than they ever were, and still on the decline.

Wall as an idealistic young man believed that these conditions had arisen partly through selfish and tyrannical individuals, such as overseers, whose job was intrinsically exploitative. He was attracted to Co-operation as an alternative to the capitalist economic structure which was geared to money-making and exploitation. Wall's concern focuses upon the alienation of individuals from each other, as much as on alienation from their work or craft. He stresses the necessity of friendship and consideration in the work situation in order to generate feelings of equality and justice between employer and workers. Wall's perhaps rather idealistic belief was rooted in Christian notions of love and brotherhood. He was at this time a regular attender at the Old King Street Baptist Church.

> Employers! Invite the confidence and trust of those who are giving their prime labour to enrich you. Show yourselves their friends, their guides. Make them your true helpers – your co-workers. It has been done successfully in France, at Paris and at Guise. Why not in Bristol? Then 'snakes' and 'tale-bearers' and 'frauds' would gradually die out. There would be no place for them. Foremen and leaders we shall always need and in the ranks of our industrial army are many qualifying for the very front of the vanguard of our future, if their manhood is not crushed out by the evils of the system under which they labour at present.[7]

Thus Wall turned to Co-operation and, whilst Secretary of the Bristol Trades Council in 1883, organized a series of talks for Autumn 1883 and Winter 1884, including one on Co-operation. He arranged for Canon Percival of Trinity College, Oxford, (one time headmaster of Clifton College) to speak at *The Star* coffee house, Old Market, where the Council ran its meetings. Percival's inspiring lecture, 'Some Ways in which Trade Unions may Help' and, later, G. F. Jones's lecture on 'Co-operation', boosted the determination and idealism of Wall and his colleagues. The outcome of these talks was that Wall and four others formed the Bristol and District Co-operative Society (the 'B and D'), establishing a small Co-op store.

In a letter to Canon Percival, dated 15 February 1884, Wall informed him of their resolution:

> You will be pleased to learn that we are making an attempt to place the co-operative principle on a practical footing in Bristol. . . . A veteran Co-operator, Mr Williamson, (who was secretary for many years of the late Bristol Industrial and Provident Co-operative Society), Mr Hams and myself talked the matter over and came to the conclusion that the time had arrived when an attempt should be made to re-establish Co-operation in the old City. . . . Any advice from you would be especially welcomed by all of us, because we know the practical interest you take in the subject and because you are an old friend of the Bristol working man.

At Wall's home in Croydon Street on Tuesday, 26 February, a small company assembled consisting of Wall and his father-in-law James White, H. A. Carter, and G. W. Ham, and, in Wall's own words, they passed 'a resolution pledging [us] to plank down one shilling each for a bundle of literature from the Co-op Union . . . to arrange for an early meeting at "The Star" . . . [and] to ask the Central Board to send down a couple of Speakers . . . to give us advice and awaken interest in the movement'.

The co-operators were loaned an office by Gilmore Barnett for subsequent meetings, having gained new recruits at the opening of the Co-operative Wholesale Society Depot. The group were then able to be in 'business', with forty-eight members and £40. The Society began its career at Houlton Street in November 1884 and Wall recorded the opening evening of the store:

> We can never forget it! The quaint shop, the small counters, the meagre supply of groceries and provisions – in all nineteen articles which had cost us £20. 'Money down on your first order', said Mr Cunningham, who waited on us at the depot. . . . The Committee, inexperienced yet willing, with white aprons tied on firmly, bustling around with . . . the importance, but also the love of a mother hen with her first brood.

The store opened for six months, two nights a week, and members of the Committee voluntarily served behind the counter. During the first quarter the average weekly trading amounted to £10 and, at the end of the first quarter, takings amounted to £130 with a 'divi' of 1s 6d. The balance was carried forward, enabling the store to open during the daytime. After nine months and a drastic reduction in the dividend and loss in trade the store-keeper was changed. John Wall, then secretary, incorporated this office with that of store-keeper and moved into the premises at Houlton Street. An improvement occurred and after a very successful meeting in Canon's Marsh Workmen's Coffee Room new members were recruited. A branch store was subsequently opened in St George Road, Hotwells and Lawrence Hill. In February 1887, the Houlton Street store moved to new premises in Newfoundland Road and became the Registered Office and Central Store.

Wall was involved with the 'B and D' for four years, working as a paid member for three. During this time he gave up the secretaryship, working on as store-keeper and accountant, but the rigorous demands of a 75-hour week led him to resign his post in the summer of 1887.

> I beg to give a fortnight's notice from Saturday next to my intention to leave your employ. My reason for taking this decisive step is simply on account of the excessive number of hours I have to devote to a conscientious performance of my official duties. . . . When I gave up the secretaryship, I was hoping with you the effect would be such a diminution of work which would enable me to accomplish the remainder in work hours. In this hope I find myself disappointed, the two journeys per week to the Stores and the Bank and now the time occupied in attending to the bakehouse have enormously increased the time I have to devote to my duties. Last week I partly remedied this by excluding myself as much as possible from Store work – the effect being that Mr Hodge and the young man were at high pressure the whole of the time, and much work such as cleaning and tidying the Store . . . had to be neglected. But notwithstanding this I had to be at the work no less than 75 hours at the lowest computation. And . . . this a Holiday Week!

Although Wall resigned from the 'B and D' he continued as a committee member, for his enthusiasm for the co-operative ideal remained strong. And in October 1888 he became involved in another co-operative venture, the Bristol Pioneers' Boot and Shoe Productive Society.

In the fall of the year Mr F. Gilmore Barnett gathered a small
company of working men together to discuss the possibility of
introducing Productive Co-operation into Bristol. . . .
[Eventually] the following scheme was adopted as expedient.
Mr Barnett agreed to lend the sum of £100 for seven years to
four men upon the express conditions.
1. That interest should be paid half yearly.
2. That 50% of the net profit should be divided amongst the
workers in proportion to their earnings. It will be readily seen
that these conditions combined business with sentiment.

In November John Wall became Secretary of the Pioneers and
they set up a small workshop in Twinnell Street, Easton, buying
machinery and materials. Initially trade was bad, but in the following August the society was registered under the Industrial and
Provident Societies Act of 1876, becoming a limited liability society.
Trade gradually improved and in 1892 the Society moved to Kings
Square. Within four years the membership increased from nine to
seventy. The Society operated at a loss, but Wall was convinced that
with careful management and increased trade they would be able
to achieve their goal of bringing dividend to custom and labour.

Wall's interest in Co-operation was not just for the material gains in
the form of the 'divi'. It was based on an idealistic yearning for a
sound and just form of economic production and distribution. The
aim of Wall's co-operative venture was to supply good quality
articles cheaply in reasonable and fair working conditions. These
conditions were dictated by the workers themselves who had
contributed a nominal sum to finance the venture.

But in 1887 he wrote to the editor of *Co-op News*, arguing that
deeper issues were involved concerning changes in attitude if Co-
operation was to succeed as an egalitarian movement:

It is not enough for Co-operators to say to the workman, 'We
employ you and pay you a fair market rate of wage. You are
therefore our servants and on the whole your hours of work
are shorter than those of the workers outside the movement.
What more do you want?' . . . What it seems to me is a bold
recognition of the sacredness of labour.[8]

Wall explained in his letter that the 'sanctity of labour' involved
not only a more equal distribution of wealth, but also of leisure, so

that the worker can 'cultivate a taste for the Fine Arts, or satisfy a literary penchant; to improve his botanical knowledge, or his linguistic attainments'. Wall saw education as the key to the moral and intellectual development of the individual, which in turn might lead to social transformation and the creation of a co-operative world. However, since elementary state education offered little more than a rudimentary training in the three R's, conducted in an authoritarian atmosphere, the working-class men and women involved in the Bristol co-operative and socialist movement were forced to educate themselves in the little spare time which they enjoyed. Robert Weare, in the 1880s, for example, regularly studied from four to six o'clock in the morning, and then for a further three hours when he returned home from the local Schweppes factory where he worked as a bottle washer and label sticker. Ernest Bevin studied during dinner breaks and was often engrossed in books while engaged in his work as a carter, driving around the country lanes on the outskirts of Bristol. John Gregory, who left school at the age of 11, was almost completely self-taught, and developed his interest in poetry through a teenage friendship with the postman poet Edward Capern. John Wall devoted the little time left to him after long, arduous working hours, tireless activity in the local co-operative and labour movement, and helping to bring up a large family, in reading and writing at home. He conceived and wrote much of his poetry and prose whilst engaged in his work, then would copy out the verses during breaks. Interviews with surviving relatives suggest that many local co-operators and socialists painstakingly built up large collections of books, usually bought second-hand, which were constantly referred to and proudly displayed in family living rooms. One prominent feature in many collections was the 'Penny Poet'; series, and some were fond of reciting at length, for example Burns and Shakespeare, to make a point or settle discussion.

Wall's intense fervour for education led him in 1883, whilst Secretary to the Bristol Trades Council, to organize evening class scholarships for working men and women. These scholarships, largely financed by the Trades Council, were to be taken at the University College. The issue produced considerable waves of controversy in the local press and one misinformed objector reveals the fearful attitude of the middle class towards higher education for the workers:

164

Sir, I see from advertisements the University college of Bristol have offered . . . to the wage earning classes 80 or more scholarships to be held at the University College itself . . . and of sufficient value to cover fees and buy books. . . . It is an offer to provide gratuitous education . . . not such education as would be had if the State . . . were to defray its cost . . . but absolutely gratuitous . . . like that of a charity school. The recipients will contribute nothing, nay they will be paid for accepting the boon. . . . Can anything be imagined more demoralising? . . . It is usually believed that one who feels he is paying his way preserves his self-respect. . . . It is the aim of most judicious philanthropists to avoid giving anything gratis . . . be it food for the body or the mind – it shall be of the best quality, and sold . . . it shall always be sold . . . to depart from this is a serious step in a downward direction.

Anti-Pauperization.[9]

This letter in response to Wall's attempt to secure a tiny wedge of the educational cake for the workers was seen by Canon Percival, at Trinity College, Oxford. He wrote to Wall offering support and supplied him with some facts with which he could respond to the 'nonsensical letter'. Wall's reply appeared in the *Bristol Times and Mirror* two days later, informing Anti-Pauperization of his errors in comprehension and logic,

Our friend talks about the scheme as being a species of 'charity', and tending to 'pauperise' those who may avail themselves of its provisions . . . he talks about 'self-reliance' and 'independence' as though these noble attributes will be entirely forfeited by those who benefit from the 'Evening Class Scholarship'. According to his theory, if 'Anti-Pauperization' was educated at either of the great schools, he has long since forfeited his right to be considered as a 'self-reliant and independent' man, because he well knows he received his education at about one half of its cost. . . . No member of the middle or upper classes enters Oxford or Cambridge without receiving lodging and education at a rate far below the actual cost.[10]

Wall's campaign for improved educational facilities for workers and their families was part of a broader set of initiatives in this area by the emerging co-operative and socialist movement in Bristol during the last decade of the nineteenth century. Adult evening classes expanded so rapidly that by 1899 they were being attended by between two and three thousand workers, and in the same year the Bristol Sunday Society was forced to hire the city's largest theatre in order to accommodate its average weekly attendance of 1,700, who listened to lectures and discussed issues of the day. The increasing importance which a growing section of Bristol's working class placed on education and learning is most clearly reflected in their demands for improvements in the quality of education provided for their children. This determination to extend educational opportunites inspired the St George's School Board, partly composed and supported by men of radical politics, to finance and operate a higher grade school in one of the poorest areas in Bristol. Despite the opposition of local conservatives who claimed that working-class parents had little or no interest in secondary education, and that they would be unable or unwilling to make the financial sacrifices involved in providing a further education for their children, the school was well supported, and established an outstanding academic record. One of the local workers who scrimped and saved to send his children to St George's School was John Wall himself. After completing her education at the school his daughter Dorothy became the first woman to take a teacher training course at the University of Bristol, a career that she followed for the rest of her life.

While Wall was concerned with the education of working-class people, he seems to have devoted a considerable amount of time to his own intellectual and literary development. In particular he used poetry and short essays to work out and express his personal thoughts and feelings about capitalism. Some of it was published in local newspapers under the pseudonym Mervyn Dauncey, but the bulk of his work went no further than his front room where he kept the mountainous collection of scraps of paper and exercise books on which he wrote everything down. One common theme in his work was the evils of competitive individualism that was unleashed by capitalism: this is clearly expressed in the poem 'The Individualist'.

THE INDIVIDUALIST

Look not into our face again, false man!
Who hast betrayed thy trust for love of gold.

Count up the tale of those thy Plan has slain –
Of needy women, men and children too;
And all to win a house upon a hill:
To write a name upon a civic roll;
Or to be mentioned in a birthday list 'Who's Who'.

Say Watt! Say Stevenson! Say all of you,
Whose brows have paled before your study lamps;
If 'twas for these ye bent your heads and worked:-
To build a wall where none before was built?
To make the poor more poor, the rich more rich?
To stamp Despair for ever on the hearts
Of homely common folk? And Murder Love? Tell me?

Tell me if 'twas for these ye gave the Loom
To us, the telegraph, the power in steam,
The apparatus to explore a mine
When Fire and Afterdamp have ruin spread,
The Locomotive, the Electric Car?
Was it for these ye sought to bind the winds
Fast to balloons, and to the gear of aeroplanes?

O Ghosts of these I name and other Ghosts,
Whose working thought on earth was Brotherhood,
Breathe not too hard against the selfish man
When he shall join you in the Sphere Beyond.
Yet if some punishment must be his due
Let him be 'cabined' in the gloom, and let
Him feel something of that he made the workers feel.

We eat of poverty – because his plan
Can pluck the fruit of life away from us:
We dwell in misery – because his plan
Reserves Life's Fullness for an Idling Class.
Then let him feel awhile, I say, the pain
We've known so long. Not for revenge, O no!
But that his Ghost at least may turn to Brotherhood.

Wall's rejection of capitalism was not rooted in any naïve yearning for a return to a pre-industrial society, for he fully recognized
the potential of modern technology. The problem was that these

technological advances were expropriated by a ruling class which exploited most workers. When Wall wrote this poem Bristol was notorious for sweated labour, and in the 'rag trade', for example, women's costumes costing 1s 1d to produce were being sold for 39s.[11] The poem clearly illustrates Wall's 'Christian socialism', for in the last stanza he does not suggest a torturous end for the entrepreneur who exploited his employees but that he should be spiritually awakened so that his soul at least may turn to 'brotherhood'.

A further criticism of capitalism – one which Wall had personally experienced – was the competition for labour between young and old. Experience of unemployment and rejection led him to write an essay, 'Too old at forty', reflecting on the psychological as well as the material evils of this type of competition.

> We become unpopular with the people who employ labour. When we answer an advertisement they look dubiously at the 'tokens of honour' appearing on our heads, the 'lines of experience' crossing our faces, the 'mellowed way' we walk into the office. And straightway they shake their heads in the peculiarly decisive way we are getting used to, 'How old did you say? My dear fellow you won't do! What we require is a young man – strong, alert. . . . Send your son along and we'll see'. . . . Of course the young must have their work to do as well . . . it is necessary for their efficient training as workmen, as citizens, as teachers, that there should be opportunities ever opening up before them. . . . It appears to me that men are 'too old at 40' or a little older, partly because of the feverish desire of some captains of industry to make a pile quickly; [and] partly because of the anxiety of some directors to secure big dividends for their shareholders. By these people human activities are made subservient to 'piles' and 'dividends'.[12]

Wall's writings, poetry, and novels constantly reiterate his desire for equality and brotherhood. He was familiar with the literary works of Shakespeare and the Romantics – Scott, Byron, Shelley; historians like Gibbon; and contemporary writers like Eugene Sue and William Morris. Although he was extremely fond of medievalism and ancient history, he was not seduced by the literature of Romantics like Keats. For example, he wrote an interesting and humorous exposition on the romantic concept of chivalry and knights in which he quotes from Scott, Masson, and Froissart. One key element in much of his writing is the condemnation of war and violence, which is in opposition to his socialist commitment to 'brotherhood'. Thus in his poetry he attacks the romantic image of medieval knights riding to battle, and also those writers who celebrate war.

THIS IS THE LAW

The sounds of soldiers' footsteps marching through a glen,
The champing bits of many steeds, the laugh of men;
And sunbeams brightly shining on the helms and spears,
But – in the villages behind them – Women's tears:

For War is not, it never can be, the great thing
Some novelists aver, some little poets sing.
It ever did, and will (this is the Law – you'll find),
Leave a broad trail of blood and ruined homes behind.

Each feud will scatter wide the seeds of later feuds,
To yield a reddened harvest for the hungry moods
Of human snarling tigers. Each onset affords
Fresh cause for hate, and ruthlessness, and jangled words.

John Wall's dream of a peaceful and harmonious society led him to write one of his greatest achievements – a historical romance, set in Thebes, which is similar to Morris's *News from Nowhere* although it is significantly a description of a *peaceful* transformation to a perfect society. However, in spite of this novel, which optimistically informs the reader of the transformation to an egalitarian society, Wall was occasionally plagued by doubt and pessimism about the future. The following poem, with its rather bitter and vehement tone, expresses this despair and suggests that one may in fact only *dream* of a socialist society:

LET ME DREAM

Let me dream of a State – happy, joyous, and full,
For the dreaming is mainly my share,
Since the Worker is thrust from that State, as a rule,
To the other of carking and care:
I know no one can, or ought, to expect

Just Life's good things, and fly from the bad,
Yet idlers of title try hard to collect
To their side every joy to be had.

Let me down – not alone for myself, there are those
Cribbed with me in the gloom. For these too
Let me dream of the Glens, and the sweet mountain rose,
And cirrus-clouds high in the blue:
In my dream there are common lands still undefiled
By the boards – PRIVATE GROUNDS. Let me dream
We can roam where the bluebells and daisies are piled
Or laugh near the loud bubbling stream.

Wall remained with the Bristol Pioneers until 1892, despite ill-health, but this co-operative venture was only able to pay a meagre and irregular wage to its workers. He supplemented this money with earnings from his own little boot shop that he set up in his front room in Croydon Street, christening it 'The Shakespeare Boot Mart'. He had a small hut at the back of the house containing his equipment for making boots and shoes, and he also did repairs. This cottage industry was to remain his principal source of income until his death in 1915.

In 1893, a period of great hardship and unemployment in Bristol's boot and shoe industry, Wall applied for a job in Nuneaton in a co-operative society, but he was unsuccessful. After that, partly as a result of his increasing sense that the co-operative movement had lost touch with its true aim of social transformation, he applied for the job of general manager in the commercial department of a local newspaper. If co-operative production was not possible then he would pursue a career in which he could rub shoulders with journalists and professional writers, and possibly become one himself. Again he was unsuccessful and the disappointment he must have felt is conveyed in some of his writing.

Between 1893 and 1908 Wall had little or no formal contact with the co-operative and socialist movement in Bristol. He devoted most of his energies to scratching a living out of the Shakespeare Boot Mart, writing more poems and short stories, and bringing up his family. Having been disappointed in public life, he retreated into a more private, family life. His dream of a new moral world was invested more and more in his children. The family became vegetarian, he spent much time teaching his children about music, poetry, and literature, and every week he took their children and his wife to the Socialist Sunday School at the Shepherd's Hall. The family soon became familiar figures in the Sunday School meetings, as Mrs Pearce recalls:

> We used to go down and watch for Mr and Mrs Wall to come in and my father used to say, 'Here comes the old schoolmaster and his wife.' So that's how we always thought of him. . . . Well he had that look about him, he had a beard and he was very genteel in his way. . . . He carried himself like that, he looked stern, yet he was very, very kind. . . . Oh we used to have some nice times. I can remember they used to have an orchestra and singing and piano playing. They used to have Dolly [John Wall's eldest daughter] and she used to do recitations . . . and there used to be a violinist, Casey, and he used to play beautiful things.

In 1908 the old co-operator – now fifty-three – joined the Bristol Socialist Society, and became actively involved in what was one of the largest and most influential SDF branches in Britain. The road that had brought him to this formal association with the socialist movement had been a long one. Chartism, in which his Bristolian father-in-law James White participated, influenced him in his youth. His awareness of poverty and inequality had been heightened when he joined the City Road Young Men's Mission and Working Association which undertook 'missionary work' in St Philip's and St Jude's, the two poorest areas in Bristol. He was brought up in a devout Baptist family and his chapel upbringing fostered in him a passion for justice, a conviction of righteousness, and a strong sense of duty which was carried over from religion into co-operation and then into socialism. For Wall these political movements were a practical expression of his Christian beliefs. His passion for a new moral world was fostered by his regular attendance at the Old King Street Baptist Chapel discussion classes which the radical Reverend James Moffat Logan held during the 1890s. And no doubt his experiences in the local co-operative movement which resulted in disappointment and a harsh struggle for survival for his family also helped to shape his emerging commitment.

By 1901 his constant moral wrestling with social and religious

171

issues led him to resign from the chapel. He wrote to Logan on 13 April 1901:

> Since the talk we had together the other day, I have communed much over the question:- ought I or ought I not to resign my membership at Old King Street Baptist chapel? You will remember I stated that I cannot understand historical facts concerning certain supernatural claims associated with the Christian religion vis the Doctrine of the Incarnation, the Gospel miracles, the physical resurrection of Jesus. . .

After lengthy discussion with Logan, Wall transferred his allegiance to another Baptist chapel but his belief in a personalized god, in moral strength derived from faith, and in the certainty of life after death were diminishing. In June 1911 he wrote in the back of the exercise book in which he had carefully catalogued the correspondence with Logan –

> Today I should not drag 'God' into the controversy. . . . With me today the 'Power' behind Nature is too big and wonderful to be personified so easily as I used to personify it. And to imagine the 'Power' takes sides with us in our ethical quarrels is not a weapon I handle today.

His last entry in the book in July 1914 a few months before his death is significant in revealing his further disaffection with orthodox Christianity and in particular the Baptist sect he had joined

> Sorting through papers again. Have taken up this book intending to tear it to pieces but halted upon reading the note of June 1911. But I still think the whole affair is of very little value beyond showing perhaps the avenues of past thought. I feel ashamed to remember the incidents that caused me to make so grave a blunder in re-identifying myself within the Baptist body.[13]

NOTES

1 Interview with Dorothy Young.
2 See J. Wall collection, deposited in Bristol Record Office.
3 See letter from Paulton 'Clickers' which illustrates the various duties Wall performed whilst secretary to the Boot Top Cutters Union – thanking him for wreaths sent from Bristol for a funeral in Paulton;

in Wall Collection. Also *The Co-operative Society Magazine*, June 1957, p. 1.

4 See MSS sent to *The Co-operative News*, especially 'The memory of May', 1910; and 'September and some problems', October 1912; in Wall Collection.

5 The two accounts, one of Bristol Pioneer Boot and Shoe Productive Society Ltd and the other of Bristol and District Co-operative Society, together with a short sketch, 'The Manufacture of Boots', appear in one book contained in the Wall Collection. They are the sources for the Co-op. narrative details in this chapter.

6 Archie Powell, 'Poet and shoemaker', in *Bristol Observer*, 21 May 1949, p. 2.

7 See Bristol Trades Council, Special Meetings Card 1883-4. 'Snakes', 'Tale-bearers', and 'Frauds' are the titles in a chapter of Wall's story 'The Murder of Ada Collins'.

8 Letter, 'Labour, capital and consumption', 16 May 1887, Wall Collection.

9 *Bristol Times and Mirror*, 1 October 1883, p. 2.

10 Letter to Wall from Percival, 2 October 1883, Wall Collection; and *Bristol Times and Mirror*, 4 October 1883.

11 *Some Facts of Bristol Life*, Christian Brotherhood Pamphlet, no. 3 (1908), p. 3.

12 J. Wall, 'Too old at forty' (1902), Wall Collection.

13 All these notes and letters are in the Wall Collection. The collection is yet to be catalogued.

Chapter 10

AN EVENT IN THE CULTURE OF CO-OPERATION: NATIONAL CO-OPERATIVE FESTIVALS AT CRYSTAL PALACE

LAWRENCE MAGNANIE

Tea Meetings, conversazione, musical evenings, 'industrial' exhibitions, festivals . . . were characteristic events in the culture of Co-operation from the mid-nineteenth century onwards. They were almost always accompanied by speeches, often reported in full in local or national co-operative publications as well as in the local press which, at its Liberal best, served as a kind of civic minute-book. The speakers would be from outside the movement, but invited onto co-operative territory, as well as from inside. The chronology is not entirely clear, but outsiders – would-be patrons – became less predominant from the mid-1890s onwards. The laying of a foundation stone, the opening of a new branch store (with meeting and reading room attached), or the Annual Meeting of a co-operative society, would not be complete without such surrounding events. They were as much a part of Co-operation as buying tea, shoes, or sugar.

The National Festival at Crystal Palace was an ambitious extension of such a culture. But it was also less than that. It was part – as was the International Co-operative Alliance – of a war of position between the 'Christian Socialist' strand of Co-operation and the Co-operative Wholesale Society, 'consumer' strand. This conflict underlay most co-operative argument during the second half of the nineteenth century, and broke – sometimes bitterly – to the surface of Co-operative Union congresses during the 1880s. Edward Owen Greening (1836–1923) was an important voice for the former, J. T. W. Mitchell (1828–95) for the latter. Greening's papers remain uncatalogued and unused in the Co-operative Union Library in Holyoake House, Manchester (an essay on Mitchell by Stephen Yeo proved to be too long for this volume and will be published separately).

The National Festivals were part of a counter-attack on the CWS by co-operators who thought that the 'principles of true Co-operation' were being abandoned in the retail and wholesale movement. The argument was not, as is commonly supposed, about 'producton' versus 'consumption'. Both sides believed in both. It was about whether, as the 'Christian Socialists' (but also Holyoake) thought, workers in co-operative fields, factories and workshops should have rights to share in the control and 'profit' of their enterprises *as workers*, or whether (as Mitchell, John Watts (1818–87) and many co-operative societies thought) the benefits of co-operation should accrue to the membership of the movement at large, being distributed at the point of *use* rather than at the point of production. It is an argument well worth studying within the revived worker co-operative movement of the 1970s and 1980s, without setting up one side as the goodies and the other as the baddies. Intricate questions of associational form are involved, of a kind which will have to be faced as soon as a co-operative 'sector' again aspires to be more than that, and to move (as the CWS had done by the late nineteenth century) beyond petty capitalism.

But it was also an argument which cannot be understood, in its historical setting, without class/regional tensions within the movement. These come through in Lawrence Magnanie's work. Northern (Manchester–Rochdale)-centred co-operators were running their own movement at this time and were proud of it. They had always suspected patrons and 'at a stroke' reformers of the Robert Owen kind, and had never despised the bit-by-bit way through to community represented by the co-operative store. This had been a class tension within the movement right back to the first series of congresses during the early 1830s. It came out in Chapter 2 of this volume. There was sectarianism on both sides, but the arguments were about something real: most of all they were about who was going to run the movement, within a set of beliefs and practices (Co-operation) where the 'who does what?' question (the division of labour) is fundamental. Works like Ben Jones's *Co-operative Production* (1894) and Catherine Webb's *Industrial Co-operation* (1904) are still worth reading as brave, practically and historically rooted attempts to move the arguments and the associational forms on.

Lawrence Magnanie's way in to the National Co-operative Festivals was an MA dissertation at Sussex on the rise and fall of the Crystal Palace as a cultural, recreational, and educational centre more generally.

The National Co-operative Festival, held annually at the Crystal Palace in London between 1888 and 1910, has been largely neglected by the movement's historians. This chapter aims to explore the development, role, and eventual demise of this event which drew so much attention from outside as well as within the movement, during these years.

The keynote of the festivals was the exhibition of co-operative productions. Edward Owen Greening (1836–1923), an indefatigable propagandist of the co-operative cause in London and the South, had been the main inspiration behind what G. J. Holyoake called this 'brilliant extension of the Exhibition idea'.[1] Exhibitions of English industry and skill were not new. They were popular events amongst the working class well before the Great Exhibition of 1851.[2] Working men had commonly been exhibitors as well as visitors to provincial exhibitions of industry before mid-century. The co-operative festivals were continuations of an established and well-known cultural form.

Greening and his collaborators aimed to promote a comprehensive demonstration of all that Co-operation was achieving and could achieve in the future. In 1886 he had been involved in the organization of the first National Co-operative Flower show, held in the Albert Hall, London.[3] A National Festival Society was formed, with Greening as secretary, to organize the first festival two years later. It took months to arrange, fifty-eight societies gave financial support, and the Portsmouth society alone sent 1,500 members. A one-day event, it was held on a Saturday in August and included concerts, speeches, athletics, vegetable and flower shows, for which hundreds of prizes were awarded, and the central exhibition of goods produced in co-operative workshops. More than 30,000 people attended.[4] A mass choir was an important feature, but the co-operative movement was as yet insufficiently organized in this area. So the majority of the 4,000 who made up the choir had to be brought in from other working-class voluntary associations, principally the temperance movement.[5]

The following year the number of societies subscribing to the festival had reached 140; these gave financial guarantees in proportion to their memberships. Funds of £1,300 were raised, compared to £313 for the previous year.[6] Festival day commenced at 9 a.m. on Saturday 24 August, and the exhibition was opened at 9.30 by Hodgson Pratt. The rest of the day's activities included a demonstration of Edison's phonograph, a testimonial to Mrs Lawrenson of the Women's Co-operative Guild, members' arts and crafts exhibitions, a gigantic flower show, athletics, and a balloon ascent. The Handel Orchestra and a choir consisting of 5,000 voices gave a concert between 4 and 6 p.m. Performing elephants, backed by a military band, entertained in the gardens, followed by a spectacular fountain display. A play was performed in the theatre at 7 p.m. while E. V. Neale delivered the presidential address in the great concert hall. As dusk fell the gardens were illuminated, and at 8.30 a floral ballet entitled 'A Golden Dream' was performed outdoors. The day ended with a bang – a great fireworks display, the crowning attraction of which was a flaming co-operative wheatsheaf. The 'hymn' used for the festival had been written the year before by Lewis Morris and bore the title, 'The Triumph of Labour'. Over 32,000 people attended.[7]

The exhibition was a deliberately highlighted part of the event, as the main organizers, men like Greening, Neale, and Holyoake, were all advocates of co-partnership and profit-sharing; hence the festival was, in a real sense, a propaganda exercise on behalf of this tendency in the movement. At the 1888 festival, exhibits included:

> shawls and skirtings from Paisley, fustians from Hebden Bridge, hosiery from Leicester, and cutlery from Sheffield, while near at hand is a huge block, composed of packets of coffee, representing the bulk actually sold every working hour by the different distributive societies in England.[8]

This was a working-class version of 1851, and the exhibits attracted even more attention when actual production processes were illustrated. At one of the very last festivals, one stand exhibited

> a model soap factory, where the article was milled, cut and stamped, and sold before the eyes of the purchaser. At another hosiery was in the process of manufacture, while at a third, the making of cigars and cigarettes was a source of considerable interest.[9]

New technology was seen as accelerating the realization of 'the co-operative commonwealth' rather than oppressing more working people. Thomas Blandford, a leading figure in the Labour Association for the Promotion of Co-operative Production which supported these festivals and exhibitions to the hilt, noted towards the end of the century that technology in itself was not a bad thing. It all depended on who controlled it, and for what purposes it was being used: 'our workers have to get the best machinery and use it for general advantage, instead of leaving it in the hands of capitalists to enrich the capitalist class still further'.[10]

The festival was also conceived as a stimulus to the growth of Co-operation in London and the South generally, a region which was a co-operative desert compared to the North of England. Moreover, it served to demonstrate the importance of Co-operation to society at large, and it was a huge success in this respect. From 1888 onwards, 'the press awoke to the fact that working-class co-operation was a power in the land, and the movement secured a large increase of public recognition and respect'.[11] The London press coverage of the festivals was exhaustive, in contrast to the relatively muted and low-key response of northern newspapers.

Greening hoped the festival would perform another function. He had started the Agricultural and Horticultural Association in 1868, to supply agricultural implements, seeds, manures, etc., on co-operative principles. He also edited its publications. The quality of ordinary people's lives and the need to maintain connections with the natural environment deeply concerned Greening. When the festival was growing by leaps and bounds in the late 1890s, he explained why he and his co-workers gave up their holidays every year in order to organize this grand holiday for co-operators. One reason was that he was 'an advocate of recreation not of idleness, and by recreation I mean re-creation. All our facilities are developed by use.'[12] Time away from work had to be used fruitfully and not wasted. Greening was very sensitive to the increasing monotony of work due to the relentless application of the division of labour; this process, according to Greening, subverted 'nature' and deformed the individual, physically and intellectually. In contrast, the Co-operative Festival, with its exhibition of co-operative productions, useful recreation and enjoyment, stood as a symbol for the possible transcendence of this alienated state. The festival was a concentrated display of beauty and gaiety, qualities virtually excluded from the lives of many working-class people, especially those forced to live in slum areas. The profusion of flowers, and the harmonized voices of thousands of men and women, showed how colourful and various life could be. It taught that what Greening referred to as the 'unredeemed ugliness' which was due to cramped, badly built houses and dirty air, was part and parcel of an oppressive social system. Co-operation offered an alternative to this barren, inhuman dullness.[13]

The emphasis of the festivals was on *excess*. Everything had to be 'Great': the largest choir, the biggest flower display, the most impressive fireworks. It gave co-operators the opportunity to meet members of other societies and demonstrated that, as in other areas, Co-operation could lead the way in entertainment. The day overflowed with spectacle and excitement, and the events were designed to appeal to a wide variety of men, women, and children. The attempt was made to draw everyone in and the festival grew steadily year by year. Cost was kept down; in the 1890s the rail fare from London came to 1s 6d including the admission fee, and for children it was half this sum. Arrangements were made with railway companies to secure reduced rates for parties from the provinces. In 1893 the festival was extended and now stretched over a period of five days, from Thursday to Saturday. By 1895 it could be described as:

> the great object lesson in co-operation. The tens of thousands of co-operators – perhaps themselves the greatest sight of all – the exhibitions of productions, the gigantic choir, the flowers and the fruits from workmen's gardens, the speaking, the sports, make up a day not to be forgotten. Nothing else helps one to realise so vividly the movement as a great living organism.[14]

The attendance in 1896 reached 41,755 for 'Festival Saturday' alone, and visitors travelled from over a hundred miles away, arriving from 8 a.m. at the Palace. New features were constantly introduced. Children's sports, musical drill, and choir contests grew in size and importance. By the late-1890s over 5,000 exhibits were sent to the flower show. The senior choir grew phenomenally as local societies were prompted to establish choirs to send to the festival. The United Choir, which sang in unison in the afternoon, numbered 10,000 in 1897.[15] Cricket matches were arranged between societies, photographic displays began to appear. A determined effort was made to maintain the interest and variety which made the festival such an astounding success.

The festival provoked a remarkable chorus of admiration for this 'newly discovered' aspect of working-class self-help from middle-class observers. Many of these individuals wanted to see the festival, and the wider movement itself, as tangible proof that a once-revolutionary working class was now respectable, well-behaved, and self-disciplined, saturated with bourgeois values. Co-operation appealed to outside observers because it gave workers a material stake in the capitalist system, and inculcated an 'improving' morality:

> Small in its inception, but earnest in its efforts, the movement has grown . . . until its adherents are numbered by millions,

and the capital invested has grown into huge proportions. The union of capital, education and earnestness, has been the motive power of the movement.[16]

But just beneath the surface of the clamorous approval which greeted the festivals lay unmistakeable anxieties. There were limits to the embrace. *The Standard* recognized the 'solid results of the most palpable and imposing kind', achieved by the movement but also warned co-operators that they would

> do well to content themselves with enlarging the limited but tangible advantages they have secured, without setting themselves up as rivals to socialists and demagogues in the pretension that they possess the secret for securing happiness and well-being to the whole of the working-class.[17]

The most common fear was that Co-operation would drive the small shopkeeper into extinction, it was 'undoubtably a dangerous rival'. Consolation was derived from the conviction that 'no system has yet been invented . . . to share proceeds equitably between money, muscle and brain'. The movement, therefore, was 'not destined entirely to crush out private enterprise'.[18] Clearly, the co-operative project had to be limited and constrained, its sphere of action precisely defined, its supporters advised not to be over-ambitious.

This view, articulated by the bourgeois press, was to some extent reinforced by the organizers of the festival. The day's events were examples of 'rational recreation', but that was in the Owenite tradition. More importantly, guest speakers invited to open the festival and the exhibition by the Labour Association, repeatedly preached the gospel of class harmony and class collaboration. Figures from outside the movement like Earl Grey and Gerald Balfour regarded Co-operation as an alternative to, and a weapon against, the twin evils of socialism and trades unionism. The Labour Association, which supported co-partnership and profit-sharing initiatives, attracted a good deal of support from employers alarmed by the labour unrest of the late 1880s and early 1890s.[19] Profit-sharing, as a method of disciplining workers and harmonizing the relationship between capital and labour, was praised consistently on the festival's platforms. Earl Grey, in his presidential address in 1900, launched a vehement attack on the Co-operative Wholesale Society, which refused to introduce profit-sharing into its productive departments. He drove a wedge between this method of co-operative production, where profits were distributed to the membership through the retail societies, and the profit-sharing enterprises beloved by paternalistic capitalists but deeply distrusted by trade unionists, in which a certain percentage of the profits made accrued to the worker. Grey argued revealingly that the latter were to be approved because they 'do not aim at being workshops entirely owned and run by the workers. They seek rather to establish a partnership between the interests of Capital, Labour and Custom, on lines which are fair to all.'[20]

Like so many of the other sympathetic supporters outside the movement, Grey had no conception of capitalism as a temporary economic system, no ambition to replace it with an egalitarian co-operative commonwealth. Although Holyoake was also active in the Labour Association, his vision was quite dissimilar. And for many working-class people the festival opened up a qualitatively different, alternative future. A co-operator from the Midlands who described the festival in the mid-1890s, regarded it in the following way:

> The Co-operative Festival, with its flowers, fruit and music, is the brightest hope of Co-operation. 6,000 young voices swelling in rhythmic harmony influenced by no fears of the future . . . is a grand and glorious sound, speaking of the future of Co-operation, voicing the first notes of that triumphal chorus which shall increase and swell until it destroys all sound of discord and strife, uniting all families, peoples and nations in everlasting peace.[21]

The meaning of the festival was contested; it could signify the principle and the desirability of immediate class-harmony or the strength and power of working-class people to transform a corrupt and brutalizing world into a new harmony, simultaneously.

Given all this creativity and initiative, why did the festival gradually contract, and then fold in 1910? The growth of the festival continued unabated until the turn of the century, but then came a set-back. Historians have linked the expansion of the railways in the mid-to-late Victorian period with greater opportunities for working-class leisure.[22] But the benefits afforded by easier transport could be quickly withdrawn; cost was crucial. From the earliest festivals,

181

railway companies had offered cheap excursions to the Crystal Palace for working people, and large parties travelled at a reduced fare. These concessions were vital if the festival was to be supported by northern societies, the main area of the movement's strength. On specially provided excursion trains, choir-singers and exhibitors were permitted to make the return journey to London for the price of a single fare. Often, exhibits were transported at low rates; advertisements were freely displayed. In 1900 these concessions were discontinued and excursion fares rose between 10 and 50 to 60 per cent, with an average of 25 per cent. The privilege of half fares for singers and exhibitors was stopped completely. This meant that for a workman, his wife and two children, travelling from Lancashire or Yorkshire, the cost of the excursion rose from 30s to £2. 10s. Moreover, Saturday excursions were cut out altogether from some towns; thirty-eight societies which had sent singers to the United Choir in 1899 were absent in 1900.[23] The railway companies argued that the increases were due to the increased costs of coal and wages and, somewhat ironically, to the congestion of traffic on Saturdays; the 'laws' of supply and demand therefore necessitated the increases. The effect on the festival was devastating, and contributed in a major way to its eventual collapse in 1910.

The reaction inside the movement was prompt and highly critical. A motion proposed at the Cardiff Congress in 1900 condemning the actions of the railway companies was passed unanimously.[24] J. C. Grey, the general secretary of the Co-operative Union, reported to Congress the following year that letters of complaint, incorporating the resolution, had been sent out to the different companies, but little had been achieved.[25] G. J. Holyoake, making a determined effort to be optimistic, wrote after the 1901 festival: 'though the paralysing hand of the railway was laid upon its excursionists and visitors it was a great Festival'.[26] However, the fact remained that the attendance was reduced to less than 29,000 and these came mostly from the London area. The choir was a mere shadow of its former self, made up of 3,000 singers.

Three years later Holyoake's daughter, Mrs Emilie Holyoake-Marsh, wrote angrily of the effects of this policy and the limitations it imposed:

The railway companies have done more to damage the great
Festival held annually in London, by raising the fares, than any

traders' society or boycotters could possibly accomplish. None know better than the wives and mothers what the increased charges mean; a small additional charge of about sixpence or ninepence each, is of importance when it is an excursion in which the whole family wish to join, and prohibitive at times when wages are scanty and work uncertain.[27]

Co-operation drew its major strength from organizing and including in its ambit whole families, and not just the male bread-winner at the point of production or the male citizen in the 'public' political sphere. But this strategy could also pose problems; small increases in cost easily undermined a recreational activity that was designed to involve women and children. This was a constant problem for co-operators, whose aspirations and desires were always limited by economic restraints. They could not do just as they pleased, otherwise the festival would have continued to expand. Scarcity of time and money, the realities of a society where ownership and control of the means of production was monopolized by a minority, and power in all its manifestations distributed in a highly unequal manner, constantly and unremittingly pushed against their project.

The festival was seriously disadvantaged, however, long before the railway companies increased their rates. This was because, as has been noted, it was originally the brainchild of, and propaganda vehicle for, advocates of co-partnership and profit-sharing. Goods produced by the Co-operative Wholesale Society, therefore, if not in fact totally excluded, were marginalized from the first festivals. This caused much acrimonious feeling and necessarily weakened the event. From about 1896 regional festivals were organized in the North and in the Midlands, and these expanded as the cost of travelling to London increased.[28] An alternative to the Crystal Palace Festival was held in Manchester, in the Botanical Gardens at Old Trafford, in August 1900, organized by the Manchester and Salford Equitable Co-operative Society. A correspondent in the *Wheatsheaf* remarked that:

> It seemed only fitting, therefore, that the Co-operative Festival should have been held here in the North, because it is the home of the mass of the working people of this country and co-operation is ideally a movement of the working classes.[29]

The festival lasted four days and was attended by about 60,000 people.[30] The aim was to present a 'thoroughly representative' exhibition of co-operative productions, and consequently CWS goods were highlighted. At the opening ceremony John Shillito defended the CWS from Earl Grey's strictures voiced at the Crystal Palace Festival that year, and maintained that the CWS was an integral part of the movement, and that the 1,250,000 members controlled its policy and elected its directors.[31]

At the Birmingham Congress in 1906 this problem was debated and a resolution passed declaring that the productive exhibition held that year would be 'representative of the whole movement'. Mr Golightly from Stratford remarked that the function of the festival had been a cause of disunion for many years, but now that the festival was in crisis the Southern Section of the Central Board had come to the conclusion that 'we need not go into details about the methods used in production and distribution'. By this time it was clear that unless the northern societies backed the festival its end was certain: 'The object of the resolution was to ask the assistance of our Northern friends, by coming to London and helping to bring this festival back to what it used to be.'[32] True, the railway fares were prohibitive, but the influence of the Wholesale could be used to restore the necessary facilities. Southern 'idealists' no longer dictated the tenor of the festivals, but by this time it was too late. Co-operators in Lancashire, Yorkshire, and the Midlands were building their own round of festivals and exhibitions, which were more accessible to their memberships. Not until the 1920s was a national festival again held in London.

Exhibitions and festivals, and a new development – pageants – held in the metropolis in the inter-war years would take us beyond the scope of this chapter, but their size and popularity can be noted. An International Co-operative Day was instituted and celebrated throughout the country from 1923 onwards. An exhibition of CWS goods held at the Crystal Palace in 1934 attracted 140,000 visitors. The pageant performed on International Co-operative Day in 1938, entitled 'Towards Tomorrow', was attended by 60,000 co-operators and was beautifully filmed. It was held at the Wembley Stadium in London and featured a dramatization, involving thousands of participants, of the history and oppression of the English working class from feudal society to the present. The author was the Communist Party member, Montague Slater. At the close the

'Internationale' was sung and thousands of people marching under a myriad of national flags filled the stadium, symbolizing the struggle for the international co-operative commonwealth.[33] Spectacle, colour, and music, and participation on a huge scale, continued to be of use to those who wished to replace competition and war with co-operation and peace.

NOTES

1 G. J. Holyoake, *The History of Co-operation in England: Its Literature and its Advocates*, London, Trubner, 1906, pp. 656–7.

2 See T. Kusamitsu, 'Great Exhibitions before 1851', *History Workshop Journal*, no. 9, Spring 1980, pp. 70–89.

3 See the *Co-operative News and Journal of Associated Industry*, vol. XVII, 35, 28 August 1886, pp. 856–7.

4 ibid., vol. XIX, 34, 25 August 1888, pp. 846–51.

5 Greening later recalled: 'When I initiated the co-operative festival I could not find in the whole movement a single choir. I had to go to the temperance movement to borrow the first choir which sang at the Crystal Palace. . . . Co-operators of all ages and both sexes had to go outside the movement for their pleasures.' Quoted in T. Crimes, *Edward Owen Greening. A Maker of Modern Co-operation*, Manchester, Co-operative Union, 1923, p. 73. For more biographical details about Greening see J. Saville and J. Bellamy (eds), *Dictionary of Labour Biography*, London, Macmillan, 1972, vol. I, pp. 136–9; and B. P. McVeich, 'Edward Owen Greening and the co-operative movement', unpublished BA thesis, University of Adelaide, South Australia, 1978. The Co-operative Union Library in Manchester has the Greening papers, an extensive and almost unused source, though shamefully, through no fault of the librarians, still uncatalogued. Consequently Greening still awaits his biographer.

6 *Co-operative News*, vol. XX, 31, 3 August 1889, p. 830.

7 ibid., vol. XX, 33, 17 August 1889, pp. 877–9.

8 *The Times*, 20 August 1888.

9 *Norwood Review*, 25 August 1894.

10 T. Blandford and G. Newell, *History of the Leicester Co-operative Hosiery Manufacturing Society Ltd.*, Leicester, Co-operative Printing Society, 1898, p. 31.

11 *Norwood News*, 25 August 1894.

12 *Labour Co-partnership*, vol. II, 9, September 1896, p. 171.

13 This was one of Greening's major preoccupations, and he wrote extensively on gardening in the *Co-operative News*, recommending, even in the early 1880s, that every society should have its own flower and vegetable gardens, which would help inculcate social habits. See vol. XIII, 3, 21 January 1882, pp. 45–5. Horticulture, a love of the countryside and natural beauty were deeply ingrained in working-

class life, and continues into our own day. For a sensitive presentation of its presence now, see J. Seabrook, *The Idea of Neighbourhood*, London, Pluto Press, 1984, pp. 94–103.

14 *Labour Co-partnership*, vol. I, 13, August 1895, p. 164.

15 ibid., vol. III, 9, September 1897, pp. 152–3. This journal, the official organ of the Labour Association, carried extensive reports on the festivals from 1894 onwards.

16 *Norwood Review*, 22 August 1908.

17 *The Standard*, 20 August 1888.

18 *Norwood News*, 25 August 1888.

19 For this body see R. A. Church, 'Profit-sharing and labour relations in England in the Nineteenth Century', *International Review of Social History*, vol. XVI, 1971; and E. Bristow, 'Profit-sharing, socialism, and labour unrest', in K. D. Brown (ed.), *Essays in Anti-Labour History*, London, Macmillan, 1974, pp. 262–89.

20 *Labour Co-partnership*, vol. VI, September 1900, p. 158.

21 *Co-operative Record of the Birmingham District*, 16, July 1896, pp. 14–15.

22 See for example H. Cunningham, *Leisure in the Industrial Revolution, 1780–1880*, London, Croom Helm, 1980, pp. 158–9.

23 A brief history of the festival containing the above information can be found in Greening's article in the *Economic Review*, XII, January 1902, pp. 87–90.

24 *Co-operative Congress Reports*, Manchester, Co-operative Union, 1900, pp. 157–8.

25 *Co-operative Congress Reports*, Manchester, Co-operative Union, 1901, pp. 38, 185.

26 *Labour Co-partnership*, vol. VII, 9, September 1901, p. 134.

27 ibid., vol. X, 9, September 1904, p. 139

28 For details of these developments see ibid., vol. VIII, November 1902, p. 117, and vol. X, June 1904, p. 84.

29 *The Wheatsheaf: A Monthly Co-operative Record*, vol. V, September 1900, p. 39.

30 *Co-operative News*, vol. XXXI, 35, 1 September 1900, pp. 974–6.

31 *The Wheatsheaf*, vol. V, September 1900, p. 42. Shillito became the chairman of the CWS when Mitchell died in 1895, and held the office until his own death in 1915.

32 *Co-operative Congress Reports*, Manchester, Co-operative Union, 1906, pp. 341–2.

33 The pageant was organized by the Watford, London and South Suburban co-operative societies, and the cast was made up of members of the Women's Co-operative Guild and other co-operative groups. A forty-minute film of the pageant is available from the CRS London Region film archive.

Chapter Eleven

CO-OPERATION AND CRISIS: GOVERNMENT, CO-OPERATION, AND POLITICS, 1917–1922

PADDY MAGUIRE

Inside and outside the co-operative movement there is probably more misunderstanding about the relations between c(C)o-operation and p(P)olitics than about anything else. Better understandings of these matters depend upon history: and heated debates on these matters within the movement always involve the exchange of historical information.

This chapter is part of wider work by its author (for which see P. Maguire, 'Politics and industrial conflict: government, employees and trade union organization 1915–1922', D.Phil. thesis, University of Sussex, 1984) in which he weaves the threads of labour's story, capital's story, and government's story in twentieth-century Britain into a single, class-riven narrative.

No one, in Maguire's story, is in control: everyone would like to appear to be. Nothing is as it seems (e.g. the threat of revolution in Britain in 1919): but as it seems – different to differently placed actors – is a fundamental determinant of what happens. Thus, the question of whether or not the co-operative movement was to be in Politics was not primarily a matter of its own choice. Once Politics (and the state) were what they had become by about 1910, a movement of any size and ambition, whether of corner-shop grocers, Lever Bros empires, local Co-operative Societies, or huge Co-operative Unions, had no alternative but to enter Parliament (or Whitehall). They were in it already, through the activities (in relation to Co-operative Societies) of those already in power. 'Centralized power', as this chapter argues, 'required centralized response, and centralized political power required centralized *political* response.' The question became *in what forms* they should be in it: and the historical narrative has been about answering that question with a greater or lesser degree of self-consciousness among the actors involved.

There were lines of least resistance. And these, for the most part, were the political lines followed. One of these was to be in Parliament as an interest, for protection against and competition with other interests.

Co-operators were aware of the need for this kind of representation from at least the 1870s onwards. J. T. W. Mitchell advocated it at Congress in 1877. Locally and nationally, moves towards Co-operative Representation Committees and Independent co-operative representation have a history parallel with (not, as is commonly supposed, subsequent to) better-known moves towards Labour representation of the same kind.

Another line was to be in Parliament as a party. This went against the grain of the movement (in the ways in which it also went against the grain of classic liberalism) in ways in which interest representation did not. But it did at least provide the basis for an oppositional stance on behalf of co-operators when there was so much opposition to them from government and private trade. The *party* form was, in the end, acceptable (as in the Co-operative Party, 1919) only when it seemed like the best way of pursuing the interest line: that is to say, the best way of protecting the co-operative movement as a vested interest against moves being made against it through the state by its competitors (see Sydney Pollard, 'The foundation of the Co-operative Party', in Asa Briggs and John Saville (eds), *Essays in Labour History 1886–1923* (London, Macmillan, 1971)). The political party as a form of organization was, to their credit, a problem for co-operators (and has remained so ever since): but it was, at least potentially, independent. Independence was a key co-operative, and wider working-class, value.

A third line was to be in Politics as the appendage of another party, namely the Labour Party, preserving the appearance of independence while losing its reality. This, after 1927, was the main line taken, with infrequent exceptions, by co-operative Politics in twentieth-century Britain. Hence the disappointing history of the Co-operative Party in twentieth-century Britain from the point of view of those hoping for a large-scale, co-operative, working-class, constructive critique of statist 'Labour' Politics (for which see T. P. Carbery, *Consumers in Politics*, Manchester, Manchester University Press, 1969).

That kind of statist, Labour Party, Politics was not all that co-operative politics had been about. There was another, largely buried, tradition from which the much misunderstood commitment to 'political neutrality' came. There was a famous phrase within the movement, taken from William Maxwell of the Scottish Co-operative Wholesale Society, that the ambition of Co-operators was 'to bring co-operation into politics and not politics into co-operation'. This would have been radical indeed, and has been a political line with such a small 'p' that it has been almost completely buried. The main inheritance from the nineteenth-century co-operative movement was (could have been) a living critique of dominant forms of Politics from a working-class point of view, through the federated practice of Co-operation. During the nineteenth century 'political neutrality' was not what many co-operative politicians in the twentieth century have supposed it to be. They have argued against it from within the Co-operative Party, Labour Party, or Communist Party as if it was neutrality from *all* forms of politics, rather than the critique of their own party forms which was latent (occasionally manifest) within it. 'Political neutrality' was not invented by the Rochdale Pioneers so that they might be left alone to become respectable grocers. It was worked out, in part during the Congresses of 1829–33, as a critique, by working people, of reformism. It was a critique of those who thought either that suffrage reform would solve working-class problems in capitalism, or that instant Community (based upon anti-religious conformity) was *the answer* (enunciated by prophets like Owen), which would transcend the messy business of producing and consuming necessities. It was to that messy business which working-class co-operators were committed as the available, material, working-class basis for bringing co-operation into politics, constructing a state within the state. Surrounding the movement with commitments to this or that religious (or secularist) or party political nostrum would, they thought, get in the way. They had, they thought, to do it themselves, and in association.

Paddy Maguire sees his period as a formative one, marking out the boundaries which have enclosed the creative politics of Co-operation. These have been boundaries between the trading/commercial side of the co-operative movement and its Political wing, and boundaries between what, in twentieth-century Britain, was to be 'legitimate', 'constitutional' Politics, and what was not.

When, in January 1921, G. D. H. Cole surveyed the state of the co-operative movement he concluded that

> Most socialists and all revolutionaries, until quite recently, have treated the Co-operative movement with patronising contempt. It was a satisfactory grocer's shop and a good savings-bank, but no self-respecting revolutionary would believe that it would ever make a big breach in the walls of capitalism.[1]

Doubtless Cole, with his background as a committed Guild Socialist and publicist of oppositional movements within the world of labour, would have included himself within the ranks of erstwhile patronizers. The causes of activists over the preceding decade or so, had been many and varied. Rarely, if ever, had the co-operative movement figured prominently in their hearts, still less in their minds, although (see Chapter 4) the 'co-operative commonwealth' had been more attractive.

Why the co-operative movement should suddenly have acceded to the pantheon of 'causes' is partly very obvious. Other such causes were receding below the horizon of realistic revolutionary expectation. The shop stewards' movements had withered in the post-war climate, with most of the leading activists finding new roles in either the Communist Party of Great Britain (CPGB) or the nascent unemployed workers' movement or, more commonly, both. Workers' control had been effectively removed from the immediate agenda both by the defeat of the miners' claims and by the increasingly anti-syndicalist orientation of the Third International. Trade union power in general was clearly waning, as employers utilized the developing slump to attack wage rates and bargaining rights. The CPGB was about to tear itself apart in the embittered debates over the rival merits of 'political' and 'industrial' struggle. The Labour Party was busily engaged in building up electoral strength and distancing itself from 'extremists'. The Triple Alliance was about to collapse in the fiasco of Black Friday. The international socialist movement was already embarked on the internecine conflicts which would so mark the inter-war period. At just this moment the co-operative movement appeared to be going 'political'. Going political, that is, in a fashion very recognizable to those who thought of politics as a separate, 'higher' sphere. It appeared to be doing so as the Co-operative Congress of that year (1921) was to consider an alliance with the Labour Party.

That particular debate will need to be returned to. It represented the culmination of a whole series of conflicts within the movement and it also encapsulated many of the tensions about what 'political' meant, at precisely the same moment as government was seeking to re-define notions of legitimate and illegitimate political and industrial actions and aspirations. For just that reason the *significance* of the co-operative movement in general, and the 1920 and 1921 Congresses in particular, went far beyond the narrowly conceived 'swing to the left' which attracted the attention of Cole and others and, momentarily, threatened to elevate the movement to the status of a recognizably oppositional *political* organization.

Those who discovered the co-operative movement as a result of its emerging Political (with a large 'P') predilections might have been surprised at the language of a delegate to the 1920 Congress on the apparently non-political question of centralization: 'Co-operators were beginning to be a menace to capitalism, and there would come a time, in view of that fact, when capitalism would carry all its forces against the movement.'[2] They might have been even more surprised at the attitude of a Liverpool NUR branch official who, in January 1917, celebrated the transfer of the branch's funds to the CWS bank as 'another brick out of the capitalist system'.[3] They would certainly have been surprised to discover that government had been keeping the movement (along with other potential or actual oppositional bodies) under surveillance since 1917. If many socialists and revolutionaries could be charged with having ignored the potential of the co-operative movement, it was not a charge which could be levelled at government.

Again, some of the reasons for government interest in the behaviour of the movement are patently obvious. The need to maintain civilian (and for civilian, largely, read working-class) support for the war, particularly during the closing eighteen months or so of the conflict, placed a premium on intelligence gathering and propaganda diffusion. Perhaps for the first time in a century the working classes in general, and working-class organizations in particular, were deemed too important (and too volatile) to be left to their own devices. Some careful and some very explicit tutoring was to be the order of the day.[4] During the long crisis of British politics, from at least the winter of 1917 to the summer of 1919, government would be particularly sensitive to changes in what it perceived as popular mentality and popular aspirations, as it engaged in an increasingly difficult balancing act: at first to maintain the impetus of the war whilst retaining the maximum support (or, at least, acquiesence) for its conduct and then to direct the peace. This meant establishing a particular variety of constitutional propriety, without unduly alienating labour from that embryonic definition. At certain moments, as in January 1918 or February 1919, government was acutely aware of just how tenuous its grip on the domestic situation could be.[5]

In the process of accommodating this crisis, government and, perhaps more importantly, semi-government intelligence/propaganda agencies had mushroomed. They were often in contradiction not just with each other but with even more diverse 'freelance', semi-official organizations like Admiral Hall's National Propaganda, the Engineering Employers' Federation's intelligence bank, the

Economic Study Club and individual companies' own networks.[6] All these agencies, with their own interests and interpretations to promote and defend, shared a common concern. That concern, simply stated, was how to monitor the beliefs and conduct of working-class organizations. They sought to influence government policy through their intelligence and/or propaganda capability. It would be no exaggeration to say that for the closing eighteen months or so of the war and the opening year or two of the peace, government was awash with 'intelligence' as to how best to cope with the alleged threat posed by evident changes in social, political, and industrial organizations.

It is scarcely surprising that the co-operative movement should be included within this convoluted intelligence net and, therefore, come to the attention of government as a potential 'problem'. The movement thus became an object to be managed as well as being viewed as a barometer of working-class feeling. After all, it represented the largest single working-class organization in Britain. Not only was it powerful and highly visible but, in common with many working-class organizations, the strains of the wartime polity and war economy had forced a reassessment of many of its working assumptions. The latter will need closer examination but for the moment it is important to stress the scale of co-operative organization. During the war membership increased from 3,053,770 to 4,131,477.[7] More importantly, to government if no one else, the activities of the movement were altering. Before the war some 80 per cent of turnover had been generated by food sales. But after the war there were signs of a shift to more ambitious designs. Between 1914 and 1921 the amount of land owned by the movement increased from 3,000 acres to 35,000 acres. In a single year it purchased in excess of 30,000 acres of Indian tea plantations and 10,000 acres of Canadian wheatland. By 1921 it could boast a total capital of £66 million and was seeking to extend its international trading links, particularly with Soviet Russia through intricate barter arrangements.[8] This was no miniscule sect which could be dismissed as eccentric and unrepresentative, nor could it be dismissed as Utopian in the customary pejorative sense.

Even more important, in a world where appearances were as politically significant as realities, was the changing role the co-operative movement appeared to be developing in the broader labour movement. Increasingly the movement signalled to labour activists much more than grocers' shops and savings banks, it signalled a more desirable form of economic organization than private enterprise. The social tensions exacerbated by the war had centred around such questions as the control of industry, the control of food supply and distribution, the rights (wrongs?) of landlords, profiteering, the conscription of wealth as well as of bodies – all issues which undermined the 'normal', 'accepted' notions of the proper organization of society as largely competitive, individualist and profit-seeking. The actions of government itself did much to underline the divide as, however reluctantly, it was compelled to control profits, rents, food distribution, housing supply and a host of other matters previously held as best left to the operation of 'natural laws'.

Divisions were highly visible as major conflicts punctuated the period, ranging from the May 1917 engineering strikes, through the quasi-insurrectionary Glasgow and Belfast strikes of February 1919, to the miners' self-confident attempt to undermine the rationale of private ownership before the Sankey Commission and on to the bitter rail strike of September 1919 and the almost endemic conflict in the coalfields. And through it all ran some very deep class antagonisms, so deep that even a 'mere' shop could belong to the other side when Manchester butchers threatened to withhold meat from striking railway workers, so deep that Brighton doctors refused treatment to the families of strikers.[9]

Hitherto dominant conceptions of the proper ordering and functioning of society were to be seriously challenged as a result of the war experience. To the Ministry of Labour it seemed quite evident (and fairly unexceptionable) that,

> There has been a marked change during the war in the public attitude towards the profit maker. The socialist cause has in consequence been much strengthened and the view that the individualist system of industry is iniquitous and intolerable has spread and intensified among working men.[10]

When even a Treasury subcommittee could draw attention to changing perceptions of the role of profits in the following terms, times could indeed be deemed to have changed:

> There is no doubt that there is a considerable feeling throughout the country – a feeling not confined to Labour alone, but

193

shared by the bulk of the middle classes – that the super-normal profits of business . . . are a proper subject of special taxation.[11]

Nowhere was that changing perception more apparent than in the relationship between the Co-operative and other Labour organizations. The Liverpool activist quoted earlier was not alone in seeing the importance of voting with one's money. By July 1920, 2,729 trade union organizations and 1,258 clubs and mutual associations were banking with the Co-operative. The number of trade union accounts alone had increased by 1,354 since September 1919 – a fact which the Home Office wished to draw to the Cabinet's attention in its weekly intelligence summary – otherwise known as the 'Reports on Revolutionary Organisations'.[12] By June 1921 some 5,550 trade unions and friendly societies were banking with the Co-operative.[13]

Time and again government papers referred to the collapse of labour discipline, to the possibilities of a labour revolt, to the aspirations of labour for a better life, for a greater role (in industry, in politics, in general).[14] It was fear of the implications of that demand which underlay a good deal of government actions and assumptions. In relation to the co-operative movement the fear had both general and particular dimensions. In general terms it was palpably a working-class organization and, therefore, potentially hostile. In the politics of crisis crude class assumptions cut far deeper, or at least were far more open, than in more 'stable' moments. Moreover, the whole ethos of the movement, both historically and materially, was in conscious opposition to private, profit-seeking industry at just the moment when that industrial structure was so clearly under attack.

There were, however, more particular reasons for government concern. First, its own dealings with the movement during the war were hardly calculated to inculcate support for its general approach. Secondly, and more crucially, was the movement's position as the country's largest grocery operation. Throughout the crisis, though for different reasons at different moments, the politics of food lay at the very heart of government concerns. In the war period it was pre-eminently a question of the price and supply of basic foodstuffs, particularly once the German submarine campaign began to bite. The price of food was a constant source of industrial disturbance and, at least after the pegging of rents, *the* source of wage conflicts. To begin with, those groups of workers powerful enough to enforce their will could be allowed to hike up wages. By the last year of the war, however, both government and employers were becoming concerned that the longer-term effects of wage inflation on unit costs would seriously jeopardize British industry's international competitiveness once the war had ended.[15] None the less wage increases, particularly when accompanied by labour shortages, did take some of the heat out of the 'food profiteering' issue. The same could not be said of the issue of food shortages. The bitterness which surrounded the question of shortages, and the government's reluctance to intervene, should not be underestimated. A characteristic complaint was voiced by the *Woolwich Pioneer*:

> For the poor, at all events, the struggle for food threatens to return to the levels of savagery. One either has to fight among scores of other women, fighting likewise, for quarters of tea and half pounds of margerine, or stand for hours outside shops in a long queue to be similarly rewarded for patience as for struggle.[16]

At certain moments, particularly in November 1917 and January/ February 1918, the food question threatened to undermine the whole war effort. In January 1918 labour exchanges were instructed to notify the Ministry of 'labour troubles likely to arise as a result of food difficulties'. In February the Minister of Munitions wanted to release additional food supplies as a response to threatened industrial action.[17] It would have been an extraordinarily apolitical grocer who could have escaped the implications of the food crisis, and the Co-operative was not just the largest retail organization in the field: it was *the* working-class grocer. The co-operative movement could not escape the implications of the food crisis. When Woolwich shop stewards demanded action on food supply, under threat of strike, it was through the Co-operative that they demanded food be distributed at cost price.[18] In itself that was hardly surprising as the local co-operative had introduced a successful rationing scheme some three months earlier.[19] Moreover, the Co-operative represented more than an efficient grocer. It also represented a non-profit-making one. And profiting from food shortages was emerging as one of the key areas of conflict between government and labour organizations.

If the co-operative movement found itself embroiled at the sharp end of the struggles over food, be it in administering rationing schemes or in finding its members discriminated against on food control committees, it found itself no less embroiled at the sharp end of the struggle over profits and the morality of 'profiteering':

> wage earners were convinced that enormous profits were being made . . . it was generally said that the war was being kept going by persons who were interested in making profits out of the war.[20]

It was partly as a result of such sentiments and partly as a deliberate bargaining strategy in the negotiations surrounding the relaxation of trade union control of working practices that the government had felt compelled to demonstrate its concern over 'profiteering' by introducing the Excess Profits Duty. Its introduction was both promoted as and largely viewed as a concession to organized labour.

How were the co-operative societies to be treated? By their own perceptions they were not engaged in the business of profit making, just the reverse. The societies' status as mutual trading associations, a status underwritten by legal judgements, was at the very core of their identity. It was at this core that the government's decision to include the co-operative societies within the scope of its excess profits provision struck.

The decision to make the societies liable to taxation of alleged profits provoked a response not dissimilar to that of other organizations during the war. As power became more centralized, and more obviously centralized, individual organizations became both more aware of that power and more inclined to attempt to influence its exercise. In particular, as it became evident that 'the control of labour now falls entirely on the Government', all sorts of different organizations sought to enter the national political arena and to develop their status as an 'interest' to be taken into account in the framing and enactment of policies which could be construed as impinging upon their particular interests.[21] Centralized power required centralized response, and centralized political power required centralized *political* response. For the co-operative movement the changing climate opened anew debates which appeared to have been settled in 1905 and 1914 – i.e. whether or not the movement should engage in 'politics'.

To a Scottish delegate to the Central Board the moral seemed obvious:

> There was a likelihood that they were about to receive their Taff Vale. . . . Organisations of profiteers had their representatives in Parliament to watch and safeguard their interests, and it was time co-operators placed themselves in a position to do the same.[22]

When the proposal for the formation of a separate Co-operative Party was put to the 1917 Congress it was carried by 1,979 to 201 votes. The position had indeed changed from that of 1905 and 1914. But it had changed in particular ways. Where *party* political allegiance had been (and still was) deemed out of court by previous congresses, *independent* political representation was now deemed essential. As in so many other areas, and doubtless against its own intentions, government action had succeeded in broadening the definition of the political to a point where a political presence could be considered essential to survival, even by the most avowed of apolitical organizations. Not, of course, that such changes went unresisted. As a Nottingham member complained in 1921, whilst noting the improved membership of his society since it had embarked on political action, it had been vehemently opposed by 'reactionaries' among the membership.[23]

The language is revealing. This was no simple opting for political organization in any narrow sense. It marked a considerable realignment in definitions, splitting along lines of 'reactionary' and 'progressive', a split in which government was firmly consigned to the ranks of the reactionaries. The formation of the Co-operative Party, and the strategy of passive resistance to taxation demands adopted by a number of individual societies, could only confirm the worst fears of government. A Sheffield co-operator believed that 'it is a question of having a movement of the workers and the Labour movement stands four square against the capitalists of the country as the co-operative movement does.'[24]

The logic of that position, in a climate of increasing antagonism between capital and labour, was spelt out in a resolution before the 1919 Congress calling for 'a federation for electoral purposes and with the ultimate object of forming a United Democratic or People's Party'. That particular resolution was amended to call for 'affiliation with the National Labour Party and the linking up of local societies with the Labour Representation Committee in their respective districts'.[25] Although both suggestions were side-stepped, as they manifestly split the membership, there could be no mistaking the direction in which a significant section wished to move. And, in 1919, that was not a direction which government could happily contemplate. The formation of a distinctive, separate and self-conscious labour constituency was a constant nightmare and one which appeared to be nearing fruition as individual labour organizations pressed home their claims through various forms of 'direct action'.

It was the threat of direct action which made the material base of the co-operative movement, far more than the political predilections of individual co-operators, of prime concern to government. And that material base led back to the politics of food. In the spring of 1918 leaders of the Barrow shop stewards' movement, which had been engaged in a running battle with employers and government since 1916 and was one of the most prominent groupings in the national shop stewards' organization, proudly announced that they had placed three of their number at the top of the poll in the local Co-operative Society elections. The reasons why they considered the event important were to prove prescient: 'If past industrial history after a war is any criterion there are bleak times ahead, *when we may be looking for food*.'[26] Food would indeed emerge as a key area of conflict in the immediate post-war crisis. Faced with large-scale industrial disturbances, government was momentarily deprived of its ultimate sanction – force. In December 1918 it had been warned that in certain industrial areas the police might not prove reliable if called on to deal with large-scale strikes.[27] By January it appeared that the army could not be relied on either, fears confirmed not just by the mutinies and half-mutinies in the demobilization camps but also by reports of left-wing efforts to infiltrate the military. Fears (and hopes) of workers' and soldiers' councils were still, after all, very much present.[28] As late as November 1919, long after the demobilization crisis had passed, Haig felt compelled to warn the Cabinet that troops could not necessarily be relied on in the event of their being deployed in industrial disputes. It would only be in 1920, and more particularly 1921, that full confidence in the military would be restored.[29]

At an early stage the government identified control of food supply as a crucial test of authority. As early as February 1919 Lloyd George was warning his colleagues (apropos the mining dispute), 'if they [the miners] chose starvation as a weapon they must not complain if society made use of the same weapon'.[30] By March the Industrial Unrest Committee was considering withholding food supplies to alienate public support from striking workers.[31] It would be no accident that the successor to the IUC would be the more aptly named *Supply* and Transport Committee. Amidst such deliberations it was scarcely surprising that the real or imagined role of the co-operatives should figure prominently. In 1921 the 1,376 retail societies generated a turnover of £320,084,000, much of it in basic foodstuffs.[32] By October, faced with a major rail dispute and the prospect of renewed conflict in the coal industry, the Home Office was recommending that government arm itself with powers to commandeer food stocks, in particular those held by co-operative societies. Such drastic measures had not been contemplated during the war, but then it had only been submarines not strikers which had imperilled food supply. The concern of the Home Office was twofold. First it appeared as if labour had equipped itself with a general staff in the guise of the TUC General Council. Secondly the Home Office believed that the Bolshevik regime 'has practically been kept alive' by the Russian co-operative movement, a movement with which the British equivalent was rapidly developing links.[33] It might also have added that in a number of instances the perception of the crucial advantage of controlling food supplies was shared by strike committees (or 'soviets' as the Leeds railway strike committee was referred to), to an extent that in at least one instance the Executive Committee of the NUR had to issue instructions to local activists not to interfere with food supply.[34] In the aftermath of the rail strike the Home Office sought to investigate the links between co-operatives and unions and came to the conclusion that it was the intention to utilize the co-operatives to feed strikers 'while the rest of the community starves'. From that perspective it was scarcely surprising that it wished for additional powers to deal with such a situation.[35] Throughout 1919 and 1920 the Home Office acted as the focus for elements within government who wished to see special legislation introduced, a demand which would receive some satisfaction with the passing of the Emergency Powers Act.

The stance of the Home Office (and of other government departments) might well be taken as alarmist, as detecting dangers where none existed. And, in a sense, that would be true. There was no grand alliance, and the general staff was soon to prove itself as divided and impotent as its precursor, the Parliamentary Committee. In a sense, though, it was not so lacking in substance. As the competing sides frequently agreed, the struggle was as much about realizing or constraining potential as about actual developments. Certainly labour activists had called loud and long for a general staff. They called, too, for co-operatives to serve as the commissariat of strikes. To put it another way, it was not only the vaguely paranoid *apparatchiks* of the Home Office who believed they had seen a (possible) future. Immediately after the rail strike W. T. A. Foot, who had played a prominent role in the railway-workers' unofficial movement and served on the strike committee, was drawing up plans for joint union and co-operative action during the next rail strike, with the co-operative disbursing food in exchange for vouchers.[36] Even before the war some labour activists had been pointing to continental experience as an indication of the greater role which could be assumed by the co-operative movement during strikes.[37]

Nor was it surprising that the co-operative movement should be expected to play such a role. The greater institutional links which had developed during the war both nationally and, more particularly, between individual union branches and the movement merely underlined the 'natural' position of the co-operative movement as a labour organization. A representative of the Central Board, in 1920, even went so far as to float the possibility of exchanging 'material aid' for unions for exemption for co-operative societies from strike action so long as they recognized union conditions.[38] By 1920, at least to government, the threat of any major strike action, be it of miners or engineers or the more generalized councils of action, carried with it the threat of co-operative support for, and involvement in, such action.[39] Nor was support necessarily confined to provisioning. The Manchester Co-operative Society, for example, wanted the movement to support the *Herald* to the tune of £10,000.[40] When the Brighton Trades Council decided to hold a public meeting to protest at the government's Irish policy, it sought the assistance of its local co-operative society in so doing.[41]

Given the increasing involvement of the co-operative movement, both in practice and in theory, in the wider world of labour politics, it could hardly be unexpected that it would be viewed as a natural opponent of government's desired order. Just as labour activists thought of a 'natural' constituency, so too did government. Not only was the co-operative movement not part of government's constituency but a part of that constituency was becoming increasingly vociferous in its attacks on co-operative practices. Although private traders had long resented the success of the movement, its developing political profile gave them an added incentive to seek government action to curb its power. By 1920, as the Ministry of Labour saw it, the Labour Party/TUC/Co-operative *entente* was proving sufficiently alarming to private traders for them to establish (or re-establish) their own organization, the Amalgamated Trades Association, to combat it.[42]

In the prevailing climate it was scarcely surprising that government should view sympathetically criticisms of an organization which was so clearly a potential enemy. And it was precisely government which could curb the co-operative movement through utilization of the weapon it had discovered during the war – taxation. It had long been a criticism made by private traders that the co-operatives enjoyed a privileged position by virtue of their legal status. It was that status which government now sought to erode. As the Cabinet committee on taxation recognized, any attempt to make the societies' dividends or surpluses liable to taxation in the fashion of private companies' profits and dividends would lead to 'open dissatisfaction on the part of a considerable body of the community'. However, such a move would have the virtue of going 'far to meet the complaint of the retail trader'. In this instance the latter consideration would outweigh the former. Indeed, it would be openly admitted that it was political rather than revenue considerations which informed the deliberations on the status of the societies.[43]

The decision even to consider making co-operative operations liable to taxation was one which could only be greeted with opposition by the movement. It was also a threat which could only further add to the demands for political representation and action. The threat dominated the 1920 Congress and deeply divided the movement. Whilst the Board attempted to negotiate with the Treasury, a number of societies, particularly in Scotland and the Midlands, wanted more direct action. In words which might have been uttered by any trade union activist, one delegate wanted to disavow 'any feelings which the members of the Board might have that the Chancellor of the Exchequer is to be impressed by the passing of mere pious resolutions'.[44] By the following year, some eighty societies had pledged themselves to resist the government's decision to impose corporation tax on undistributed surpluses.[45]

Even as Congress was debating the taxation position, the Liverpool Society moved a resolution, 'That this Congress is of the opinion that the time has now arrived for the affiliation of the Co-operative Party and the Labour Party, both locally and nationally.'[46] As in 1917, the threat of government intervention in the affairs of the movement gave a fillip to those who already desired more positive action. As one Liverpool delegate saw it, 'We shall have the Commonwealth after we have kicked this Parliament out.'[47] Unlike the situation in 1917 it was now evident that there was an organized group in favour of political action. By November 1920 there was a left-wing caucus devising its own 'slate' for Board elections and a number of societies were actively lobbying in advance of the 1921 Congress's consideration of political affiliation with Labour.

They were not the only ones to mobilize. The lead up to the Congress was marked by an intensive press campaign against 'politics' being allowed to sully the apolitical purity of the movement. The intensity of the campaign convinced supporters of the Liverpool resolution to add to their list of demands the creation of an independent co-operative newspaper.[49] They might have considered that an even more pressing necessity had they been aware that by this stage, through various organizations, the government possessed a highly sophisticated machine for directing the content of the press. At its peak the Supply and Transport Committee could boast the ability to dispatch 1,700 briefs *daily*.[50] Not surprisingly, the unofficial co-ordinator of the government's propaganda machine, Frederick Guest (the Liberal Chief Whip) saw it as his function to accentuate divisions within labour organizations, as 'Our biggest gain with them is always to drive in this wedge.'[51]

Divisions within the movement there clearly were. The Congress split almost exactly in half, with a considerable number expressing their opposition not to political action *per se* but to alliance with a specific party. The resulting vote showed 1,682 in favour of alliance with the Labour Party and 1,686 against. An amendment against political alliance in general had been lost by the much larger margin of 1,953 to 1,199.[52] By the time Congress held its deliberations, however, the real crisis had passed. Government was rapidly retreating from overt (and from much, though not all, covert) involvement in labour affairs. It had succeeded in attaining a degree of political and industrial stability which had seemed unrealizable in 1919. To a degree, too, it had succeeded in establishing its own definition of political and industrial propriety. In that sense, no doubt, those interested would have been heartened by the objection of one delegate to affiliation – simply that the Labour Party was about class and the co-operative movement was above class. In a fashion, albeit an incomplete one, government was in the business of defining politics as a specialist, narrow, professional area best left to politicians and not to 'ordinary' people.

Just as Congress was about to debate affiliation, the *Economist* observed of the movement's failing performance that it had much to do with 'the way in which political matters have lately overwhelmed the main purpose of co-operation'.[53] Presumably, the even more spectacular decline of private companies was solely attributable to the rapid deterioration of the domestic and international economy. The intended message was clear. Business and politics did not, and should not, mix. In a sense that was also the conclusion of the Congress, but only in a very partial sense. Throughout 1921 individual societies played an active (and sometimes financially crippling) role in the mining dispute. The movement now possessed a political arm and, whatever the constitutional niceties, the realities of electoral politics as well as feelings of class-based affinity dictated that that body would need to relate to the Labour Party both locally and nationally. Equally, the movement had developed clear links with unions, links which would not simply disappear. Its activists were still committed to a particular vision of society. The very year after Congress had so narrowly rejected affiliation, the Women's Co-operative Guild was calling for the creation of an independent newspaper which would serve not just the movement but the Labour Party and the TUC. It linked that demand to a call for the movement to campaign for the election of a 'Co-operative and Labour Government'.[54]

If the politics of crisis had not totally altered the shape and direction of the movement, it had certainly not been left unmarked. As would again be discovered in the 1930s, however much it might be wished that politics and politicians could be excluded from the movement they both had a recurrent habit of including themselves. Indeed, it might be said that politicians appreciated the politics of Co-operation far more than did co-operators. In the crisis of British politics at the end of the First World War they also appreciated it far more successfully.

NOTES

1 *New Statesman*, 15 January 1921. Cole might almost have been caricaturing himself, having written somewhat earlier that 'The sphere of Co-operation has definite bounds, and it is evident that though the movement may double or treble the volume of its trade, it will remain, in essentials, pretty much what it is now. It will continue alongside Capitalism; but it will do nothing to overthrow it.' G. D. H. Cole, *The World of Labour*, Hassocks, Harvester Press, 1973 (reprint of 1919 text (originally published 1913)), p. 341.

2 Co-operative Congress Report, 1920.

3 *Railway Review* (journal of the NUR), 19 January 1917.

4 From late 1916 a number of back-bench MPs had been pressing government to engage in educational propaganda. That would come to fruition, albeit in a piecemeal fashion, under Lloyd George's ministry.

5 At such moments ministers would openly express fears of imminent revolution, 'stop the war strikes', insurrection, and similar 'Russian phenomena'.

6 A number of attempts to co-ordinate domestic intelligence/propaganda were (unsuccessfully) made; e.g. Lloyd George Papers, F/79/11/1, memorandum of 10 December 1917 and Cabinet (hereafter Cab) 24/114, CP 2100, 12 November 1920.

7 A. Bonner, *British Co-operation*, Stockport, Co-operative Wholesale Society, 1961, p. 143.

8 G. Crossick, 'Shopkeepers and the state in Britain, 1870–1914' in G. Crossick and Heinz-Gerhard Haupt (eds), *Shopkeepers and Master Artisans in Nineteenth Century Europe*, London, Methuen, 1984, p. 248. *New Statesman*, 15 January 1921.

9 *Daily Herald*, 3 October 1919. Brighton Trades Council Minutes, October 1919.

10 Cab 24/87, GT 8059; Ministry of Labour Weekly Report (hereafter MLWR), 27 August 1919.

11 Cab 27/101, TX 7, February 1920.

12 Cab 24/108, CP 1564; Home Office Intelligence Report (hereafter HDI) 61, 1 July 1920.

13 *Economist*, 25 June 1921. The movement was growing rapidly. Be-

tween 1919 and 1920 its turnover increased by 20 per cent. In the following year it increased by a further 23½ per cent. *Economist*, 26 March 1921.

14 See a 1918 memorandum in Steel Maitland Papers, GD/193/395/L.

15 As late as January 1918 the Engineering employers had been willing to accept 100 per cent Excess Profits Duty in exchange for firmer government action to control labour.

16 Cab 24/30, GT 2457; MLWR 31 October 1917.

17 Ministry of Labour 2/428/A/468/18, draft instructions to labour exchanges, 16 January 1918. War Cabinet (hereafter WC) 339–4, 5 February 1918. The Ministry of Munitions even considered it unwise to hold production-boosting works meetings as 'criticism of both price and shortage of food has been vigorous'. Ministry of Munitions 5/52/30/79, summary report of meetings, 26 January 1918.

18 Cab 24/40, GT 3441, MLWR 23 January 1918.

19 Cab 24/30, GT 2457, MLWR 31 October 1917.

20 WC 305–14, 24 December 1917.

21 Cab 24/57 GT 5013, MLWR 3 July 1918.

22 Co-operative Congress Report, 1917.

23 Co-operative Congress Report, 1921.

24 Co-operative Congress Report, 1921.

25 Co-operative Congress Report, 1919.

26 *Solidarity*, May 1918, emphasis in original. Cf. *Workers' Dreadnought*, March 1918 and *Solidarity*, March 1918.

27 Cab 24/71, GT 6425, 2 December 1918.

28 General Childs to Cabinet, WC 522–1, 30 January 1919. For fears about using army electricians during a strike, see WC 527–1, 5 February 1919. For doubts about the reliability of the military during the rail dispute, LG/F/30/3/24. For a general discussion of the military situation, WC 514–7, 8 January 1919.

29 Memorandum from Haig, Cab 24/93 CP 111, 6 November 1919. The military authorities had their own reasons for wanting to avoid involvement; K. Jeffery and P. Hennessy, *States Of Emergency*, London, Routledge & Kegan Paul, 1983, chs 1 and 2.

30 WC 530–4, 10 February 1919.

31 Cab 27/59, Industrial Unrest Committee 14–2, 12 March 1919.

32 Ministry of Labour, *Gazette*, November 1922.

33 Cab 24/20, GT 8304, HDI 24, 8 October 1919.

34 *The Times*, 1 October 1919. Cab 27/61 SC 73, 2 October 1919.

35 Cab 24/90, HDI 26, 23 October 1919.

36 Cab 24/101, CP 902, 25 March 1920 and MLWR 22 October 1919.

37 Cole, *World Of Labour*, pp. 342–3.

38 W. Millerchip to 1920 Congress, Report 1920. From 1917 the United Advisory Council of Trade Unionists and Co-operators (consisting of six representatives of the TUC's Parliamentary Committee and six from the Central Board) had, at least in theory, acted as a liaison body; F. Hall and W. P. Watkins, *Co-operation*, Manchester, Co-operative Union, 1953 edn, pp. 344–7.

39 e.g. Cab 24/110, CP 1706, Report on Revolutionary Organisations 65, 29 July 1920; *New Statesman*, 9 October 1920; *The Times*, 16 April 1921.

40 Cab 24/107, HDI 59, 17 June 1920.

41 Brighton Trades Council Minutes, 9 February 1921.

42 Cab 24/98 GT 613, MLWR 11 February 1921.

43 Cab 27/101 TX 7, February 1920. The Commission accepted that they had 'considered the matter at somewhat greater length than is warranted by its importance from an Income Tax point of view'. They also accepted that the proposed changes would not result in 'any great increase of revenue'. *Report of the Royal Commission on the Income Tax*, 1920, Cmd. 615, paras 537 and 566.

44 Co-operative Congress Report, 1920.

45 Co-operative Congress Report, 1921.

46 Co-operative Congress Report, 1920.

47 Co-operative Congress Report, 1922.

48 Cab 24/114 CP 2067, 4 November 1920.

49 In the end the 1922 Congress would support a co-operative paper but one specifically not including in its remit support for the Labour Party and the TUC.

50 Cab 23/38, Cabinet Conference (91), 13 April 1921.

51 Frederick Guest to Lloyd George, 15 April 1920, LG/F/22/1/29.

52 Cab 24/123, CP 2956, 21 May 1921; Co-operative Congress Report, 1921.

53 *Economist*, 14 May 1921.

54 Ministry of Labour, *Gazette*, August 1922.

Chapter Twelve

LIMITS TO MUTUALITY: ECONOMIC AND POLITICAL ATTACKS ON CO-OPERATION DURING THE 1920s AND 1930s

NEIL KILLINGBACK

The enormous growth of the co-operative movement during recent years [means that] an ever-increasing volume of trade is yearly passing out of the taxable area and becoming a menace to the state by making it more and more difficult for the Chancellor of the Exchequer to balance the nation's accounts. (National Chamber of Trade, *Evidence to the Royal Commission on the Income Tax*, 1919)

The declared policy of the Wholesale Societies is to establish new manufacturing departments or absorb existing businesses in a determination to eliminate the profit maker. (Raeburn Committee, *Report*, 1933)

The policy of the Co-operators has been openly declared to be the elimination of the profit-maker and the capitalist middleman. The recent advance of the movement is the measure of its success. (*The Economist*, 20 May 1933, p. 1126)

Working with material from outside the co-operative movement, Neil Killingback's work ('The politics of small business in Britain during the 1930s', D.Phil. thesis, University of Sussex, 1980) has listened to those in twentieth-century Britain who thought Co-operation more powerful than many co-operators did. As in Chapter 11, the concern is with class conflict over associational form: on what terms were working people, if at all, to be allowed to do the same things, to make the same relations, as capitalists? On what terms was mutuality to be allowed within the public, state demesne, contested as that public territory increasingly was by the organizations of private capital as well as by those of would-be private labour? The fundamental insight of this chapter, highly relevant to the new co-operators of the 1970s and 1980s, is that legal incorporation of working-class associations is, in its very nature, a limitation upon mutuality. It can and probably will be used in radical Right attempts to destroy that mutuality altogether. Laws present themselves as conveniences, but can only be built upon in the interests of Co-operation if their inconveniences are also realized. In 1931 the Grocers' Federation put their opposition to the co-operative movement this way:

> A Socialist Commonwealth in the United Kingdom . . . is the ideal of a dreamer, not of practical men who realise that the past prosperity of the British Empire has been built up by private enterprise and that its continuance has been jeopardised by making the community undertake to far too great an extent responsibilities which should rest mainly upon the individual.

In order to weaken Co-operation, radical, political attempts were made in the inter-war period in Britain to assimilate its forms to those of private, 'individualistic' capitalism. Such a process of assimilation was an active struggle against the co-operative movement, rather than (or as well as) the collusive will, or abdication, of that movement. As Neil Killingback shows here, mutuality is acceptable (even beautiful) to the powers that be, as long as it remains small and unambitious.

Lord Graham, the 1987 President of the Co-operative Congress, told the 1987 History Workshop at the Co-operative College that the movement was still in a major period of struggle:

> no one gets more depressed or more infuriated with our performance than those of us who are deeply immersed in it, either as a professional, or an activist, or both. There is no doubt that we live in dangerous times. There are forces out there determined to snuff us out.

Mutual organizations for distribution and production – formed by working people with little personal capital – have competed with the capitalist economy on a considerable scale in nineteenth- and twentieth-century Britain.

A Financial Secretary to the Treasury, Hore-Belisha, acknowledged the threat. In 1933 he was reported as saying:

> Co-operative societies should be placed on the same footing as trading companies bearing income tax as normally computed. There must, he argued, be some limit to the principle of mutuality. If the whole country were covered by co-operative societies the Revenue would receive no income tax at all. It was the government's duty to see that all individuals and corporations in similar circumstances and performing the same tasks should be treated with equality before the law.[1]

During the first three decades of this century, co-operative societies were attacked on two fronts. A political campaign started by small shopkeepers in the industrial North in the wake of the Great Depression, spread to all sections of the capitalist class. In 1933 it achieved legislative success. At the same time economic action was taken by private enterprise to limit mutual trading and control free competition by fixing prices.

This chapter will focus on these two campaigns. It will show that co-operative societies did not decline spontaneously because they were inherently less efficient than capitalist forms. I will propose that they were pushed down because they were successful, perfectly 'rational', but from labour's point of view. Co-operative societies, it will be argued, were attacked because they threatened the cosy protectionism set up by manufacturers and shopkeepers and because they challenged capitalist forms of distribution. They were seen as a major problem: alternatives to the capitalist order at least as resilient as trade unions or the Labour Party. It will be shown how co-operative societies were made to accept capitalist definitions of economic activity, which in time thwarted their development.They remained: but the principle of mutuality weakened.

Consolidation of the Industrial and Provident Societies Acts in 1893 set the legal conditions for the twentieth-century development of the co-operative movement. Societies had to have unrestricted membership beyond a minimum number. The law encouraged expansion by making them open. As a matter of principle, co-operative societies were distinguished from joint-stock companies because the societies provided a limited return on capital invested. Registration under the Acts reflected other differences. Every member of a society held one vote independent of personal holdings in the society; the surplus of mutual trading was distributed – through the 'divi' – on the basis of the total spending of a member with the society during a set period.

Governments had come to their own view on the nature of co-operation. Members usually had low incomes such that they qualified for exemption from income tax. Accordingly, co-operative societies were exempted payment of income tax under Schedules C and D as long as they allowed unlimited membership. Moreover, the particular economic nature of co-operative trading was distinguished from profit-making. G. D. H. Cole summed up the situation as follows:

It was laid down that exemption from income tax should be restricted to societies which placed no limitation on entry of new members, and it was in addition specified that the exemption should not extend to the profits of trade with non-members. Co-operative Societies remained liable to income tax under Schedules A and B, income from ownership or occupation of land, and individual co-operators whose incomes were above the exemption limit were taxable on the interest accruing to them from share or loan capital in Co-operative Societies. What did become established was that 'dividend on purchases' as distinct from interest on shares or loans, was not taxable income, because the co-operative trading 'surplus' could not be correctly regarded as 'profit'.[2]

The law, however, concealed a contradiction. The Industrial and Provident Societies Acts incorporated societies, i.e. defined them as separate legal entities distinct from their members. Societies were to continue to function under the law independently of changes in leadership and membership. Members were granted limited liability in return. These were, already, limitations on, or particular definitions of, mutuality. In these respects, co-operative societies had the same legal status as joint-stock companies while not in fact being the same forms.

The first rumblings of discontent with this situation were voiced by shopkeepers in the grocery trade with the onset of the Great Depression. Local associations of grocers in the North campaigned for a boycott of co-operative societies by private manufacturers.[3] W. H. Lever encouraged them and then helped to form a national federation of grocers' associations in 1891. It remained in the North until 1914. His company became Unilever.

The Great Depression unleashed the spectre of over-production and tumbling prices. Unfettered competition no longer guaranteed success. The market had to be controlled to ensure profitability. Raymond Williams charts this turnaround by private business in *The Long Revolution*:

> After the Depression, and its big falls in prices, there was a more general and growing fear of productive capacity, a marked tendency to reorganise industrial ownership into larger units and combines, and a growing desire to organise and where possible control the market. Advertising then took

on a new importance and was applied to an increasing range of products, as part of the system of market control, which at full development, included tariffs and preference areas, cartel quotas, trade campaigns, price fixing by manufacturers, and economic imperialism.[4]

From that time forward, private enterprise concentrated increasingly on supplying the demands of the home market. Co-operative societies, however, blocked the extension and easy establishment of resale price maintenance. Nevertheless, it spread. The resale price of foods, light-bulbs, shoe leather, car tyres, electrical goods, bicycles, and even cement was fixed by the manufacturer. At the turn of the twentieth century price-fixing was in its infancy but by the 1930s it was fully grown. A study of British commerce noted that in 1900 only 3 per cent of all spending by consumers went on price-fixed goods, but by 1938 it had reached around 30 per cent.[5] Fixed prices guaranteed profits for even the least efficient trader; increasingly so as consumers' needs and wants were being fashioned by advertising into requests for brand names. Margarine became 'Stork' and vacuum cleaners became 'Hoovers'.

In practice price maintenance involved restraint of trade. Retailers who refused to accept fixed prices did not get any more supplies. Co-operative societies endured boycotts or accepted price-fixing and sold goods at their set price with no 'divi' being calculated on their sale.

The ending of 'perfect' competition was investigated by two governments between the wars but neither acted. The law gave its blessing. On the other hand, the tax position of co-operative societies was frequently scrutinized.

A Treasury Committee (The Ritchie Committee) investigated the regulations of the income tax in 1905. The Chancellor of the Exchequer ordered an extension of its brief to discover if co-operative societies were favoured by any undue exemption.[6] Representatives from three small shopkeepers' organizations from the North gave evidence independently.[7] All demanded that co-operative societies be taxed to the full. They feared the expansion of the movement and made it into a scapegoat, responsible for their own economic decline. One organization proposed a special tax for co-operative societies that included taxing 'divi' payments and refusing members rebates despite their liabilities.[8] Representatives of medium and big business – including the London and Birmingham Chambers of Commerce – ignored the issue.[9]

The Chairman and Board of the Inland Revenue dismissed the shopkeepers' demands. In their view co-operative societies did not make profits as they were associations engaged in mutual exchange. The Deputy Chairman of the Inland Revenue stated the liberal view of social progress:

> It is important to bear in mind that in principle it is not the society that is ultimately taxed as a unit, but the individual members composing it. Whatever the aggregate profits may be, every member whose total income from all sources does not exceed £160 a year is entitled, like the ordinary trader, to be relieved from the payment of Income Tax on his share of the profits.[10]

The Ritchie Committee accepted the status quo. They reaffirmed the principle of mutuality in the face of several members' claim that significant trade took place between societies and non-members. This allegation was frequently made despite the fact that the Board of the Inland Revenue estimated the societies' trade with non-members to be less than 2 per cent of total sales in evidence to the Royal Commission on Income Tax in 1919. The Co-operative Union disputed their assessment, putting the figure at less than ½ per cent. The penalties of legal incorporation in the strict sense were not to be imposed. The implications of societies being seen as separate entities from their members were not pressed home.

Co-operative societies continued to grow and extend their markets. During the First World War they supplied public and government contracts. As they did so, consternation spread among private businesses and opinion in the Conservative Party hardened against them. Limits to mutuality were urged. As Bonar Law – Chancellor of the Exchequer in 1917 – said:

> I believe these societies have done a great deal of good in the country but they are doing an exceedingly large share of the retail trade of the country; and although they do not make profits in the ordinary sense, it comes to this, that that immense share of the trade is done without paying the share to the Revenue which is borne by other traders. I think that is something that ought to be remedied. I think members of

Co-operative Societies themselves will see that that is not quite a reasonable position, and that some arrangements later on will be possible which will make it fairer from that point of view. . . . I sympathise with retail traders in connection with this matter[11]

Mutual trading, it increasingly appeared, was acceptable only when it operated on a small scale at the margins of the economy.

The growing importance of domestic markets after 1918 presented private businesses with problems. They were disorganized and the markets were still very much regionally differentiated. Working-class consumption, although not fully exploited, was satisfied to a considerable extent by co-operative societies.

In 1920 co-operative societies accounted for 18 to 20 per cent of the total national sales of groceries and provisions. Membership rose to 4.5 millions by 1920, but over 10 million consumers had been registered for sugar rations with the co-operative societies in 1919. Average sales per member remained constant at £20 per year for the inter-war years.[12] Co-ops were well organized, using mass distribution techniques efficiently. In response to this economic success, a campaign against Co-operation spread to all sections of British business.

The common concern of private capitalists re-emerged during the deliberations of the Royal Commission on Income Tax in 1919–20.

The enormous growth of the co-operative movement during recent years . . . [means that] an ever-increasing volume of trade is yearly passing out of the taxable area and becoming a menace to the state by making it more and more difficult for the Chancellor of the Exchequer to balance the nation's accounts.[13]

Since its inaugural meeting in 1900, the National Chamber of Trade had demanded that co-operative societies should be taxed on the same grounds as private, limited liability companies. Every year they reaffirmed their demand.

Other small-business organizations scattered around the country wanted to go further. In their opinion the 'divi' paid out to members should be taxed as unearned income. As a result, they believed that Co-ops would reduce their prices and so go bankrupt.

213

Their aim, as put by the National Traders' Defence League, was clear: 'One thing we would gain would be that within nine or twelve months thereafter there would be no Co-operative Societies.'[14]

Organized small businesses looked upon mutual trading as the cause of their economic decline. A new organization, the Middle Classes' Union, sworn to defend the economic position and social status of the middle classes, added its support. Speaking to the Royal Commission, Mr W. Allen viewed the taxation position of co-operative societies as privileged, an erroneous assertion as members of the Royal Commission pointed out.[15]

In 1919 the owners of multiple-shop companies and department stores joined the campaign. Co-operative societies should be taxed as if they were limited liability companies. 'If this exemption from tax continues, I think it will divert business from the limited company form of trading into the Co-operative Society form.'[16]

Such a step would have denied co-operative societies an important source of capital for investment and expansion. But neither the extent nor the strength of business opinion moved the civil servants of the Treasury and Inland Revenue. They saw no need to change the law.

The Report of the Royal Commission was another matter. It showed that the liberal view of progress was weakening. The majority report of the Commission ignored mutuality and solely defined co-operative societies as separate legal entities distinct from their members. Registration under the law meant incorporation.

> We have taken the view that a registered Co-operative Society cannot be regarded merely as a group of individuals; it is as much a separate entity as any other body of persons. If the transaction of purchase and sale were complete when a purchase from the society is effected by a member, then the whole of the surplus arising on sales to members would be taxable profit. We think, however, that the transaction is not really completed until the society has decided what discount it can allow on the aggregate purchases of the member and has paid to him that discount in the form of a 'dividend' on purchases. In other words, the so-called 'surplus' on members' purchases is not really a surplus at all; it is the result of a book-keeping balance made for the purpose of determining what portion of the nominal purchase price has been returned to the shareholder. When that discount or rebate on purchase

price has been returned to the purchaser, we are of opinion that the surplus remaining in the hands of the society is a true trading profit.[17]

On this basis all returns not divided out were profits from trade. The Report also recommended that the 'divi' should not be taxed, not because of the individual co-operators' circumstances, but because it was a trading expense of the society. Co-operative societies, then, were seen as dynamic and successful. The basis for this success, in the opinion of members of the Commission, was maximization of profit. Success in the economy must, they thought, indicate the existence of capitalist social relations. Co-operative societies merely used a particular economic calculation in their accounts. In all other respects they were identical with capitalist forms. They should not be exempt, therefore, from taxation under Schedules C and D.

For one leading economist of the time, the Report did not go far enough. Sir Josiah Stamp submitted a joint appendix in which he tried to confine mutuality to small spaces separate from what he called the 'ordinary economic sphere'. Mutual associations were small and economically unimportant, outside the market.

> 'Mutuality' is most marked where the services can be withdrawn from the ordinary economic sphere, and rendered more or less independent of competitive prices and business conditions. It is therefore at its strongest when the persons are few in number and known to each other, so that they are less dependent upon purely commercial tests, and it is also dominant where the services rendered can only be enjoyed in common and are not competitively available. Mutuality is thus most complete in the case of clubs where members pay (ultimately 'at cost price') for services and advantages which are hardly obtainable in an open market. Mutuality, as a test of whether the advantages enjoyed were 'income' or not, was also very complete in the early days of Co-operative Societies.[18]

Seven other members of the Royal Commission, including economist A. C. Pigou, contended that co-operatives were both separate legal entities and mutual associations. They could not agree with the majority's report that co-operative societies should be taxed under Schedules C and D of the income tax. The exemptions, they argued, should continue because they reflected the low incomes of the members of the societies. Mutual trading – more precisely the surplus so generated – did not, in their view, incur income tax. They did add, however, that if there were a corporation tax levied, then co-operative societies would be liable.[19]

The inter-war years proved decisive for the political campaign against co-operative societies. They expanded; their membership grew; they moved into southern parts of England; they introduced sophisticated production and distribution methods; they acted as travel agents, and in some stores they sold fur coats. Membership doubled between 1914 and 1938 – from 3 million to 6.5 million – while the number of societies decreased through amalgamation. Overall, the societies increased their share of all retail trade by 2½ per cent (this was much less than the chain stores).

It was not surprising that the fears of the small shopkeepers and manufacturers grew. The opposition of big business was more expedient. Introduction of a corporation tax in 1920, levied on Co-ops and companies, satisfied their demands for 'taxation' of the co-operative societies. Their organizations returned to the attack when the Labour government removed the regulation four years later.

Back-bench Conservative MPs frequently pursued the question of the 'privileges' of co-operative societies. In 1925, Lt.-Col. Sir F. Hall asked Churchill to remove the exemptions granted to them. Churchill refused, no doubt with the delicate political situation on his mind. The defeat of the trade unions in 1926/7 heartened the Conservative campaigners. Their pressure brought about a Treasury investigation in 1927, but both civil servants and Chancellor reiterated that a stable society needed large-scale, open, unlimited associations of working people. Through them they could increase their incomes and wealth. Winston Churchill told Parliament:

Those enterprises which are owned by people who are below the Income Tax limit – owned by a large number of persons of whom few are liable to Income Tax – have undoubtedly an advantage, an inherent advantage, over those which are owned by people who are not below the Income Tax limit. This advantage, enjoyed with the formidable power of massed capital on a vast scale, constitutes a formidable menace to the ordinary trader; but I do not see how you can make any greater change in the way in which the Income Tax laws of this country are administered than if you were to invade the primary rights, the primary advantages to those who are themselves in such a small way that they are beneath the Income Tax limits. Those rights appear to be, and I do not see in what way they can be altered by or impaired by any extra burden being thrown upon their possessions in respect of their interest in co-operative societies. The fact remains that people who have not risen to a certain standard of income are immune from Income Tax and if they chose to band themselves together into societies, Parliament has long considered that their immunity was in no way wise to be impaired.[20]

This was the last occasion, however, that the Treasury, its Chancellor, and the Civil Service stated these views.

The co-operative movement seized the opportunity presented with the election of a Labour Government in 1929 to challenge private enterprise head-on. Capitalist interests had successfully – and increasingly – checked competition since the turn of the century.[21] Manufacturers refused to supply co-operative societies with some goods; an action most prevalent among newspaper publishers. The societies wanted an end to this imperfect competition. They were confident of their ability to compete in a free market. In response to their political agitation, inside and outside the government, a committee under the Lord Chancellor and the President of the Board of Trade was set up to investigate restrictive trade practices. It was a half-hearted affair from the beginning. It avoided discussion of the extent and effects of price maintenance[22] and its report vindicated price-fixing and boycotts. This initiative cost the co-operative societies dearly for they had challenged the capitalists' quest for economic stability. By attempting to open a debate about free trade, the co-operative movement precipitated another offensive on its tax position.

By 1930, the multitude of small-traders' organizations had banded into the National Organizations Co-ordinated Committee (NOCC) specifically to attack co-operative societies. Their campaign was supported by press barons Rothermere and Beaverbrook. The formation of the National Government committed to economic orthodoxy and the national interest provided their opportunity,

despite Ramsay MacDonald's election pledge that there would be
no taxation of the Co-ops while he was Prime Minister.[23]

During the debate on the 1932 Budget, Chamberlain announced
that he was setting up an 'impartial committee' to investigate the
position of co-operative societies and their income tax liabilities. 'It
is not a question of revenue that is concerned', he told the House,
'It is a question of equity.'[24] He was referring to the undistributed
reserves of the co-operative societies, their fund of capital for
expansion. But there was another reason for his action. The
government had a responsibility to defend political order. It could
not allow the dissatisfaction of the commercial middle classes to
grow into economic despair and then be mobilized for authoritarian
ends. As he told Parliament:

> The Government approached this subject without prejudice
> . . . they do think it is highly undesirable that our system of
> taxation should give rise to a burning sense of injustice,
> whether ill or well founded, on the part of any section of the
> community.[25]

Organizations of small and large businesses in both production
and distribution lined up to give evidence to the 'impartial'
Raeburn Committee. An editorial in *The Grocer* asked for united
support for the NOCC in order to see the day when 'the societies
[would be] paying their fair share towards the national income.'[26]

The National Traders' Defence League, while supporting the
NOCC, elected to give its own evidence; but their objective was the
same. The ability of co-operative societies to compete against private
enterprise in production, distribution and service was seen as indi-
cating development beyond mutuality. It was no surprise that the
Grocers' Federation complained to the BBC that a broadcast on the
history of Co-operation was advertising mutuality, and that if the
BBC put out the programme it would be advocating a different
economic belief. The Greater London Council of Grocers' Associations thought that subversive elements were at work in the BBC.
The lecture was not broadcast.[27] In 1931 the Grocers' Federation
put it this way:

> A Socialist Commonwealth in the United Kingdom . . . is the
> ideal of a dreamer, not of practical men who realise that the
> past prosperity of the British Empire has been built up by

private enterprise and that its continuance has been jeopardised by making the community undertake to far too great an extent responsibilities which should rest mainly upon the individual.[28]

Co-operative societies, in the view of private capitalists, had become too big and too successful. Their dynamism questioned the mystique of business acumen and competence, erected on the beliefs of individualism, which served to legitimate social differences. The only way forward for capitalists was to explain economic success by managerial organization and the economies of large-scale activities. The Scottish Federation of Grocers and Merchants put their opinion to the Raeburn Committee:

> How can a miner, or other resident for instance in a remote country village, or the average customer at their shops, have any practical control of what have now become huge and highly organised trading concerns?[29]

And there was another dimension of co-operative societies which troubled capitalists: power and authority was shared equally and democratically. Every member had a vote which carried the same weight. Wealth could not buy additional power. Members of the Raeburn committee could not accept this extension of democratic theory into economic activity. They reported:

> The purchaser acting as one of the body of members still cannot exercise over any part of the undistributed surplus a greater degree of control than attaches to the vote to which as a member he is entitled. He may be outvoted . . . [and as] each member has one vote, his voting power bears no relation whatever to the amount of his contribution.[30]

The evidence and submissions from the small-traders' organizations reproduced the earlier patterns. Yet the complaints of the numerous organizations were confused. Some alleged that co-operative societies 'overpriced' their goods, so preventing the 'poor' from shopping at their stores. Other organizations accused co-operative societies of cutting prices and 'unfair' trading by paying out the 'divi'. Officials from the National Traders' Defence League openly expressed their fears in reply to questions from members of the Raeburn Committee:

Your case is that the consumer prefers that method of purchase and we ought to prevent it? – Yes, if you put it that way.[31]

You want general legislation applicable to all people, not specially to Co-operative Societies? – That is within the province of the Government. We are only, as you might say, attacking the Co-operative Societies.[32]

The organizations of big business suggested to the Raeburn Committee that the recommendations of the majority on the 1920 Royal Commission on the Income Tax be implemented. Unlike the small-traders' organizations, they did not propose a specific tax for co-operative societies. They wanted them taxed as if they were limited liability companies.

Throughout the earlier history of the campaign, civil servants had stressed the importance of mutuality in considering the tax position of co-operative societies. In their evidence to the Raeburn Committee, however, officials from the Board of Trade and the Inland Revenue stated that registration under the Industrial and Provident Societies Act made each society an independent legal entity. Consequently, the trading surplus and the 'divi' resulted from profit-making, not mutuality. As they said, the 'divi' is a 'contingent trade discount rather than a share of profits'.[33] The Chairman of the Inland Revenue was equivocal in front of the Raeburn Committee, but privately he viewed co-operative societies as identical to limited liability, joint-stock companies. He told the Chancellor of the Exchequer, 'the pure doctrine of mutuality has no relevance in the case of *incorporated* trading concerns like Co-operative Societies'.[34] The campaign instigated by a few isolated traders' organizations at the end of the nineteenth century – with which successful manufacturing and distributive businesses allied on expedient grounds in the twentieth century – had, by the 1930s, gained support from the Civil Service and members of the government.

The Raeburn Committee ignored the demands of small shopkeepers for a special tax to be levied on co-operative societies. It recommended that the income tax law be changed to remove the provisions that exempted the societies from taxation under Schedules C and D. They should be taxed, it proposed, in respect of all their trade. The 'divi' should be treated as a trade expense of the society.[35] These proposals meant that every society would become liable for taxation on its undistributed 'profits' regardless of the individual tax position of any of its members.

The government faced a dilemma. Outside Parliament the co-operative movement had mounted its own campaign against any tax changes. It had forced Labour Party leaders to promise to keep the status quo; and after the formation of the National Government it circulated a monster petition and made the issue an electoral consideration. During the first years of the National Government, by-election results went in favour of the Labour Party with the taxation of co-operative societies featuring on the hustings. Inside the Cabinet, Chamberlain looked for a solution which would satisfy the shopkeepers without further prejudicing the government with the public. The National Government was trying to create economic conditions that encouraged private enterprise. His Cabinet colleagues did not necessarily follow this current of opinion but there was no inclination by ex-Labour Party ministers to protect mutuality and co-operative societies.

The Cabinet hoped to resolve the issues raised by the Raeburn Committee report in secret for several reasons. Chamberlain was not satisfied that its proposals fitted the political demands of the time. In his opinion, there was a danger that too punitive measures against co-operative societies would cause financial hardship to members on low incomes which were below the tax limit. The Inland Revenue had already proposed a special scheme for just this situation; societies could pay out interest to members without deduction of income tax (private companies, however, deducted it first). If not, said officials, the Inland Revenue would be overwhelmed with repayment claims from individual co-operators.[36]

Moreover, there were dangers that the Labour Party would revive its fortunes and gain support from co-operators. Already the campaign mounted by the co-operative movement worried the government and its officials. A petition was being circulated by the movement and co-operators sent in their own protests. Civil servants said that these letters amounted to a 'flood' and they told Cabinet ministers that there was little evidence of public support for the case of small and big business. Such was the scale of popular discontent with any change of the taxation law to the detriment of the co-operative societies that members of the Inland Revenue considered mounting a smear campaign against the societies. They could cite evidence, they said, of a worker in a CWS factory being forced to sign the petition.[37]

The Cabinet wanted to avoid publishing the evidence and report of the Raeburn Committee most of all because they thought it provided ammunition for the co-operative movement's campaign. Representatives of small shopkeepers had spoken so savagely against the co-operative societies that the Cabinet thought that their views might swing public opinion over to the societies and so limit the field of political action. The Chairman of the Board of the Inland Revenue warned Chamberlain not to publish any material from the Raeburn Committee meetings. He said:

> the Committee allowed representatives of all the interested bodies to attend the meetings with the result that some of them could not contain themselves and interjected comments of their own. A further argument against publication is that it would certainly assist the Co-operative Movement to obscure the issue by attacking particular portions of the evidence.[38]

This matter brought out tensions in the Cabinet. Sir John Simon – who had told Parliament in 1926 that the General Strike was illegal – supported the government in public, but he argued privately that the exemption clauses should continue. He told Chamberlain that there was no difference between the 'divi' and undistributed reserves – they came from mutual trading. Simon's views on mutuality and co-operative trading were being used by A. V. Alexander – a Co-op leader and MP – in the campaign against the Raeburn Committee. Simon told Cabinet that taking powers to tax the undistributed reserves of co-operative societies was inconsistent with the principle of mutuality. Furthermore, he said to them, the Raeburn Committee proposals involved taxing the total investments of co-operative societies not their income.[39] Simon believed co-operative societies to be partnerships of their members and not legal entities.[40] He felt that the government would lose political support if it went ahead, but he accepted that they had to act. While expressing his loyalty to Chamberlain, he told him:

> I am, therefore, personally in for a devil of a time in my own constituency where most of my best supporters are co-operators, and where they are accustomed to regard me as a man of my word.[41]

Sir John Simon was alone in Cabinet. The two former Labour MPs, Thomas and MacDonald, sided with Baldwin, Viscount Hailsham, and Chamberlain in favour of action for reasons of political expediency. Conservative back-benchers were demanding a change in the tax position to make co-operative societies pay. They resented the pressure and success of the co-operative movement's campaign.[42] Thomas and Macdonald informed their Cabinet colleagues that they were prepared to sacrifice their seats in support of taxing the co-operative societies. It was a secondary issue, they said; the important one was the political stability of the country on the international stage.[43] The National Government had to be kept in office. Chamberlain reminded the Cabinet that there was no budgetary need for change but it was necessary to resolve the grievances of small shopkeepers. Any lasting discontent among these voters, said Chamberlain, might make them susceptible to 'alternative ideas'.[44]

The Chancellor appealed to the co-operative movement to compromise. He suggested a number of schemes as options to the proposals of the Raeburn Committee, but they all included removal of the tax clauses. During these negotiations A. V. Alexander, MP and other leaders of the Co-operative Party and Congress were prepared to make a deal with Chamberlain. For a time it was mooted that Budget Day be delayed. The leaders of the co-operative movement found it difficult to persuade their members to compromise but this did not prevent Alexander from suggesting a scheme whereby all retail societies would be taxed on their trade with non-members and the 'profits' they made on their investments.[45] But Hayward, another leading member of the movement's delegation, saw Alexander's scheme as double taxation, although he confirmed that he still wanted agreement. Other proposals were brought forward by both sides. Chamberlain suggested a scheme which he thought would protect mutuality by imposing two taxation liabilities on retail societies while relieving the wholesale societies of a tax burden. The co-operative movement side rejected it and Chamberlain soon lost faith with the idea when his civil servants pointed out that the retail societies might increase their 'divi' or convert more shares into loan capital and so reduce their taxable income. They also told him that this scheme would cut down the revenue taken from co-operative societies in comparison with the present policy.

Facing increasing pressure from the Conservative Party, Chamberlain realized that he could no longer be seen to prevaricate. He could not afford to be considered as colluding with the co-operative movement, particularly as the shopkeepers were not going to get taxation of the 'divi'. He decided to act on the basis of the Raeburn Committee proposals and made the evidence and report public.

Ramsay MacDonald was criticized fiercely by the Labour Party over the proposals. He had pledged at the election that there would be 'no taxation of the Co-ops' while he was Prime Minister. What he really meant, he said after the 1933 Budget, was no taxation of the 'divi' and this was protected in the Budget.

An enabling resolution was drafted for the Budget debate, thereby perpetuating the myth that the change was a simple financial measure. Small traders got another concession; they could pay their income tax in half-yearly instalments from then on. The price for working people was sweetened by a penny off a pint of beer. The cost of these two measures was to be covered by the extra revenue brought in by the removal of tax exemption under Schedules C and D on co-operative societies. 'For the sake of quite a small revenue', said *The Economist*,

> the Government is apparently prepared to incur a wholly disproportionate amount of political unpopularity, besides running the risk of encouraging the co-operative societies to evade taxation by unsound methods of finance. It may be lawful to tax them; it is hardly expedient.[46]

The legislation introduced in the 1933 Budget assimilated mutual organizations to joint-stock companies. For tax purposes, they were supposed to be the same, and so the trading surplus of a society was equivalent to the profits of a private business. The 'divi' became a trade expense. But unlike the private companies, co-operative societies did not have to deduct tax at source when paying out to members. In other words, special provision was again granted to the societies because of the nature of their membership. And more, the 'divi' was exempted from tax – by way of being a trade expense of the society – but the sums placed to reserve by a society were taxed even though their source was common. The result was that co-operative societies were now liable to an increased tax burden under Schedules C and D of the income tax.

This change did not satisfy the small shopkeepers. They wanted a more proscriptive tax levied on mutuality. Only then would their economic position be secure.[47] They did not have enough support for this measure either from successful capitalists or leading politicians. Newspaper magnates (Beaverbrook and Rothermere) championed them throughout this period. Beaverbrook circulated pamphlets to numerous traders' organizations which outlined a plan to prevent the growth of co-operative societies by a new law which would restrict their sales. Rothermere had much the same idea. At one point he told the small traders that their political salvation rested with Oswald Mosley and the British Union of Fascists. In 1934, the *Daily Express* cited Rothermere – with approval – on the dangers of mutuality:

> Like a small swelling that has grown into a dangerous tumour, the co-operative movement is eating at the heart of British retail trade. . . . It is imperative that any further extension of co-operative retail societies should be restricted by law. . . . I urge large retail traders everywhere to press Members of Parliament for legislation forbidding the establishment of new retail co-operative societies except under licence from a central authority. . . . Any that may be authorised should pay three times the ordinary rate.[48]

British small businesses had opposed the co-operative societies since their beginnings in the nineteenth century. This opposition had been a major force in leading to organization among them. They turned co-operative societies into scapegoats for their economic decline. As with their German counterparts in the same period, they objected to the success of mutual trading. In Britain, however, small shopkeepers and manufacturers achieved a political victory within the parliamentary system against mutuality and the co-operative movement. The Conservative Party remained loyal and able to defend the interests of shopkeepers. It published, in its *Agents Journal*, the political and economic reasons for the attack on co-operation:

> There must be some limit to the idea of mutuality and when a Society, or series of Societies, has a turnover of hundreds of millions of pounds it is impossible to identify any particular purchaser with the principle of mutuality. . . . When you

come to these vast organisations which have been built up to their present size, you are dealing with something that goes much further than the mere joint purchase or sale by a group of individuals. . . . There can be no difference today between the position of a Co-operative Society and an ordinary trading company.[49]

NOTES

1 *The Law Times*, vol. 175, 3 June 1933, p. 428. See also 'Taxation of co-operative societies. Notes for a speech', *Conservative Agents Journal*, July 1933, pp. 224–5.
2 G. D. H. Cole, *A Century of Co-operation*, Manchester, Co-operative Union, 1944, p. 122.
3 H. Levy, *Retail Trade Associations*, London, Kegan Paul, 1942, p. 18.
4 R. Williams, *The Long Revolution*, London, Chatto & Windus, 1961, pp. 200–1.
5 J. B. Jeffreys, *Retail Trading in Britain 1850–1950*, Cambridge, Cambridge University Press, 1954, pp. 53–4. Other studies on the extent of price maintenance include J. D. Kinpers, *Resale Price Maintenance in Great Britain*, Wageningen, Dunkkerig, 1950, and B. S. Yamey (ed.), *Resale Price Maintenance*, London, Weidenfeld & Nicolson, 1966.
6 *Report of the Departmental Committee on Income Tax*, Cmnd 2575, 1905 (The Ritchie Committee).
7 They were the Federation of Grocers' Associations, the Association of Trade Protection Societies, and the Central Board of Traders' Defence Associations.
8 R. Walker, representative of the Central Board above. His evidence encompassed the views of the Drapers' Chamber of Trade, the British Federation of Confectioners' Associations, and the St Helens and District Fruit and Potato Traders' Association.
9 R. Lake spoke for the manufacturers' section of the London Chamber. Arthur Chamberlain spoke for his city's Chamber.
10 *Evidence to the Ritchie Committee, Appendix X*, p. 45.
11 96 H.C. Deb 5s, c277, 17 July 1917.
12 Jeffreys, op. cit. pp. 55–8.
13 *Royal Commission on the Income Tax: Minutes of Evidence*, Cmnd. 288, 1919, p. 976 para. 19921. Evidence from the National Chamber of Trade which had been formed by amalgamating small traders' organizations with the Traders' Defence Association.
14 ibid., p. 871, para. 17858.
15 ibid., p. 703, para. 14215. Mr May put him straight. Mrs Knowles offered condolence.
16 ibid., p. 908, para. 19921. Joint evidence from the Retail Distributors' Association and the United Kingdom Association of Multiple Shop Proprietors.

17 *Royal Commission on the Income Tax: Report*, Cmd 615, 1920, p. 120, para. 551.
18 ibid., p. 166. Reservation submitted by Professor J. C. Stamp and Wm McLintock.
19 ibid., pp. 163–4. Reservation submitted by C. W. Bowerman, Wm Brace, E. E. Nott-Bower, N. F. Warren Fisher, H. J. May, Wm Graham and A. C. Pigou.
20 219 H.C. Deb 5s, c628–9, 27 June 1928.
21 S. Pollard, *The Development of the British Economy 1914–1950*, London, Edward Arnold, 1962, p. 182; 30 per cent of retail trade in 1938 was covered by resale price maintenance.
22 *Report on Restraint of Trade*, Board of Trade, 1931.
23 MacDonald made his pledge in his Seaham constituency following much public discussion on this issue. He was fortunate to have the wiles of Chamberlain to protect him.
24 265 H.C. Deb 5s, c2073, 12 May 1932.
25 264 H.C. Deb 5s, c1433, 19 April 1932.
26 *The Grocer*, 23 April 1932, p. 70.
27 *The Grocer*, 24 October 1931, p. 65; 10 October 1931, p. 91; 17 October 1931, p. 60.
28 *The Grocer*, 3 October 1931, p. 76.
29 *Raeburn Committee, Evidence*, p. 48, para. 354.
30 *Raeburn Committee, Report*, Cmnd. 4260, 1933, p. 8, para. 20.
31 *Raeburn Committee, Evidence*, p. 66, para. 532. C. W. Clark.
32 ibid., p. 70, para. 605. R. Walker.
33 ibid., p. 11, para. 39.
34 PRO T171/306. Letter from Sir P. J. Grigg.
35 *Raeburn Committee, Report*, p. 9, para. 25. It is worth noting that the Raeburn Committee took as its yardstick for assessing mutuality the activities of enormous insurance companies, viz., New York Life Insurance and the Municipal Mutual Insurance Limited. The investors in these companies were seen as identical to co-operators.
36 ibid., p. 10, para. 26.
37 PRO CAB 23/75, 28 (33)1, 13 April 1933.
38 PRO T171/306. Taxation of cooperative societies.
39 PRO CAB 23/76, 30 (33)1, 24 April 1933.
40 PRO T171/306. Letter from Sir John Simon to Chamberlain, 3 May 1933.
41 ibid.
42 PRO CAB 23/75, 28 (33)1, 13 April 1933.
43 PRO CAB 23/76, 33 (33)1, 5 May 1933.
44 PRO T171/306. Meeting between Chamberlain and delegation from the Co-operative Movement (Alexander, Hayward, Palmer, and Cooper).
45 ibid., Confidential letter from Alexander to Chamberlain.
46 *Economist*, 20 May 1933, p. 1126.
47 *The Times*, 22 May 1933, p. 10. Report on the views of the NOCC.
48 *Daily Express*, 1 February 1934. See also W. Fox, *Who Attacks the Co-ops*,

Labour White Paper, no. 52, June 1934, and *The British Shoeman*, March 1934, p. 449.

49 'Taxation of co-operative societies. Notes for a speech', *Conservative Agents Journal*, July 1933, pp. 224–5.

Chapter Thirteen

ON THE USES OF 'COMMUNITY': FROM OWENISM TO THE PRESENT

EILEEN AND STEPHEN YEO

Inheriting the first, compulsory term of the Sussex MA course in History from John Harrison in 1977, we tried to re-think it. The aim was to make a course which students with different interests and backgrounds could take, and which would have conceptual as well as empirical interest. We came up with a course which has been developing ever since: 'Keywords and Key Concepts in Social History: Social History in Keywords and Key Concepts'. This essay is a product of that course, and owes a great deal to many cohorts of students.

In the course we focus on a cluster of ways of seeing human aggregates: *class, mass, people, public, community*. Each of them has been fundamental in the history of British culture and society. We try to look at each of them theoretically, but also, through them, to develop manageable lines of associated research (for example on community associations in the 1920s, or the language of Owenism in the 1820s). Each of the keywords has a cluster of usages around it: 'the working class', 'the working classes', 'the middle class', 'the classes versus the masses', 'mass society', 'community politics', 'community association', 'the mass of the comunity', 'the general public', 'public opinion', 'the people', 'the community at large', 'people's halls' . . . and so on.

All of the keywords have been more than ways of seeing: they have been influential as ways of living, acting upon others. They have been ways of seeing with particular, class locations at particular times, with particular uses and functions for those who employ them, and with power to constrain and to shape the ideas and actions of those about whom and by whom they are used. They also refer to material realities, changing over time. They are never purely 'ideological', whatever that may mean. They are in fact 'historical categories' in the sense proposed by E. P. Thompson for class, rather than 'theoretical categories' in the sense proposed by some 1970s Marxisms. They are interesting categories precisely because they lead straight into questions fundamental to the development of modern

229

capitalisms as well as questions fundamental to the development of social history as a discipline. They also lead into complicated questions concerning language itself about which historians have recently become exercised.

This chapter is a preliminary foray into a huge area of work. If anyone would like to help with *community* or any of the other four keywords we use in the course, work sheets on each of them are available from us at Sussex.

'You can't get away from the word "community" nowadays.' This is what the East Sussex Youth and Further Education Officer said when showing us literature on the National Federation of Community Associations in 1977. It was a time when we were active in 'community politics' and wanted to try to understand them better.

Turning the clock back 150 years, 'community' was also very visible. Co-operators and socialists were using it during the early nineteenth century in order to convey a vision of a new moral world: their antagonists were attacking it as a code-word for everything destructive and immoral. 'Community' has had an extraordinary capacity – and for a very long time – to carry opposed meanings. As a keyword it has been conspicuous in – and constitutive of – social conflict in Britain for at least 500 years. 'Community' seems unusually serviceable as a signifier for what human beings are and can become, and is thus an 'essentially contested concept'.[1]

One of its earliest and most enduring areas of meaning has had to do, quite simply, with the state. Britain was the earliest centralized nation-state in Europe and one strand of 'community' use expresses this. In the fourteenth century, '*the* community' (usually with the definite article) meant the realm and every individual in it. By the early nineteenth century, and particularly in the debate about the reform of the franchise, the community denoted either the state or civil society or all of the inhabitants or groups composing them. Phrases like 'all classes of the community' were frequent. Some voices, like W. A. Mackinnon in 1828, used 'nations or communities' interchangeably in ways which have become very familiar during the twentieth century.[2] In this area of meaning, the community *already exists*, has perhaps existed from time out of mind. It certainly pre-dates and does not depend upon the activity of the inhabitants for whom it is supplied, from above: it is made for people, not by them.

At another extreme, 'community' has meant a positive quality of social relationship. Since at least the sixteenth century, this sense of 'community' which goes back to the Latin *communitatem* (fellowship) has indicated the characteristic of holding something in common, a feeling of common identity and, most positively of all, a quality of mutual caring in human relations. This sense of community as mutual support has also been extended to mean an actual group of people practising community in a part or the whole of their social lives. The Digger view of twofold community contains both these elements: a shared spirit of love and consonant arrangements of material life. 'If ever the Creation be Restored', Gerard Winstanley insisted in *A New Yeers Gift* for 1650,

this is the way which lies in this Two fold power:

First *Community of Mankind*, which is comprised in the unity of spirit of Love, which is called Christ in you, or the Law written in the heart, leading mankind into all truth, and to be of one heart and one mind.

The Second is *Community of the Earth*, for the quiet livelihood in food and raiment without using force, or restraining one another: These two Communities, or rather one in two branches, is that true Levelling which Christ will work at his more glorious appearance.

This kind of community requires the continual practice of mutual support from the people within it: it is community made *by* people *for* themselves. It is not provided or defined by an already existing ruler or state.

These poles of definition mark two boundaries in an old linguistic field. In this chapter we will be particularly interested in attempts, definitely visible from the mid-nineteenth century onwards, to fuse or to confuse the two opposites and to attach warm feelings about mutuality and fellowship to unequal social arrangements which are structured from above and which often involve the state. These attempts go through 'community', illustrating well the way that keywords have of opening up or closing down avenues of understanding and action in particular social settings. We will explore three important usages of 'community' – as mutuality, as service, and as the state. Our presentation cannot be chronologically neat, because the history has not been. We shall be moving backwards and forwards in time trying to listen for the ambiguities and contradictions which riddle each usage, creating the enduring and structured complexity within which, if we want to stay with the keyword, we still have to manoeuvre today.

COMMUNITY AS MUTUALITY

In the early nineteenth century, Owenite socialists and co-operators achieved a near-monopoly over the keyword in its sense as a positive, self-made quality of social relationship. They were not the only group to use it in this sense nor did they only use it in this sense, but they dominated and developed the idea of community as mutuality. Between 1829 and 1845, they built a nation-wide, largely working-class movement which carried a vision of communities of mutual co-operation and which had an intellectual influence on working people out of all proportion to its numbers. They also turned community into a dirty word for their opponents who raged splenetically that the socialists had 'substituted "community" for Christianity' and really meant by community 'one vast brothel'.[3] The early socialists and co-operators were incorrigible inventors of new words using *commun-* as a root, including such words as commun-ionists, commun-ists, commun-itarians.

Socialists and co-operators used 'community' to open up thinking on three levels: visionary, critical, and constructive. First, they used community to convey a vision of a fully liberated humanity living in supportive social relations. Neither the present working class nor labouring poor needed to be idealized. William Hawkes Smith, a Birmingham socialist, urged people to think of themselves,

> not as a *class* or caste of WORKERS, but as human beings, capable of infinite improvement; and to whom, under wise arrangements, work – labour – sufficient for the production of every reasonable enjoyment, physical or intellectual, may be so reduced, as to form only a pleasant and healthful recreation.[4]

It was community which would constitute such 'wise arrangements'. The early socialists thought about the social relations necessary to unlock human potential. Committed to a thoroughgoing environmentalism (what they called the doctrine of the influence of circumstances on human character), the socialists were determined to 'surround each other with circumstances' which embodied the ethical precept 'love thy neighbour as thyself' or the motto 'all for each, each for all'. They focused on the whole range of social relations within which people live, not only those of economic production. As part and parcel of this, communitarian socialism made more space for concern with gender and family relations involving women and children than have other types of socialism relying more on keywords like 'class' and 'masses'. In the socialist community, the family principle was to be extended beyond blood ties. The project was 'the enlargement of home': 'single families with separate interests' were to be eliminated so that 'communities . . . with one interest . . . arranged as one family' might flourish.[5]

If community was to remake all human relations, then what was to be remade had to be understood. A second layer of early-nineteenth-century community sensibility contained an analysis and critique of the opposite of community, namely the competitive system as a whole. 'Community' does not always, as Marxists sometimes suppose, conceal the nature of class relations. Communitarian socialists produced an extensive analysis of domination and sub-ordination, with a focus on economic production, but also an awareness of the distribution of religious, educational, cultural, sexual, and sometimes state power. Along with their analyses of the power of capital over labour, went their concern with the power of priests and teachers (moralists of contradiction) to shackle the mind. They were eager to make working people the active producers of an understanding of their own potential. Hence their fecundity as coiners of words, all grasping at a different kind of co-operative as opposed to competitive knowledge, at a *social* science.[6]

Thirdly, the counterpoint between the present and a different possible future in community set up a dynamic tension. The perceived distance between what is and what could be, created a pressure towards construction to bridge the gap. The language of class has not always opened up this dynamic space. There were, however, deep class rifts within the movement about how to move across the space. Reformers from above, like Owen, advocated community 'at a stroke' and looked to businessmen and govern-ment for funds. Working-class socialists tended to think more in terms of going through co-operative trading and manufacture into community, bit by bit. In 1834 Senex had great hopes 'that such a unity of the labourers . . . must effect a very great change in the community . . . a change without which the word "community" has long been to us, Brethren, and must remain, a word of insult'.[7]

The resonance of 'community' remained long after socialists and co-operators had lost faith in any settlements on the land. Although discouraged by the Owenite experience from having much faith in self-sufficient communities, it was William Morris who most clearly perceived the need to educate desire in order to get people to hope and to act. He was very self-conscious about the use of words and understood the visionary value of 'community':

> I must confess great sympathy for those who look longingly on the scheme of a community. Miserable as the life of the workers now is *they get used to it*; their standard of life is so low that any slight bettering of 'living to toil that they may toil to live' quiets them and gives a new lease of life to the present system of oppression. If it were but possible to give them new hopes by showing them, even imperfectly, what the life of a community might be, and how it would develop our energies and create new pleasures for us.[8]

Morris employed the language of 'community' to great effect, in lectures like 'Monopoly: or How Labour is Robbed', in which he asked his listeners to conceive of an utterly different social order from their own and to start acting upon it: 'here, then, is our reasonable community'.

COMMUNITY AS SERVICE

Soon after the failure of the Queenwood community, a main focus of socialist activity between 1839 and 1845, middle-class men and women began to develop a second key version of community, as service: service, often through voluntary association, but service to a constructed, public entity.

Local Liberal leaders first created this meaning in response to the socialist practice of community. But it also featured in twentieth-century Labour Party politics and can be identified with politicians like Clement Attlee, Hugh Gaitskell, and with many would-be progressives in modern Britain. Community as service was important to professional men like doctors and lawyers, who grew rapidly in numbers from the mid-nineteenth century onwards, and who tried to establish their legitimacy by stressing their competence to treat social disease and their service to individual clients and to the community. Middle-class women, trying to move out of the home into public work, presented themselves as social mothers doing self-sacrificial service to the poor and to the community. These men and women also co-operated to reinforce each other's service role, especially in the area of public health, where women supposedly sweetened medical inspection, while doctors upgraded traditional philanthropic visiting into scientific activity. Professionalization, science, and service came together once again in early academic sociology's concern with community in Britain and America.[9]

The notion of community as service could thus be explored through any number of movements or individuals from the mid-nineteenth century onwards. In this section of the chapter, we will first examine how this usage came into being in reaction to working-class practices of community. Then we will characterize community as service mainly by contrast with community as mutuality. To help do this, we will make a large chronological leap in order to foreground the Community Association movement of the 1920s and 1930s as a convenient epitome. We will show how the movement contained impulses from above and from below, just as did Owenite socialism and co-operation, impulses which came into conflict over the notion and even over the word 'community'. Then, using the case of the Community Associations, we will again indicate how middle-class people have invoked community as service to displace working-class mutuality or militance.

The socialist movement in the 1830s officially aimed to found communities in the countryside. But the desire to live a form of community *now* and the need to accumulate funds over a long period of time led to other kinds of local initiatives. However small-scale, these local initiatives often had great ambition and saw themselves as part of large transformations. Many early co-operative societies saw themselves as the germ of a new social order:

> When the capital was accumulated sufficiently, the society may
> purchase land, live upon it, cultivate it themselves and
> produce any manufactures they please, and so provide for all
> their wants of food, clothing and houses. The societies will
> then be called a community.

Later, there was a vision of local societies, with the Co-operative Wholesale Society as their aggregate, becoming the 'closed community' or 'state within a state'. William Openshaw of the London branch of the CWS, in a speech as President of the National Co-operative Festival in 1907, said:

> Almost every variety of the necessaries of life was now co-operatively produced but co-operators had a long way to go before they reached the end they had in view, viz. to become a practically self-supporting and self-employing community, co-extensive with the limits of the civilised world.[10]

The early socialists created Halls of Science, multi-purpose cultural centres, owned and controlled by working people, where socialists and others could practise their own versions of education, recreation, and religion. All the halls contained libraries and reading rooms. Such local cultures continued on in the co-operative movement through the second half of the nineteenth century and well into the middle of the twentieth.

The halls were independent and imposing enclaves of working-class territory. They were intrusive to the bourgeoisie who wished to shape the public sphere according to their own rules and property-based modes of access. In Manchester, the symbolic as well as the actual headquarters of industrial capitalism in 1840, the Hall of Science had the largest meeting rooms. After initial reactions of violent hostility (including arson and prosecution), the capitalists who had gained control of the urban boroughs began to take a different approach. Unable to accept independent working-class action, which by definition excluded them, these Liberals created forms of community which included and privileged themselves. They developed a strategy of counter-provision which involved supplying rival cultural institutions in more imposing buildings, creating a new zone of 'public' territory and appropriating keywords like 'community', 'common', 'co-operation' for the new *civitas*.[11] They moved in on the co-operative movement, getting as close as they could, as patrons, presidents, speech-givers, legislators, reformers . . . giving it their own definitions so successfully that most outside historians have confused these definitions with the reality of the working-class movement itself.

Mid-nineteenth-century civic leaders tried to transcend conflict and create community by making the municipality (as a city-state) into an object of service. Through service in local government and voluntary associations, public life was to bring 'the community', in the sense of everybody within the local state, into 'community' in the sense of a new kind of caring union. In the words of the Reverend Dale of Birmingham, where the 'civic gospel' received its clearest formulation in the 1860s, 'new ideas about municipal life and duty were pressed on the whole community'. The Reverend Dawson spoke of the Birmingham Public Library movement as

> capable of bringing about a better union of classes. . . . There could not be anything more valuable than men [sic] finding rallying points at which they might forget sectarianism and political economy, which they did not half understand, and find a brotherhood removed from the endless grovellings, and the bickerings. . . . This then was the new corporation, the new church, in which they might meet until they came into union again.

In 1857, Dawson welcomed the opening of Calthorpe Park in a phrase which seemed to echo Robert Owen's Association of All Classes of All Nations when he found the scene 'most animating, there being an association of all classes of the community, each being determined on enjoyment'.[12]

Community was to be created by public facilities notionally available to all classes. These would displace or absorb similar facilities supplied by working people for themselves. Bought for a song from the socialists, the Manchester Hall of Science became the first free Public Library in Britain and was hailed as the product of a 'common effort for a common purpose . . . that public domain for mental culture which is the joint heritage and ought to be the common enjoyment of rich and poor'.[13] These fine words must not obscure the fact that this idea of 'common' was displacing mutuality with hierarchy. A full history of public libraries would also need to explore the differences between the huge libraries (and halls) of co-operative societies in many cities and the succeeding town libraries (and town halls), and discover the sense in which the latter were takeover bids for the former, often using Carnegie money. But it is safe to say that in bringing the public facilities into being and then in running them, bourgeois men had decisive power. The Public Subscription Committee which often raised the funds was multi-class, but it was divided into a complement of wealthy donors, a large body of affluent subscribers and a separate 'Working Men's Committee'. The resulting hospitals, libraries, town halls, and parks were turned over to local government to be made into state 'services'. They were never controlled, or actively produced, by the users. This was very much a version of community provided through the service of middle-class governors and philanthropists for the people, however much energetic participation in it was urged and however much it was recommended with the rhetoric of mutuality.

Indeed a key feature of community as service and a clear contrast to working-class mutuality has been the continuing middle-class attempt to harmonize social relations without disturbing inequalities of class or gender power. A characteristic project of middle-class groups has been to marry the two oldest definitions of 'community' and to conceal, or, as they would see it, transcend, social antagonism. They have tried to force a union between the community as supplied from above with its basically unequal social structures and community created from inside with its supportive and more ethical human relations. The transforming agency was to be their own *voluntas* expressed in service to a formal entity (e.g. the municipality or a Community Association) together with equivalent though unequal working-class participation. This strand of community thinking has remained strongly committed to locality (the city rather than the nation) and to voluntary effort. But the emphasis has been on co-ordinating voluntary and state activity so that, despite the presence of democratic and visionary anti-state rhetoric, the state has been left in place and in control. Ernest Barker, a member of the National Council for Social Service and the chief ideologue of the Community Association movement, drew upon the whole radical rhetoric of essential Englishness (including the Saxon precedent and the Norman Yoke) to celebrate 'Voluntary Community and a New Democracy', even calling the Community Centre 'a "moot-stow" for their deliberations'. But however representative, Barker argued that a Community Association was 'not a unit of local government, and does not attempt to replace the Local Authority' (which usually, he noted, filled people with massive apathy).[14] This view differed from working-class anti-statism which sought to constitute a (new) state (of affairs) through its own associational activity.

Community Associations formed in the new, sprawling, post-1919 estates built by local Councils. Partly inspired by the Garden City movement and by the desire to give the returning military heroes healthy homes, then deformed by the need to build on the cheap, these estates came into existence rapidly.[15] They were as large as existing cities and composed only of working-class people. Middle-class groups dedicated to social service took the initiative in forming Community Associations. Both in Manchester and Liverpool, the University Settlements played a leading role in launching these 'suitable centres of a strong community life'. The Settlement movement enabled graduates, particularly single women, to continue to live in a collegiate way while undertaking regular social service to the poor. Other affiliates had the word 'Service' prominently displayed in their names: the local Council of Social Service, the Personal Service Society, and the Service Club for the Unemployed. Also involved was the New Estates Community Committee, part of the National Council of Social Service and composed of representatives from voluntary bodies, and from local and central government.

People seeing community as service have often been preoccupied with formal institutions and with constructions in the literal sense – buildings as the symbol and the location of community life. We have noted the mid-nineteenth-century bourgeois concern with public buildings. Community Associations put a lot of energy into fund-raising and into lobbying local Councils for a Community Centre or Community Hall. Not least, this building was necessary to provide a venue for middle-class service. Ernest Barker made this point in a somewhat anxious but tactful way:

> It took all sorts to make a world; whereas a world in a new Housing Estate was an artificial world, not as big and broad as it might be. That was not its own fault. It was made so by the local authorities. It naturally wanted to be independent, and not to be patronised from the outside. That was good; but on the other hand such a little world did need help, comfort and a widening of interest which could be given from outside, because in that way it was not wide enough. These two considerations had to be joined together; and the Community Centre could help greatly towards such a consummation. Many outside people wanted to come to them in a spirit of good fellowship, and to add to that good neighbourliness which was their own creation and achievement.[16]

On the Norris Green estate in Liverpool, the Hall was needed as the place where the Personal Service Society could arrange low-interest loans, the Mothers' Welfare Clinic give birth-control advice, and the Service Club for the Unemployed do its woodworking.

In a similar way, some British and American sociology at the time, in contrast to Tönnies to whom we will return, reserved the concept 'community' precisely for 'more formal and less intimate' social relations and institutions. As Robert Park of the Chicago School put it, 'the community, then, is the name that we give to this larger and more inclusive milieu, outside of ourselves, our family and our immediate neighborhood where the individual maintains not merely his existence as an individual, but his life as a person'.[17] The Liverpool University Department of Social Science, which did research into the new estates, shared this understanding. One study stated:

> A community is constituted of neighbourhoods of different kinds, from the unskilled-labourer neighbourhood to the professional class neighbourhood. It requires playing fields, and a group of public buildings, churches, schools, a shopping centre and a community hall in a centralised position.

Commitment to this public construction of 'community' was seen as the most developed human activity, because it signified a sense of concern beyond selfish interest. The citizen, as L.T. Hobhouse, the first British Professor of Sociology, would have agreed, was the true human being.

The idea of community as service was usually located away from economic production, in leisure life after work. As Park of Chicago, an advocate of Community Centres, put it, 'politics, religion, and community welfare, like golf, bridge and other forms of recreation, are leisure-time activities and it is the leisure time of the community that we are seeking to organize'.[18] This was another contrast with the socialist vision, where production of every kind, including economic production and production of family life, was to be reorganized in order to embody community. The locus of community shifted in middle-class thinking between the middle and end of the nineteenth century. At first, wealthy local Liberals felt that community, patterned on patriarchal family relations, could permeate many civic activities and voluntary organizations, and even be present in some aspects of factory life. Everywhere, however, it was reserved for the public territory of men. By the twentieth century, the division between work and leisure had become conceptually as well as geographically more complete. The characteristic bourgeois attempt to separate work from life (as in suburbs) had got well under way alongside attempts to moralize and redeem work through revalued 'leisure'. Council estates in the 1920s were first built as dormitories without places of work or even shops. One of the main grievances of the new tenants – leading them to undertake estate agitations (associations) which were then enclosed within the bricks and mortar of Community Centres – was that work was too far away from the estates and trams too infrequent and expensive.

Although situated where people had their homes, the middle-class view of community with its stress on service within formal organizations tended to restrict working-class women and to displace their communities. Women's informal networks of relatives and neighbours were a continuing experience of mutual aid. But Community Associations, while purporting to answer the sexism of Working Men's Clubs, had few women officers in their committee structures and few women writers for the CA newspaper. It is true that groups like the Women's Co-operative Guild and the Townswomen's Guild did affiliate, for example, to the Norris Green Community Association in Liverpool and that this Association started a benevolent fund to give members 'a little immediate help'. But the Community Associations never seemed to relate to the neighbourhood networks among women which provided economic and emotional support so important for survival.[19]

Sometimes middle-class women tried to absorb poor women's networks into a notion of community in which social workers and their service was indispensable. Helen Bosanquet was an activist in the Charity Organisation Society and, together with the Women's University Settlement, a pioneer proponent of training for social workers in Schools of Sociology and Social Economics. She argued that social workers would have to coerce into being the very family and neighbourhood networks which were already there and on which the poor had always relied. She inflated the service of social workers at the expense of poor people's sacrifice:

the unceasing sacrifice of patiently unintelligent women and selfishly unintelligent men is of little use to the community. It does not rise to the level of self-sacrifice, for there is seldom anything voluntary about it; it is submission to the brute forces round them.[20]

Only much later, in the 1950s, did the pendulum swing the other way. Just when social services, public housing and private materialism seemed to be undermining the informal networks in fact, groups like the Institute of Community Studies resurrected these neighbourhood networks in theory as the 'traditional' (and desirable) working-class community.[21]

The example of Bosanquet and other women social workers illustrates a key feature of most of the middle-class practice of community. This was the inability to leave independent working-class mutuality alone and the recurrent attempt to absorb it or replace it with a practice designed to make middle-class service indispensable. This was the case even where the mutual aid was informal, as in the case of women's networks, and perhaps even more the case when mutuality was organized into formal and sometimes militant associations. Community as service has been continually invoked in and against situations of working-class militancy. We have seen how the civic leaders of the mid-nineteenth century tried to replace, and in some cases to take over, the cultural initiatives of militant working-class movements. Community Associations did not appear in a vacuum. In the wider context of the industrial militancy of the 1920s, tenants had organized themselves into independent Tenants' or Residents' Associations. Middle-class progressives raised the banner of community in reaction to these groups. And tenants resisted it, for example in Middlesex and in Liverpool.

The Larkhill and North-East Liverpool Tenants' Association started work in 1921 when tenants discovered that one key would open any door on a particular road. A deputation visited the Housing Committee to get this changed. Once formally constituted in 1922, the Association acted as a tenants' trade union, pressing the Corporation about rents, contracts and decorations. Besides this area-union collective bargaining function, the Association organized educational and recreational activity. Some activists even envisioned the Tenants' Associations replacing political parties in a new state consisting of local and national parliaments with representatives from consumers' and producers' organisations.[22] In Watling, Middlesex, a Residents' Association (WRA) was formed at the end of 1927 after vicious attacks on the new estate in the local press. The WRA pressed the London County Council for necessary facilities like a meeting-place and also began generating schemes of co-operation and mutual aid, like a loan and share-out club and collective lawn-mowing.

At the same time, a Watling Association was formed, chiefly by people from Hendon and Mill Hill who resented the lower class of newcomer, who were 'interested in the welfare of Watling' and who wanted a large house for a community centre (a house which the Watling tenants had already turned down because the LCC would not allow a drinking licence). These suburbans had a direct line to Sir Wyndham Deedes of the New Estates Community Committee. 'After a series of struggles' which went directly through the word 'community' (which the WRA resented) – and not without the deepest suspicion – a merger of the two groups was eventually agreed, with the 'external group of friends' calling themselves 'the local Community interest'. They carried the keyword around as their own and met with resistance to the point where the resulting community centre was called the 'Watling Centre', 'the word "community" being somewhat out of favour in 1932-3'.[23]

In Liverpool, the keyword 'community' was repeatedly used to try to defuse a conflict situation and to contain union-like solidarities. Here the local Council of Social Service tried to head off the Tenants' Associations by recruiting them into a Liverpool Community Committee in 1927. The same Council of Social Service, together with the University Settlement, pressed for a Community Council on the Norris Green estate, an initiative heartily endorsed by the national New Estates Community Committee. The keyword 'Community' was deliberately chosen, as Barker made clear:

> We welcome with open arms Tenants' Associations if they are democratically organised for the general social welfare of their estates over and above bodies dealing with questions of the relation of landlord and tenant. But the title 'Tenants' Association' does perhaps suggest as the basis of your union that you are a tenant, and have a landlord confronting you, and that there is antagonism between landlord and tenant. I know the Tenants' Associations transcend their names. They are in effect Community Associations. But I have a sneaking preference for the title 'Community'. It has a deep human effect – that you have a neighbourhood feeling towards each

other as good neighbours, and that you are going to act together for good purposes as good neighbours.[24]

In Liverpool, the Community Committee was riven with tension. Individual Tenants' Associations were also resistant to being absorbed into any Community Council or Community Association, arguing that the Community groups 'have yet to prove their value as a means of watching over the interests of their members as tenants and ratepayers'.

Ever since that time, tenants have often detected and disliked the view of community imposed from above. A sociologist studying a Sheffield estate in the 1960s heard complaints like 'some make a community of it. They have a club. I shouldn't like to see it made a community. I'd like to see it free for everyone.' One respondent saw 'community' as 'no fences allowed and kids and dogs all over the place like a Butlin's Holiday Camp'. A Barbadan immigrant living near Manchester during the 1970s recalled his experience of village life back home and its *gemeinschaft* mutuality: 'we never heard the word "community" '. In Britain he did, and he observed how typically it was captured by priests and others who said

> 'I am it.' And these people are lifted and carried shoulder high, and people go and report to them, and these people are responsible to a man, not to a community. That's not a community, it's a locality. I feel that our little village had a lot on other places, because we could trust each other, because we felt that sooner or later, 'I'm going to need you, and if you can't trust me, I can't trust you. And if you can't trust me, you're going to say "Now bugger off" when I really need you.' The thing about 'community' is that it's a posh name like sociology.[25]

The middle-class embrace had so corrupted the keyword that some working people who had experienced fuller mutuality of an informal kind had trouble using the word 'community' to describe it. Similarly more formal working-class associations had difficulty in using the keyword in post-Owenite times, not only because of the difficulties of sustaining self-supporting communities, but because middle-class groups had used it to displace working-class activity in many episodes from the mid-nineteenth-century civic takeovers to the twentieth-century Community Associations. Another development making 'community' increasingly problematic for working people was its increasing use in connection with the national state.

COMMUNITY AS STATE

The earliest area of meaning of 'community' became highly visible again from the late nineteenth century onwards. If, in the fifteenth century, the role of the king in relation to the inhabitants and interest groups in his realm was being defined, so in the late nineteenth century the role of the state in relation to social life was an issue high on many middle- and working-class agendas. The use of 'community' in relation to the state has been conspicuous ever since. By the 1970s, many agencies and programmes funded by central or local government were tagged with the keyword: while now in the 1980s 'community' is also being used to name schemes like 'community care' which aim to dismantle the Welfare State.[26] It would be simplistic to make the chronology too neat, but community as state did, in part, succeed and replace community as service in the same way that the latter replaced community as mutuality. Replacement is the wrong word in a social history of keywords and concepts where survivals and contests are as evident and as important as innovations. Raymond Williams's categories of dominant, emergent, and residual (developed to understand the history of literary forms), are perhaps more helpful.[27] One can certainly watch emergent practices of community as state displacing dominant practices of community as service in the projects of important groups of middle-class activists, for example those who moved through the Settlement Houses in the 1880s – 90s into the Civil Service during the 1906 Liberal administration.

The links between the community, the state, and the nation were forged in a complicated setting. The atmosphere crackled with ethical energy but was also heavy with the menace of perceived threats from outside and within. The 'Great Depression' of the 1870s had cast grave doubts on Britain's ability to compete against vigorous young rivals like Germany and America. Anxiety reached crisis point at the turn of the century. After several decades of investigation of poverty in towns, revelations about the poor physical condition of army recruits to the Boer War seemed to show that the British race, nation, and empire were in danger. Ruling-class alarm was used by other groups, including organized labour and middle-class progressives, to press for an expanded role for the state. This expansion in turn helped to create a whole cadre of middle-class professionals, women as well as men, who often had a deep commitment to service but also a vested interest in more national, state-oriented understandings of community, and who found influential employment as state servants (including teachers and social scientists as well as administrators and managers) in our own time.[28]

'The community' and especially 'the community as a whole' were key phrases in the discourse of such people. In an age of majority democracy (from 1867 but particularly after 1918 when all men over the age of 21 and some women over 30 had the vote) the community could mean much more than simply the state and its inhabitants. Now the community could be seen as the citizenry, possessing, determining, and licensing the legitimate interests of the nation. It could be presented as the embodiment and the arbiter of the public good. This keynote was amplified by collectivists who, in the words of Collini, craved

> a new ethical spirit in social relations, a stronger sense of community and of the duties of its members to each other. In the most general terms, they went on to argue that the state as the political expression of the community should embody the 'new moral world' in its legislation.[29]

However, critics of collectivism, both from the left and from the right, were quick to expose the dangers of abstraction and the ease with which politicians (and government officials) could manipulate this idea of community. Conservative Hilaire Belloc's insistence in *The Servile State* (1911) that 'the community is an abstraction and the politician a reality' was endorsed by socialist Victor Grayson who hoped to move 'the instruments of production into the hands of the Community': 'Mr. Belloc pulls up at the word "community" and excitedly interjects "the politicians"! Under existing circumstances we confess we can find no very honest or effective answer to his interjection.'[30]

The new legitimating construct of 'the community' was quickly used to contain independent working-class action, and has been wielded in this context ever since. The community could be erected as an overriding tribunal of appeal to discredit militant working-class activity by making it seem separate, antagonistic, sectional, and selfish. A movement of language in this direction, propelled by late-nineteenth-century collectivists, got an enormous impetus in the First World War, especially from 1917, a moment of intense working-class presence when Bolshevism was not safely quarantined in One Country. Government ministries and the owners of the tabloid press (the two coalescing in Lord Beaverbrook) deliberately fashioned a discourse to bring militancy into disrepute. To convey an interest more legitimate and comprehensive than labour's, they used a barrage of words including 'community', which have done service ever since: the community (public) at large, the general public, the national interest, the (great) British people (public), the community as a whole. Stanley Baldwin, addressing the House of Commons on 6 August 1925 after giving way to the miners on Red Friday, used the '(whole) community' over and against the strikers:

> If the will to strike should overcome the will to peace temporarily . . . let me say that no minority in a free country has ever yet coerced a whole community. The community will always protect itself, for the community must be fed, and it will see that it gets its food. And let me just say this too: I am convinced that, if the time should come when the community has to protect itself with the full strength of the Government behind it, the community will do so, and the response of the community will astonish the forces of anarchy around the world.

This construct of 'the community' has overriding authority. It is very abstract. Usually it is coupled with some very concrete grouping (in Baldwin's statement the government) which will take action on its behalf. While this version of the community contains great numbers of people, it is unclear how they can articulate their own views or take their own actions. Numbers unlimited are included but presented in a passive pose needing outside agents to decipher and carry out their will. How these often self-appointed agents are to be accountable to the community is never clear. Sometimes 'the masses' who comprise the community are portrayed as unable to act for themselves because of inherent incapacity (moral, racial, psychological, educational, or whatever) rather than because of the social situation or system.[31] In all cases some characteristic twentieth-century agents, who have defined them this way, then have to step in and speak for them: the state (government, bureaucrats, political parties), newspaper magnates, consumer kings, and social science experts. Labour politicians have also inhabited this structure of thought and claimed to represent the community. So Arthur Henderson, 'sceptical of the unions' capacity to take the "broad view" ', asserted that 'Labour is in politics, not in the interests of a class, but to further the interests of the Community as a whole.'[32] So Ramsay MacDonald, in his *Parliament and Democracy* (1920), saw 'the community' as reaching 'the stage when it must begin to protect itself and its freedom by the organisation of its production'. Full of 'its', he urged that 'it must absorb into its system the voluntary organisations which have been formed for similar purposes by groups in the capitalist community'. 'Voluntary organisations' here included the labour movement.

To capture this abstraction of 'the community' has been, in our own time, a high prize indeed. Unlike community as mutuality, it allows a minority enormous power over the language and facts of community which affect a great majority. Particularly in the hands of the state, the power can conscript, outlaw, and coerce: it can attach the warm resonance of the keyword to projects which are compulsory and punitive. Thus poll taxes can be called 'community contributions', approved schools, 'community schools'. Home Office projects to deal with problems of inner-urban public order can be called Community Development Projects (the same name given to imperial projects in the colonies). Real people living in real places can be excluded from belonging to any community at all:

> One may police [Brixton and Handsworth] by a radically
> revised book; one may play football and embrace community
> leaders; but it is so much bandaging if, beneath the surface,
> there are groups who belong to no community, who roam
> only a vast wasteland. It is they who fired Handsworth and
> they who lit Coldharbour Lane.[33]

The police can then be seen as the creators of community: 'Community policing is conscious aid given by the police to build up the community where it is weak or non-existent.'

This extremely dominative practice of community is different from the statist understanding which, particularly in the 1960s and 70s, opened the way for some popular participation in planning and released some inconvenient, and militant, mutuality from below.[34] It is also very different from community as service, even though both functioned and often intended to displace action from below. The most coercive statist notions of the community do not attempt to create more caring human relations; social ethics are of little concern. Nor is service as a way of life or associative effort, even of an unequal kind, of much concern. The contrast between the two extremes of community from above (coercion and service) was spotlighted in the crisis of 1917, when both were very active, and, however conflicting, could reinforce each other in containing community from below. In that year, the Royal Commission of Enquiry into Industrial Unrest reported in record time and, interestingly, produced diagnoses and remedies saturated with community as service assumptions.

Focusing on one of the most turbulent areas, the mining valleys of South Wales, the Commissioners bemoaned the absence of community in language reminiscent of mid-nineteenth-century civic leaders:

> the civic and corporate life of the community has suffered owing to the absence of 'town centres' and of any conveniently centralised institutions. For instance, dignified municipal buildings are extremely rare: not a single municipally maintained public library is to be found in the central Glamorgan block of the coalfield. . . . There are, it is true, many working men's institutes, most of them with collections of books attached to different collieries; there are also many clubs, but we believe not a single trade union or co-operative hall for large gatherings and with offices for various labour organisations. Finally, the Rhondda has an abundance of cinemas and music halls, but not a single theatre. Owing to this absence of municipal centres and centralised institutions, the development of the civic spirit and the sense of social soli-darity – what we may in short call the community sense – is seriously retarded.[35]

It was less plausible than in the case of 1920s housing estates for those outside these Welsh areas to call them 'cultural deserts' or – as in the case of 1980s inner-city blacks – to see Welsh miners as 'groups who belong to no community, who roam only a vast waste-land'. To do the Commissioners justice, the vigour of what they were trying to replace could not be kept entirely out of their language. A safer idea of culture was to replace the strong informal community of the miners (never acknowledged by the Report) and the vigorous independent educational activity of the Central Labour College (funded by the unions) and the Independent Labour Party branches (which both impressed and alarmed the investigators). The Commissioners called for a broad and humanistic technical education, stressing work as 'a form of public service' and industry as 'a co-operative effort'. The Commissioners chose the university as 'the centre of the life of the community gathering to itself its aspirations and hopes, fulfilling its deepest need and ever shaping it to nobler purposes': extension classes were to spread everywhere. But neither the technical training nor the university, both of which became para-state services, could be provided by working people for themselves. The 1917 Report contained much Liberal appreciation of human dignity and of the need for working people to see themselves 'in the affairs of the community as partners, rather than as servants'. This was certainly a more generous discourse than the exactly contemporary statist construct of independent labour as enemies of the community. But the whole underlying drift was still towards removing the independent bases which could make possible future working-class power.

The discourse of community from above, even when it has allowed for working-class participation, has been difficult to articulate on behalf of labour. From the late nineteenth century, an interesting variant of the idea that the state represented the community has been the continuing use of 'the community' to mean the citizens or the consumers, in a corporate vision of industrial life. This usage featured in the case for co-partnership, against working-class co-operation, and in the writings of collectivists like the Webbs and even the New Liberal L. T. Hobhouse, who were fascinated by the labour movement and who made blueprints for containing its commitment to independence within polities of producers, consumers, and citizens. This attempt at containment was visible in the proceedings of the Sankey Commission on the Coal Industry in 1919. The Commissioners kept pressing the idea of an overriding community interest of consumers upon spokesmen for the miners, who clearly had trouble in distinguishing themselves from the community or its interest. Thus a hostile questioner attacked W. Straker, the Secretary of the Northumberland Miners' Association, about his proposal for the nationalization of the coal mines:

8794. I put it to you that the danger of your scheme would be that instead of the profits from the coal mining going into the pockets of the shareholders would they go into the pockets of the miners?

– No. Instead of the profits of the industry going into the pockets of the few, as it does at the present time, it would go to the whole community, including the miners.[36]

None the less the miners did half-heartedly accept the state as the custodian of the community interest and, as a result, included one significantly less democratic element within their plans. While half the members of all governing boards of the industry were to be chosen by and accountable to the Miners' Federation (the constitutional machinery for keeping them accountable was carefully detailed), the remainder were to be appointed by a Minister of Mines to 'look after the interest of the community'. Little was said about how these political or civil service appointees could be made accountable to consumers. It would seem that the real, if unintended, effect was to reinforce a construction of a passive community, in the pockets of 'spokesmen' (in the end politicians), but with no meaningful powers of control. Many labour leaders have colluded in this usage, then and since, as if giving up on the hard and very detailed task of contesting emergent statist notions of community, using available working-class traditions of mutual ideas and constitutional forms. Thus Arthur Henderson, already an opponent of domestic syndicalism, insisted in 1917 that 'capital and labour had often in the past, in the settlement of their differences by lock-out or strike, forgotten that there was a third party, the community, whose interests were being seriously endangered' and urged that 'the state should act as a buffer between two warring sections'. Unless 'the state' in this context was simply to mean him and men like him 'representing' labour, this sentence cries out for detailed, specific communal invention.[37]

CODA

Such invention will be needed more and more. It does not look as though statists – with their Community Everything – will abandon the keyword 'community': it would therefore be inadvisable for anyone else who believes in what 'community' could be to drop its other, genuinely communal possibilities. As Engels wrote to Bebel in March 1875,

The state is merely a temporary phenomenon which Socialists can use in the revolutionary struggle . . . as soon as genuine freedom is established, the state as such ceases to exist. We suggest that the word 'state' should be replaced in the Gotha Programme by the word 'community' (*Gemeinwesen*) which is a good old German word and may be regarded as the equivalent of the French word 'commune'.[38]

Communal invention will be needed against a tendency within capitalism, noticed by Raymond Williams, Roland Barthes, and others, to suck human labour out of the language – draining away the details, the minutely constructed particulars, the active sense of people producing.[39] 'Community' has pulled and can still pull against such abstraction, although as we have shown, it can and does get abstracted.

The social history of language can help. But only if all the contradictions and counter-currents are left exposed. There is one obvious danger in the way we have arranged the history here. From mutuality to service to the state as a degenerative sequence, if you identify, as we do, with the mutual beginning of that sequence, might serve to recommend a *return* as the way forward, back to the. . . , back to mutuality. But there is now no way back to any kind of simplicity, any kind of magical 'time before' or original unity – even though the idea of such a time, which clings close to the word 'community', is valuable fuel for finding ways forward. Any effective, indeed any possible state of mutual affairs, or co-operative state, will have to be unimaginably complex: complex, not simple co-operation constructed through real conflicts in and around community.

Just to take one difficulty in one, intellectually very influential and tempting, way back, Ferdinand Tönnies's *Gemeinschaft und Gesellschaft* (1887). One of the most important and unresolved conflicts running through the definition of community as mutuality concerns that key formation: the family.

As we have seen, in order to depict the relations of community as loving, emotional, affirming, supportive, and as the opposite of oppressive, contractual, instrumental, and competitive, some model of family relations has often been invoked and then generalized. Contradictory models of the family have been used. At the two extremes, the family can either be patriarchal, involving marked inequality between members and genders, or more egalitarian. In his seminal work, Tönnies formalized the contrast which was increasingly being felt between the human relations of community and the contractual relations of capitalism and the state. He described *gemeinschaft* (community) relations as being rooted in natural will, instinct, and feeling, and especially in 'reciprocal binding sentiment' which led to 'mutual furtherance and affirmation'. He depicted the social reality of the *gemeinschaft* of blood, locality, and friendship in terms of an idealized feudal system and a model of the patriarchal family with a pattern of authority which pervaded all social relations. Tönnies also detected another potential in feudalism 'based on the equality of brothers and sisters', but this did not come to dominance. For Tönnies there was no contradiction between mutuality and inequality of power. So long as the more powerful party maintained an attitude of benevolence and tenderness, there was no problem. However, once the more powerful party began abusing his position, the relationship, by definition, ceased to be mutually affirming and stopped being *gemeinschaft* – a definitional sleight of hand![40]

Perhaps it is not surprising that an intellectual from a rich peasant family in Schleswig Holstein should not be preoccupied with any inconsistency between patriarchy and community. But it is significant that the same contradiction has often remained undetected and unresolved within more socialist strands of community thinking. While it has been easy to use the imagery of an egalitarian family to remake economic, political, and religious relations, it has seemed one of the hardest things to extend the analysis and root out oppressive patriarchy in the families where people actually live. The Diggers of the seventeenth century were able to construct an equal family of humankind by moving both figures of authority, the Father and the Mother, into metaphysical realms, calling them God and the Earth, and leaving human men and women to be equal as brothers and sisters. Yet Gerard Winstanley still thought of the husband as the master of the human family.[41]

We have few models to work with here, only continuing preoccupations, continuing contests. But 'community', with its inherited emphasis on the quality of relationship and its familial imagery, has at least served to keep such conflicts exposed. They do not get buried, as they have been within statist traditions. In the early socialist and co-operative movement there was 'the social father' Robert Owen, who clung to a version of patriarchy which gave special weight to age and to himself, and who always looked to the rich and to the state for the funding of his schemes. But there was also a recently rediscovered feminist contingent, brought to life in Barbara Taylor's work, attacking the characteristics of the bourgeois and working-class family which sustained the social psychology and the institutions of the competitive system. Not only were nuclear families part of the apparatus of private property, but they made habits of domination and subordination seem a normal and natural part of life. 'Every family', insisted William Thompson,

> is a centre of absolute despotism, where of course intelligence and persuasion are quite superfluous to him who has only to command to be obeyed: from these centres in the midst of which all mankind are now trained, spreads the contagion of selfishness and love of domination through all human trans-actions.[42]

Working women echoed the words of this maverick Irish landlord by calling themselves 'the slaves of slaves'. Communities of mutual co-operation would rescue this situation, not by abolishing family, but by extending kinship beyond blood ties to all. As an American communitarian very clearly put it, 'the great problem of socialism is whether the existence of the marital family is compatible with that of the universal family which the term "Community" signifies'.[43] It is by staying with and working through community, rather than abandoning it in a fit of modernizing pique, that we may construct real spaces to realize and resolve such 'great problems' in the way of 'universal family'.

NOTES

1 Auberon Waugh commented in *The Sunday Telegraph*, 17 November 1985, 'Listening to a sermon in church a few years ago I counted 24 uses of the word "community" and only 3 references to God.' For essentially contested concepts, see S. Collini, *Liberalism and Sociology*, Cambridge, Cambridge University Press, 1979, p. 15; W. B. Gallie, 'Essentially contested concepts', *Proceedings of the Aristotelian Society*, 1955-6, vol. 56, pp. 167–98; A. Macintyre, 'The essential contestability of some social concepts', *Ethics*, no. 84, 1973, pp. 1–9.
2 W. A. Mackinnon, *On the Rise, Progress and Present State of Public Opinion in Great Britain and Other Parts of the World*, London, 1828, reprinted

Shannon, Irish University Press, 1971, p. 31. *Oxford English Dictionary* for earlier statist definitions. P. Corrigan and D. Sayers, *The Great Arch. State Formation as Cultural Revolution*, Oxford, Basil Blackwell, 1985, and Q. Skinner, *The Foundations of Modern Political Thought*, Cambridge, Cambridge University Press, 1978, vol. 2, pp. 352–3, for the development of the forms and the idea of the state. James Mill, *An Essay on Government*, 1820, reprinted: New York, Liberal Arts Press, 1955, for an early example of the use of 'the Community' in the debate about the vote. Prime Minister Asquith on women for a later example: *Speeches*, London, Hutchinson, 1927, pp. 175, 183.

3 *Coventry Standard*, reprinted in *New Moral World*, 19 May 1838.

4 W. Hawkes Smith, ibid., 31 December 1836.

5 R. Owen, *Book of the New Moral World*, 1844, reprinted: New York, Kelley, 1970, pt. 6, p. 48.

6 E. Yeo, 'Social science and social change', unpublished PhD thesis, University of Sussex, 1972, ch. 2; W. Thompson, *Labour Rewarded*, London, 1827, for an analysis of 'competitive political economists' and the 'co-operative school'.

7 *The Pioneer*, 10 May 1834.

8 *Commonweal*, September 1885, p. 87; 'Monopoly etc.' in *Collected Works*, London, Longman, 1914, vol. xxii, pp. 248–9.

9 These themes will feature in E. Yeo's forthcoming *Social Science, Class and Gender in Britain, 1789–1914* to be published by Virago Books.

10 *The Co-operator*, 1 May 1828; *Labour Co-Partnership*, September 1907, p. 137. We owe the Openshaw reference to Pete Gurney.

11 For working-class halls and civic counter-attractions, see E. Yeo, 'Culture and constraint in working-class movements, 1830–1855', in E. and S. Yeo (eds), *Popular Culture and Class Conflict, 1590–1914*, Brighton, Harvester Press, 1981, pp. 177–8. For the bourgeois vision of civic service, S. Yeo, *Religion and Voluntary Organisation in Crisis*, London, Croom Helm, 1976, ch. 2.

12 A. W. W. Dale, *The Life of R. W. Dale of Birmingham*, London, Hodder & Stoughton, 1899, p. 403; Dawson quoted in E. P. Hennock, *Fit and Proper Persons. Ideal and Reality in Nineteenth Century Urban Government*, London, Edward Arnold, 1973, p. 75.

13 Quoted in A. Briggs, *Victorian Cities*, London, Odhams, 1963, pp. 199–200.

14 *Norris Green Life*, June 1937, pp. 14–15, reprinting his address to the 8th Annual New Estates Conference in London.

15 M. Swenarton, *Homes Fit For Heroes. The Politics and Architecture of Early State Housing in Britain*, London, Heinemann, 1981. For the vision, see W. L. Creese, *The Legacy of Raymond Unwin: a Human Pattern for Planning*, Cambridge, Mass., Harvard University Press, 1967. Unwin, a devotee of William Morris and the Labour Church, ultimately became Chief Technical Officer for Building and Town Planning at the Ministry of Health, facilitating the council estates which, in fundamental ways, contradicted his ideals. His career illustrates how

professionalization and state intervention worked against community produced from below. For jerry-building which offended craftsmen, see A. Paul, *Hard Work and No Consideration*, Brighton, QueenSpark, 1981.

16 E. Barker, 'Tenants' and Community Associations', *The Flowing Tide*, Liverpool, Council of Social Service, vol. 1, no. 1, July 1938, p. 36. *Norris Green Life*, March 1936, p. 13, March 1937, p. 14, April 1937, p. 16.

17 R. E. Park, E. W. Burgess, and R. D. Mackenzie, *The City*, Chicago, University of Chicago Press, 1925, pp. 104, 106; University of Liverpool, Department of Social Science, *Population Problems of New Estates with Special Reference to Norris Green*, Liverpool, Liverpool University Press, 1939, p. 48; Collini, op. cit., p. 216.

18 Park *et al.*, op. cit., p. 117.

19 *Norris Green Life*, January 1937, p. 7. *The Wilbraham World: The Official Organ of the Wilbraham Association*, vol. 1, no. 1, December 1932 – vol. 2, no. 12, April 1935, in the Manchester Central Reference Library, is a rich source for the aspirations of a high-minded Community Association on a Manchester estate. From 1929 to 1935 their secretary was Emily J. Jenkinson; see her Utopian dream of what the Wilbraham estate could be like in 1999 in *The Wilbraham World*, vol. 1, no. 3, p. 29, and her disappointed departing letter in *WW*, December 1934. 'A change of heart in their neighbours' seemed to be what the Wilbraham Association was trying to achieve, although there is also evidence, for example from Wythenshawe (*WW*, June 1934), of tenants' union/area union impulses at work.

20 H. Bosanquet, *Rich and Poor*, London, Macmillan, 1899, p. 103; *Social Work in London, 1869-1912*, London, 1914, reprinted Brighton, Harvester Press, 1973, pp. 403-4.

21 e.g., P. Wilmott, *The Evolution of a Community. A Study of Dagenham after Forty Years*, London, Routledge & Kegan Paul, 1963, p. 109, the follow-up study to Wilmott and M. Young, *Family and Kinship in East London*, London, Routledge & Kegan Paul, 1957. S. Laing, *Representations of Working-Class Life, 1957-1964*, London, Macmillan, 1986, pp. 37ff, for genres of community study in the 1950s.

22 James Smith, *Tenant Associations*, Liverpool, Larkhill and North-east Liverpool Tenants' Association, 1931, pp. 4, 13. Wary of the name 'Community', he coupled it with resonant working-class radical language when he called for 'a People's Hall, or Community Centre', p. 18. For an earlier phase of tenant organization, D. Englander, *Landlord and Tenant in Urban Britain 1838-1918*. Oxford, Clarendon Press, 1983. Being 'consulted both by national and local governments upon everything which concerns the residents' seemed to be the limit of the Wilbraham Association's vision; *The Wilbraham World*, vol. 2, no. 1, May 1934, p. 2.

23 The Watling material is taken from E. Sewell Harris and P. N. Molloy, *The Watling Community Association: The First Twenty-One Years*, n.d.. In very different, pacificist, circles, *Reconciliation* (March 1938, p.

79) commented five years later, ' "Community" is becoming one of those hard-worked words'; quoted in M. Ceadel, *Pacifism in Britain*, London, Oxford University Press, 1980, p. 292.

24 Barker, op. cit., p. 34. H. R. Poole, *The Liverpool Council of Social Service*, Liverpool, 1960, p. 57. Liverpool Council of Social Services, *Annual Report*, 1930, p. 21. Smith, op. cit., pp. 9–10.

25 'Once there was a way', *Lifetimes*, no. 4, Manchester, Institute of Advanced Studies, n.d., pp. 4, 15–16. This is a publication of a Federation of Worker Writers and Community Publishers affiliate.
P. A. Baldock, 'Tenants' voice: a study of council tenants' organisations with particular reference to those in . . . Sheffield, 1961–1971', unpublished PhD thesis, University of Sheffield, 1971, pp. 5:12–19.

26 For an excellent discussion of the 'community' strategy in the late 1960s and 70s, C. Cockburn, *The Local State. Management of Cities and People*, London, Pluto Press, 1977. In the 1980s government-funded schemes still have the keyword: e.g. The Community Programme (for the unemployed) and Community Policing.

27 R. Williams, *Marxism and Literature*, London, Oxford University Press, 1977.

28 For the growth of the 'professional managerial class', S. Yeo, 'Notes on three socialisms – collectivism, statism and associationism – mainly in late nineteenth- and early twentieth-century Britain', in C. Levy (ed.), *Socialism and the Intelligentsia 1880–1914*, London, Routledge & Kegan Paul, 1987. B. B. Gilbert, *The Evolution of National Insurance in Great Britain: The Origins of the Welfare State*, London, Michael Joseph, 1966; Anna Davin, 'Imperialism and the cult of motherhood', *History Workshop Journal*, no. 5, 1978.

29 Collini, op. cit., pp. 66–7.

30 *The Clarion*, 21 July 1911. Thanks to Ian Bullock for this reference.

31 For the structured coupling of the masses and leaders, see S. Yeo, 'On the uses of "Apathy" ', *European Journal of Sociology*, vol. 15, 1974.

32 Quoted in R. McKibbin, 'Arthur Henderson as Labour leader', *International Review of Social History*, vol. xxiii, 1978, p. 91.

33 *The Guardian*, 13 September 1985; *The Times*, 13 April 1981, for Community Police.

34 Cockburn, op. cit., pp. 123–9, 139–57, discusses how both the Community Development Projects and the Neighbourhood or Community Councils got out of hand and were closed down.

35 Commission of Enquiry into Industrial Unrest, No. 7 Division, *Report of the Commissioners for Wales, including Monmouthshire*, Parl. Sess. Papers, 1917–18, vol. xv, Cd. 8668, pp. 12, 19, 28, 30.

36 *Coal Industry Commission, Reports and Minutes of Evidence on the First Stage of the Inquiry*, 1919, Cd. 359, pp. 343–4, also question 8778; 8975, p. 352 for Robertson, Scotland; 9335, p. 366 for Hartshorn, South Wales, answering in the same vein. Straker's loathing of the centralized bureaucratic state and idea of proper accountability, 8812–13,

p. 344, 8441ff, p. 335. S. and B. Webb, *Industrial Democracy*, 2 vols, London, Longman, 1897; L. T. Hobhouse, *The Labour Movement*, 2nd edn, London, Unwin, 1898.

37 19 February and 19 June 1917 remarks quoted in McKibbon, op. cit., p. 90.

38 W. O. Henderson (ed.), *Engels*, 1967, p. 137.

39 A theme in much of Wiliams's work since *The Country and the City*, London, Chatto, 1973; R. Barthes, *Mythologies*, trans. and ed. A. Lewes, London, Cape, 1970, pp. 137-47.

40 F. Tönnies, *Community and Society (Gemeinschaft und Gesellschaft)*, trans. and ed. C. Loomis, New York, Harper & Row, 1963, pp. 41-7. For Tönnies in historical context, A. Mitzman, *Sociology and Estrangement. Three Sociologists of Imperial Germany*, New York, Knopf, 1973.

41 'The True Levellers Standard Advanced', 'The Law of Freedom in a Platform or True Magistracy Restored', in G. H. Sabine (ed.), *The Words of Gerard Winstanley*, New York, 1965, pp. 265, 545. For more freedom allowed women by theological equality, K. Thomas, 'Women and the Civil War sects', *Past and Present*, no. 13, 1958, and C. Hill, *The World Turned Upside Down*, London, Temple Smith, 1972, ch. 15.

42 W. Thompson in *The Co-operative Magazine*, August 1826. B. Taylor, *Eve and the New Jerusalem. Socialism and Feminism in the Nineteenth Century*, London, Virago, 1983.

43 C. Lane, quoted in J. H. Noyes, *History of American Socialisms*, 1870, reprinted New York, Hillary House, 1966, p. 143.

INDEX

259